W9-CRR-557

College

Accounting

A. B. Carson, PhD, CPA
Professor of Accounting, University of California, Los Angeles

Arthur E. Carlson, PhD
Professor of Accounting, Washington University, St. Louis

Clem Boling

Eighth Edition

Published by South-Western Publishing Company
Cincinnati   •   Chicago   •   New Rochelle, N.Y.
Dallas   •   Burlingame, California

preface

College Accounting is designed for students of accounting, business administration, and secretarial science. An understanding of the principles of business accounting is essential for anyone who aspires to a successful career in business, in many of the professions, and in numerous branches of government. Those who manage or operate a business, its owners, its prospective owners, its present and prospective creditors, governmental taxing authorities, and other government agencies have need for various types of information. Accounting systems are designed to fill the needs. The particular practices followed are tailored to meet the requirements and the circumstances in each case. However, the same accounting principles underlie the practices — just as the same principles of structural engineering apply to the construction of a one-car frame garage and a fifty-story steel and concrete office building.

This eighth edition of College Accounting continues the pattern of earlier editions — explanations of principles with examples of practices. Numerous forms and documents are illustrated. Because the terminology of accounting is undergoing gradual change, the currently preferred terms are used throughout the textbook. Diagrams and color are used both to facilitate understanding and, in the case of many of the color illustrations, to conform to practice. The arrangement of the subject matter in Part 1 has been altered to present the application of fundamental principles to a personal service enterprise before the accounting for a merchandising enterprise is explained and illustrated. To facilitate the exposition of the principles of accrual accounting, the subject of notes and interest is treated before the sequence of chapters dealing with the application of the accrual basis of accounting to a retail merchandising business. Because the discussion of practices requires several references to modern data processing procedure, an appendix treating "Automated Accounting Systems and Procedures" is included.

The textbook is organized to facilitate the use of various supplementary learning aids. Each chapter consists of one or more study assignments. A workbook containing correlated practice assignments is available. Each workbook *report* includes an exercise on principles and one or more problems bearing on the material discussed in the related section of the textbook. Additional accounting problems to be used for either supplementary or remedial work are included following Chapters 5 and 10. In addition to the workbook, two completely new practice sets are available: the first involves the accounting records of a professional man (Howard C. Miller, an architect); the second involves the accounting records of a retail appliance store (The Adams Appliance Store). These sets provide realistic work designed to test the student's ability to apply his knowledge of the principles of accounting gained from studying the textbook and completing the workbook assignments.

A comprehensive testing program is provided. Tests are available for use following completion of Chapters 2, 5, and 10. Upon completion of each practice set, a test is used to determine the student's ability to interpret the records and financial statements intelligently.

The authors acknowledge their indebtedness and express their appreciation to the considerable number of accounting instructors, business executives, accountants, and other professional people whose suggestions contributed to the preparation of this textbook.

A. B. C.

A. E. C.

C. B.

contents / *part one*

part one / *contents*

chapter one

the nature of business accounting

The purpose of business accounting is to provide information about the financial affairs of an enterprise to the individuals, agencies, and organizations who have the need and the right to be so informed. These interested parties normally include the following:

(a) The **owners** of the business — both existing and prospective.

(b) The **managers** of the business. (Often, but not always, the owners and the managers are the same persons.)

(c) The **creditors** of the business — both existing and prospective. (*Creditors* are those who furnish or supply products and services "on credit" — meaning that payment need not be made immediately. The creditor category also includes banks and individuals who loan money to the business.)

(d) **Government agencies** — local, state, and national. (For purposes of either regulation or taxation — sometimes both — various governmental agencies must be given certain financial information.)

The preceding list of four classes of users of financial information applies to virtually every business enterprise. In connection with many businesses, some or all of the following also make use of relevant information: customers or clients, labor unions, competitors, trade associations, stock exchanges, commodity exchanges, financial analysts, and financial journalists.

The information needed by all of the users is not identical, though most want data regarding either results of operations — net income or loss — for a recent period, or financial status as of a recent date, or both. In addition to these requirements, a variety of other financial information may be wanted. The exact requirement depends upon who wants it and for what purpose. As might be expected, the demand for the most and greatest variety of financial information comes from the managers of the business. They constantly need up-to-the-minute information about many things.

The accountant has the task of accumulating and dispensing needed financial information. Since his activities touch upon nearly every phase of business operation and financial information is communicated in accounting terms, accounting is said to be the "language of business." Anyone intending to engage in any type of business activity is well advised to learn this language.

Since accounting relates to so many phases of business, it is not surprising that there are several fields of specialization in accounting. Some major fields are tax work, cost accounting, system design and installation, and budget preparation. Many accountants have but one employer; whereas, others become qualified as public accountants and offer their services as independent contractors or consultants. Some states license individuals as *Public Accountants* or *Registered Accountants*. All states grant the designation *Certified Public Accountant* (CPA) to those who meet various prescribed requirements, including the passing of a uniform examination prepared by the American Institute of Certified Public Accountants. Public accountants perform various functions. One of their major activities is *auditing*. This involves testing and checking the records of an enterprise to be certain that acceptable policies and practices have been consistently followed. In recent years, public accountants have been extending their activities into what is called "management services" — a term that covers a variety of consulting assignments. Specialization is common among members of the accounting profession. Tax work is one important specialty.

All of the foregoing comments have related to accounting and accountants in connection with profit-seeking organizations. Since there are thousands of nonprofit organizations (such as governments, educational institutions, churches, and hospitals) that also need to accumulate financial information, thousands of accountants are in their employ. These organizations also engage public accountants. While the "rules of the game" are somewhat different for nonprofit organizations, much of the record keeping is identical with that found in business.

the accounting process

Accounting Defined

A widely quoted definition of accounting is

> . . . the art of recording, classifying, and summarizing in a significant manner and in terms of money, transactions and events which are, in part at least, of a financial character, and interpreting the results thereof.[1]

Recording traditionally has meant writing something by hand. Much of the record keeping in accounting still is manual, but for years typewriters and many varieties of so-called "bookkeeping machines" (which, typically, combine the major attributes of typewriters and adding machines or desk calculators) have been in use. Today the recording sometimes takes the form of holes punched in certain places on a card or a paper tape, or of invisible magnetized spots on a special type of tape used to feed information into an electronic computer.

Classifying relates to the process of sorting or grouping like things together rather than merely keeping a simple, diary-like narrative record of numerous and varied transactions and events.

Summarizing is the process of bringing together various items of information to determine or explain a result.

Interpretation refers to the steps taken to direct attention to the significance of various matters and relationships. Percentage analyses and ratios often are used to help explain the meaning of certain related bits of information.

---

[1]*Accounting Research and Terminology Bulletins, Final Edition*, "No. 1 — Review and Résumé" (New York: American Institute of Certified Public Accountants, 1961), p. 9.

Accounting and Bookkeeping

Accounting involves records design, policy making, data analysis, report preparation, and report interpretation. A person involved with or responsible for these functions may be referred to as an accountant. Bookkeeping is the recording phase of the accounting process. The person who records the information in the books of account may be referred to as a bookkeeper. Sometimes the accountant also serves as the bookkeeper, an experience that may be of great value to him.

Accounting Elements

If complete accounting records are to be maintained, all transactions and events that affect the accounting elements must be recorded. The accounting elements are *assets*, *liabilities*, and *owner's equity*.

Assets. Properties of value that are owned by a business are called assets. Properties such as money, accounts receivable, notes receivable, merchandise, furniture, fixtures, machinery, buildings, and land are common examples of business assets. *Accounts receivable* are unwritten promises by customers to pay for goods purchased on credit or for services rendered. *Notes receivable* are formal written promises by debtors to pay specified sums of money at some future time.

It is possible to conduct a business or a professional practice with very few assets. A dentist, for example, may have relatively few assets, such as money, instruments, laboratory equipment, and office equipment. But in many cases, a variety of assets is necessary. A merchant must have merchandise to sell and store equipment on which to display the merchandise, in addition to other assets. A manufacturer must have materials, tools, and various sorts of machinery, in addition to other assets.

Liabilities. An obligation of a business to pay a debt is a business liability. The most common liabilities are accounts payable and notes payable. *Accounts payable* are unwritten promises to pay creditors for property, such as merchandise, supplies, and equipment purchased on credit, or for services rendered. *Notes payable* are formal written promises to pay creditors or lenders specified sums of money at some future time. A business also may have one or more types of *taxes payable*.

Owner's Equity. The amount by which the business assets exceed the business liabilities is termed the owner's equity in the business. The word "equity" used in this sense means "interest in" or "claim of." It would be quite reasonable to call liabilities "creditors' equity," but this is not customary. The terms *proprietorship*, *net worth*, or *capital* are sometimes used as synonyms for owner's equity. If there are no business liabilities, the owner's equity in the business is equal to the total amount of the assets of the business.

In visualizing a business that is owned and operated by one person (traditionally called the proprietor), it is essential to realize that a distinction must be made between his *business* assets and liabilities and any *nonbusiness* assets and liabilities that he may have. The proprietor will certainly have various types of personal property, such as clothing; it is probable that he will have a home, furniture, and a car. He may own a wide variety of other valuable properties quite apart from his business. Likewise the proprietor may owe money for reasons that do not pertain to his business. Amounts owed to merchants from whom food and clothing have been purchased and amounts owed to doctors and dentists for services received are common examples. Legally there is no distinction between his business and nonbusiness assets nor between his business and nonbusiness liabilities, but since it is to be expected that the formal accounting records for the enterprise will relate to the business only, any nonbusiness assets and liabilities should be excluded. While the term "owner's equity" can be used in a very broad sense, its use in accounting is nearly always limited to the meaning: business assets minus business liabilities.

Frequent reference will be made to the owner's investing money or other property in the business, or to his withdrawal of money or other property from the business. All that is involved in either case is that some property is changed from the category of a nonbusiness asset to a business asset or vice versa. It should be apparent that these distinctions are important if the owner is to be able to judge the financial condition and results of the operations of his business apart from his nonbusiness affairs.

The Accounting Equation

The relationship between the three accounting elements can be expressed in the form of a simple equation:

$$\text{ASSETS} = \text{LIABILITIES} + \text{OWNER'S EQUITY}$$

When the amounts of any two of these elements are known, the third can always be calculated. For example, C. J. Wilson has assets in his business on December 31 in the sum of $21,800. His business debts on that date consist of $300 owed for supplies purchased on credit and $400 owed to a bank on a note. The owner's equity element of his business may be calculated by subtraction ($21,800 − $700 = $21,100). These facts about his business can be expressed in equation form as follows:

$$\text{ASSETS} = \text{LIABILITIES} + \text{OWNER'S EQUITY}$$
$$\$21{,}800 \qquad \$700 \qquad\qquad \$21{,}100$$

For Mr. Wilson to increase his equity in the business, he must either increase the assets without increasing the liabilities, or decrease the liabilities without decreasing the assets. For him to increase the assets and owner's equity without investing more money or other property in the business, he will have to operate the business at a profit.

For example, if one year later the assets amount to $32,900 and the liabilities to $1,300, the status of the business would be as follows:

$$\text{ASSETS} = \text{LIABILITIES} + \text{OWNER'S EQUITY}$$
$$\$32,900 \qquad \$1,300 \qquad\qquad \$31,600$$

However, the fact that Mr. Wilson's equity in the business increased by $10,500 (from $21,100 to $31,600) does not prove that he made a profit (often called *net income*) equal to the increase. He might have invested additional money or other property in the business. Suppose, for example, that he invested additional money during the year in the amount of $4,000. In that event the remainder of the increase in his equity ($6,500) would have been due to profit (net income).

Another possibility could be that he had a very profitable year and withdrew assets in an amount less than the amount of profit. For example, his equity might have been increased by $15,000 as a result of profitable operation, and during the year he might have withdrawn a total of $4,500 in cash for personal use. This series of events could account for the $10,500 increase. It is essential that the business records show the extent to which the change in owner's equity is due to the regular operation of the business and the extent to which increases and decreases in owner's equity are due to the owner's investing and withdrawing assets.

Transactions

The activities of an enterprise which involve the exchange of values are usually referred to as *transactions*. These values are expressed in terms of money. Buying and selling property and services are common transactions. The following typical transactions are analyzed to show that each one represents an exchange of values.

TYPICAL TRANSACTIONS	ANALYSIS OF TRANSACTIONS
(a) Purchased equipment for cash, $250.	Money is exchanged for equipment.
(b) Received cash in payment of professional fees, $125.	Professional service is rendered in exchange for money.
(c) Paid office rent, $100.	Money is exchanged for the right to use property.
(d) Paid a debt owed to a creditor, $300.	Money is given in settlement of a debt that may have resulted from the purchase of property on credit or from services rendered by a creditor.
(e) Paid wages in cash, $90.	Money is exchanged for services rendered.

(f) Borrowed $1,000 at a bank giving a 6 percent interest-bearing note due in 30 days.

A liability known as a note payable is incurred in exchange for money.

(g) Purchased office equipment on credit, $200.

A liability known as an account payable is incurred in exchange for office equipment.

Effect of Transactions on the Accounting Equation

Each transaction affects one or more of the three accounting elements. For example, the purchase of equipment for cash represents both an increase and a decrease in assets. The assets are increased because equipment is acquired; the assets are decreased because cash is disbursed. If the equipment were purchased on credit, thereby incurring a liability, the transaction would result in an increase in assets (equipment) with a corresponding increase in liabilities (accounts payable). Neither of these transactions has any effect upon the owner's equity element of the equation.

The effect of any transaction on the accounting elements may be indicated by addition and subtraction. To illustrate: assume that David Bennett, an engineer, decided to go into business for himself. During the first month of this venture (May, 1967), the following transactions relating to his business took place:

An Increase in an Asset Offset by an Increase in Owner's Equity

Transaction (a). Mr. Bennett opened a bank account with a deposit of $3,000. This transaction caused his new business to receive the asset cash, and since no business liabilities were involved, the owner's equity element was increased by the same amount. As a result of this transaction, the equation for the business appears as follows:

$$\left.\begin{array}{c} \underline{\text{ASSETS}} \\ \text{Cash} \\ \text{(a) } 3{,}000 \end{array}\right\} = \left\{\begin{array}{c} \underline{\text{LIABILITIES} + } \end{array}\right. \begin{array}{c} \underline{\text{OWNER'S EQUITY}} \\ \text{David Bennett, Capital} \\ 3{,}000 \end{array}$$

An Increase in an Asset Offset by an Increase in a Liability

Transaction (b). Mr. Bennett purchased office equipment (desk, chairs, file cabinet, etc.) for $2,600 on 30 days' credit. This transaction caused the asset office equipment to increase by $2,600 and resulted in an equal increase in the liability accounts payable. Amending the foregoing equation by this (b) transaction gives the following result:

ASSETS			LIABILITIES	+ OWNER'S EQUITY
Cash +	Office Equipment		Accounts Payable	David Bennett, Capital
Bal. 3,000				3,000
(b)	+2,600	=	+2,600	
Bal. 3,000	2,600		2,600	3,000

An Increase in One Asset Offset by a Decrease in Another Asset

Transaction (c). Mr. Bennett purchased office supplies (stationery, carbon paper, pencils, etc.) for cash, $350. This transaction caused a $350 increase in the asset office supplies that exactly offset the $350 decrease in the asset cash. The effect on the equation is as follows:

	ASSETS			LIABILITIES + OWNER'S EQUITY	
	Office	Office		Accounts	David Bennett,
Cash +	Equipment +	Supplies		Payable	Capital
Bal. 3,000	2,600			2,600	3,000
(c) − 350		+350	=		
Bal. 2,650	2,600	350		2,600	3,000

A Decrease in an Asset Offset by a Decrease in a Liability

Transaction (d). Mr. Bennett paid $1,000 on account to the company from which the office equipment was purchased. (See Transaction (b).) This payment caused the asset cash and the liability accounts payable both to decrease $1,000. The effect on the equation is as follows:

	ASSETS			LIABILITIES + OWNER'S EQUITY	
	Office	Office		Accounts	David Bennett,
Cash +	Equipment +	Supplies		Payable	Capital
Bal. 2,650	2,600	350	=	2,600	3,000
(d) −1,000				−1,000	
Bal. 1,650	2,600	350		1,600	3,000

An Increase in an Asset Offset by an Increase in Owner's Equity Resulting from Revenue

Transaction (e). Mr. Bennett received $900 cash from a client for professional services. This transaction caused the asset cash to increase $900, and since the liabilities were not affected, the owner's equity increased by the same amount. The effect on the equation is as follows:

	ASSETS			LIABILITIES + OWNER'S EQUITY	
	Office	Office		Accounts	David Bennett,
Cash +	Equipment +	Supplies		Payable	Capital
Bal. 1,650	2,600	350	=	1,600	3,000
(e) + 900					+ 900
Bal. 2,550	2,600	350		1,600	3,900

A Decrease in an Asset Offset by a Decrease in Owner's Equity Resulting from Expense

Transaction (f). Mr. Bennett paid $200 for office rent for May. This transaction caused the asset cash to be reduced by $200 with an equal reduction in owner's equity. The effect on the equation is as follows:

ASSETS				LIABILITIES + OWNER'S EQUITY	
	Office	Office		Accounts	David Bennett,
Cash +	Equipment +	Supplies		Payable	Capital
Bal. 2,550	2,600	350	=	1,600	3,900
(f) − 200					− 200
Bal. 2,350	2,600	350		1,600	3,700

Transaction (g). Mr. Bennett paid a bill for telephone service, $21. This transaction, like the previous one, caused a decrease in the asset cash with an equal decrease in owner's equity. The effect on the equation is as follows:

ASSETS				LIABILITIES + OWNER'S EQUITY	
	Office	Office		Accounts	David Bennett,
Cash +	Equipment +	Supplies		Payable	Capital
Bal. 2,350	2,600	350	=	1,600	3,700
(g) − 21					− 21
Bal. 2,329	2,600	350		1,600	3,679

The Financial Statements

A set of accounting records is maintained to fill a variety of needs. Foremost is its use as source data in preparing various reports including those referred to as *financial statements*. The two most important of these are the *income statement* and the *balance sheet*.

The Income Statement. The income statement, sometimes called a *profit and loss statement* or *operating statement*, shows the *net income (net profit)* or *net loss* for a specified period of time and how it was calculated. A very simple income statement relating to the business of David Bennett for the first month's operation, May, 1967, is shown below. The information it contains was obtained by analysis of the changes in the owner's equity element of the business for the month. This element went from zero to $3,679. Part of this increase, $3,000, was due to the investment of Mr. Bennett. The remainder of the increase, $679, must have been due to net income, since Mr. Bennett had made no withdrawals. Transaction (e) involved revenue of $900; transactions (f) and (g) involved expenses of $200 and $21, respectively. Taken together, these three transactions explain the net income of $679.

DAVID BENNETT, ENGINEER
Income Statement
For the Month of May, 1967

Professional fees......................		$900
Expenses:		
Rent expense........................	$200	
Telephone expense...................	21	221
Net income for month....................		$679

The Balance Sheet. The balance sheet, sometimes called a *statement of financial condition* or *statement of financial position*, shows the assets, liabilities, and owner's equity of a business at a specified date. A balance sheet for Mr. Bennett's business as of May 31, 1967, is shown below. The information it contains was obtained from the accounting equation after the last (g) transaction.

DAVID BENNETT, ENGINEER
Balance Sheet
May 31, 1967

Assets		Liabilities	
Cash......................	$2,329	Accounts payable..........	$1,600
Office supplies............	350	Owner's Equity	
Office equipment..........	2,600	David Bennett, capital.......	3,679
	$5,279		$5,279

NOTE: In order to keep the illustrations of transaction analysis, the income statement, and the balance sheet as simple as possible at this point, two expenses were ignored, namely, office supplies used and depreciation of office equipment.

Report No. 1

A workbook is provided for use with this textbook. Each practice assignment in the workbook is referred to as a report. The work involved in completing Report No. 1 requires a knowledge of the principles developed in the preceding study assignment. Before proceeding with the following assignment, complete Report No. 1 in accordance with the instructions given in the workbook.

the double-entry mechanism

The meanings of the terms asset, liability, and owner's equity were explained in the preceding pages. Examples were given to show how each business transaction causes a change in one or more of the three accounting elements. The first transaction (a) shown on page 7 involved an increase in an asset with a corresponding increase in owner's equity. In the second transaction (b), an increase in an asset caused an equal increase in a liability. In the third transaction (c), an increase in one asset was offset by a decrease in another. In each of the transactions illustrated, there was this *dual effect*. This is always true. A change (increase or decrease) in any asset, any liability, or in owner's equity is always accompanied by an offsetting change within the accounting elements.

The fact that each transaction has two aspects — a dual effect upon the accounting elements — provides the basis for what is called *double-entry bookkeeping*. This phrase describes a recording system that involves the making of a record of each of the two aspects that are involved in every transaction. Double entry does not mean that a transaction is recorded twice; instead, it means that both of the two aspects of each transaction are recorded.

The technique of double entry is described and illustrated in the following pages. This method of recording transactions is not new. Double entry is known to have been practiced for at least 500 years. This long popularity is easily explained since the method has several virtues. It is orderly, fairly simple, and very flexible. There is no transaction that cannot be recorded in a double-entry manner. Double entry promotes accuracy. Its use makes it impossible for certain types of errors to remain undetected for very long. For example, if one aspect of a transaction is properly recorded but the other part is overlooked, it will soon be found that the records are "out of balance." The bookkeeper then knows that something is wrong and can check his work to discover the trouble and can make the needed correction.

The Account

It has been explained previously that the assets of a business may consist of a number of items, such as money, accounts receivable, notes receivable, merchandise, equipment, buildings, and land. The liabilities may consist of one or more items, such as accounts payable and notes payable. A separate record should be kept of each asset and of each liability. Later it will be shown that a separate record should also be kept of the increases and decreases in owner's equity. The form of record kept for each item is known as an _account_. There are many types of account forms in general use. They may be ruled on sheets of paper and bound in book form or kept in a loose-leaf binder, or they may be ruled on cards and kept in a file of some sort. Following is an illustration of a standard form of account that is widely used:

ACCOUNT									ACCOUNT NO.	
DATE	ITEMS	POST. REF.	✓	DEBITS	DATE	ITEMS	POST. REF.	✓	CREDITS	

Standard Form of Account

This account form is designed to facilitate the recording of the essential information regarding each transaction that affects the account. Before any entries are recorded in an account, the title and number of the account should be written on the horizontal line at the top of the form. Each account should be given an appropriate title that will indicate whether it is an asset, a liability, or an owner's equity account. The standard account form is divided into two equal parts or sections which are ruled identically to facilitate recording increases and decreases. The left side is called the debit side, while the right side is called the credit side. The columnar arrangement and headings of the columns on both sides are the same except that the amount column on the left is headed "Debits" while that on the right is headed "Credits." The Date columns are used for recording the dates of transactions. The Items columns may be used for writing a brief description of a transaction when deemed necessary. The Posting Reference columns and the (√) columns will be discussed later. The Debits and Credits columns are used for recording the amounts of transactions.

The three major parts of the standard account form are **(1)** the title (and, usually, the account number), **(2)** the debit side, and **(3)** the credit side. To determine the balance of an account at any time, it is necessary only to total the amounts in the Debits and Credits columns, and calculate the difference between the two totals. To save time, a "T" form of account is commonly used for instructional purposes. It consists of a two-line drawing resembling the capital letter T and is sometimes referred to as a skeleton form of account.

TITLE

Debit side	Credit side

"T" Account Form

Debits and Credits

To debit an account means to record an amount on the left or debit side of the account. To credit an account means to record an amount on the right or credit side of the account. The abbreviation for debit is Dr. and for credit Cr. Sometimes the word _charge_ is used as a substitute for debit. Increases in assets are recorded on the left side of the accounts; increases in liabilities and in owner's equity are recorded on the right side of the accounts. Decreases in assets are recorded on the right side of the accounts; decreases in liabilities and in owner's equity are recorded on the left side of the accounts. Recording increases and decreases in the accounts in this manner will reflect the basic equality of assets to liabilities plus owner's equity; at the same time it will maintain equality between the total amounts debited to all accounts and the total amounts credited to all accounts. These basic relationships may be illustrated in the following manner:

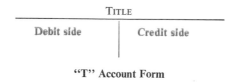

ASSETS	=	LIABILITIES + OWNER'S EQUITY
DEBITS	=	CREDITS

ASSET ACCOUNTS		LIABILITY ACCOUNTS	
Debit to record increases (+)	Credit to record decreases (−)	Debit to record decreases (−)	Credit to record increases (+)

		OWNER'S EQUITY ACCOUNTS	
		Debit to record decreases (−)	Credit to record increases (+)

Use of Asset, Liability, and Owner's Equity Accounts

To illustrate the application of the double-entry process, the transactions discussed on pages 7–9 will be analyzed and their effect on the accounting elements will be indicated by showing the proper entries in "T" accounts. As before, the transactions are identified by letters; dates are omitted intentionally.

An Increase in an Asset Offset by an Increase in Owner's Equity

Transaction (a). David Bennett, an engineer, started a business of his own and invested $3,000 in cash.

CASH		DAVID BENNETT, CAPITAL	
(a) 3,000			(a) 3,000

Analysis: As a result of this transaction the business acquired an asset, cash. The amount of money invested by Mr. Bennett represents his equity in the business; thus the amount of the asset cash is equal to the owner's equity in the business. Separate accounts are kept for the asset cash and for the owner. To record the transaction properly, the cash account was debited and David Bennett's capital account was credited for $3,000.

An Increase in an Asset Offset by an Increase in a Liability

Transaction (b). Purchased office equipment (desk, chairs, file cabinet, etc.) for $2,600 on 30 days' credit.

OFFICE EQUIPMENT		ACCOUNTS PAYABLE	
(b) 2,600			(b) 2,600

Analysis: As a result of this transaction the business acquired a new asset, office equipment. The debt incurred as a result of purchasing the office equipment on 30 days' credit is a liability, accounts payable. Separate accounts are kept for office equipment and for accounts payable. The purchase of office equipment caused an increase in the assets of the business. Therefore, the asset account Office Equipment was debited for $2,600. The purchase also caused an increase in a liability. Therefore, the liability account Accounts Payable was credited for $2,600.

An Increase in One Asset Offset by a Decrease in Another Asset

Transaction (c). Purchased office and drawing supplies (stationery, carbon paper, pencils, etc.) for cash, $350.

CASH				OFFICE SUPPLIES	
(a)	3,000	(c)	350	(c)	350

Analysis: As a result of this transaction the business acquired a new asset, office supplies. However, the addition of this asset was offset by a decrease in the asset cash. To record the transaction properly, Office Supplies was debited and Cash was credited for $350. (It will be noted that this is the second entry in the cash account; the account was previously debited for $3,000 when Transaction (a) was recorded.)

It is proper to record office supplies as an asset at time of purchase even though they will become an expense when consumed. The procedure in accounting for supplies consumed will be discussed later.

A Decrease in an Asset Offset by a Decrease in a Liability

Transaction (d). Paid $1,000 "on account" to the company from which the office equipment was purchased. (See Transaction (b).)

CASH				ACCOUNTS PAYABLE			
(a)	3,000	(c)	350	(d)	1,000	(b)	2,600
		(d)	1,000				

Analysis: This transaction resulted in a decrease in the liability accounts payable with a corresponding decrease in the asset cash; hence, it was recorded by debiting Accounts Payable and by crediting Cash for $1,000. (It will be noted that this is the second entry in the accounts payable account and the third entry in the cash account.)

Revenue and Expense

The owner's equity element of a business or professional enterprise may be increased in two ways as follows:

(a) The owner may invest additional money or other property in the enterprise. Such investments result in an increase in both the assets of the enterprise and in the owner's equity, but they do not further enrich the owner; he merely has more property invested in the enterprise and less property outside of the enterprise.

(b) Revenue may be derived from sales of goods or services, or from other sources.

As used in accounting, the term _revenue_ refers to an increase in the owner's equity in a business resulting from transactions of any kind except the investment of assets in the business by its owner. In most cases, the increase in owner's equity due to revenue results from an addition to the assets without any change in the liabilities. Often it is cash that is increased. However, an increase in cash and other assets can occur in connection with several types of transactions that do not involve revenue. For this reason, revenue is defined in terms of the change in owner's equity rather than the change in assets. Any transaction that causes owner's equity to increase, except investments in the business by its owner, involves revenue.

The owner's equity element of a business or professional enterprise may be decreased in two ways as follows:

(a) The owner may withdraw assets (cash or other property) from the enterprise.

(b) Expenses may be incurred in operating the enterprise.

As used in accounting, the term _expense_ means a decrease in the owner's equity in a business caused by a transaction other than a withdrawal by the owner. When an expense is incurred, either the assets are reduced or the liabilities are increased. In either event, owner's equity is reduced. If the transaction causing the reduction was not a withdrawal of assets by the owner, an expense was incurred. Common examples of expense are rent of office or store, salaries of employees, telephone service, supplies consumed, and many types of taxes.

If, during a specified period of time, the total increases in owner's equity resulting from revenue exceed the total decreases resulting from expenses, it may be said that the excess represents the _net income_ or net profit for the period. On the other hand, if the expenses of the period exceed the revenue, such excess represents a _net loss_ for the period. The time interval used in the measurement of net income or net loss can be chosen by the owner. It may be a month, a quarter (three months), a year, or some other period of time. If the accounting period is a year, it is usually referred to as a _fiscal year_. The fiscal year frequently coincides with the _calendar year_.

Transactions involving revenue and expense always cause a change in the owner's equity element of an enterprise. Such changes could be recorded by debiting the owner's equity account for expenses and crediting it for revenue. If this practice were followed, however, the credit side of the owner's equity account would contain a mixture of increases due to revenue and to the investment of assets in the business by the owner, while the debit side would contain a mixture of decreases due to expenses and to the withdrawal of assets from the business by the owner. In order to calculate the net income or the net loss for each accounting period, a careful analysis of the owner's equity account would be required. It is, therefore, better practice to record revenue and expenses in separate accounts. These are called *temporary* owner's equity accounts because it is customary to close them at the end of each accounting period by transferring their balances to a *summary* account. The balance of this summary account then represents the net income or net loss for the period. The summary account is also a temporary account which is closed by transferring its balance to the owner's equity account.

A separate account should be kept for each type of revenue and for each type of expense. When a transaction produces revenue, the amount of the revenue should be credited to an appropriate revenue account. When a transaction involves expense, the amount of the expense should be debited to an appropriate expense account. The relationship of these temporary accounts to the owner's equity account and the application of the debit and credit theory to the accounts are indicated in the following diagram:

OWNER'S EQUITY ACCOUNT

Debit to record decreases (−)	Credit to record increases (+)

EXPENSE ACCOUNTS		REVENUE ACCOUNTS	
Debit to record increases (+)	Credit to record decreases (−)	Debit to record decreases (−)	Credit to record increases (+)

It is important to recognize that the credit side of each revenue account is serving temporarily as a part of the credit side of the owner's equity account. Increases in owner's equity are recorded as credits. Thus, increases in owner's equity resulting from revenue should be credited to revenue accounts. The debit side of each expense account is serving temporarily as a part of the debit side of the owner's equity account. Decreases in owner's equity are recorded as debits. Thus, decreases in owner's equity resulting from expense should be debited to expense accounts.

Use of Revenue and Expense Accounts

To illustrate the application of the double-entry process in recording transactions that affect revenue and expense accounts, the additional transactions completed by David Bennett, an engineer, will be analyzed and their effect on the accounting elements will be indicated by showing the proper entries in "T" accounts. These transactions represent a continuation of the transactions completed by David Bennett in the conduct of his business. (See pages 14 and 15 for Transactions (a) to (d).)

An Increase in an Asset Offset by an Increase in Owner's Equity Resulting from Revenue

Transaction (e). Received $900 in cash from a client for professional services rendered.

	CASH				PROFESSIONAL FEES	
(a)	3,000	(c)	350		(e)	900
(e)	900	(d)	1,000			

Analysis: This transaction resulted in an increase in the asset cash with a corresponding increase in owner's equity because of revenue from professional fees. To record the transaction properly, Cash was debited and an appropriate account for the revenue was credited for $900. Accounts should always be given a descriptive title that will aid in classifying them in relation to the accounting elements. In this case the revenue account was given the title Professional Fees. (It will be noted that this is the fourth entry in the cash account and the first entry in the account Professional Fees.)

A Decrease in an Asset Offset by a Decrease in Owner's Equity Resulting from Expense

Transaction (f). Paid $200 for office rent for one month.

	CASH				RENT EXPENSE	
(a)	3,000	(c)	350	(f)	200	
(e)	900	(d)	1,000			
		(f)	200			

Analysis: This transaction resulted in a decrease in the asset cash with a corresponding decrease in owner's equity because of expense. To record the transaction properly, Rent Expense was debited and Cash was credited for $200. (This is the first entry in the rent expense account and the fifth entry in the cash account.)

Transaction (g). Paid bill for telephone service, $21.

	CASH				TELEPHONE EXPENSE	
(a)	3,000	(c)	350	(g)	21	
(e)	900	(d)	1,000			
		(f)	200			
		(g)	21			

Analysis: This transaction is identical with the previous one except that telephone expense rather than rent expense was the reason for the decrease in owner's equity. To record the transaction properly, Telephone Expense was debited and Cash was credited for $21.

The Trial Balance

It is a fundamental principle of double-entry bookkeeping that the amount of the assets is always equal to the sum of the liabilities and owner's equity. In order to maintain this equality in recording transactions, the sum of the debit entries must always be equal to the sum of the credit entries. To determine whether this equality has been maintained, it is customary to take a trial balance periodically. A *trial balance* is a list of all of the accounts showing the title and balance of each account. The balance of any account is the difference between the total debits and the total credits to the account. Preliminary to taking a trial balance, the debit and credit amounts in each account should be totaled. This is called *footing* the amount columns. If there is only one item entered in a column, no footing is necessary. To find the balance of an account it is necessary only to determine the difference between the footings by subtraction. Since asset and expense accounts are debited for increases, these accounts normally have *debit balances*. Since liability, owner's equity, and revenue accounts are credited to record increases, these accounts normally have *credit balances*. The balance of an account should be entered on the side of the account that has the larger total. The footings and balances of accounts should be written in small figures just below the last entry. A pencil is generally used for this purpose. If the footings of an account are equal in amount the account is said to be *in balance*.

The accounts of David Bennett are reproduced below. To show the relationship to the fundamental accounting equation, the accounts are arranged in three columns under the headings of Assets, Liabilities, and Owner's Equity. It will be noted that the cash account has been footed and the balance inserted on the left side. The footings and the balance are printed in italics. It was not necessary to foot any of the other accounts

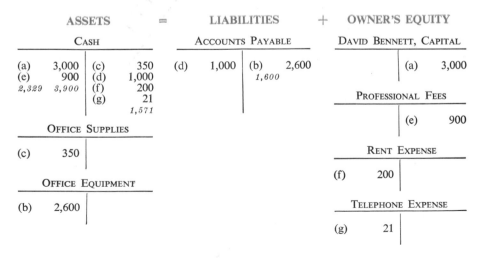

because none of them contained more than one entry on either side. The balance of the accounts payable account is shown on the credit side in italics. It was not necessary to enter the balances of the other accounts because there were entries on only one side of the accounts.

A trial balance of these accounts is shown below. The trial balance was taken on May 31, 1967; therefore this date is shown in the third line of the heading. The trial balance reveals that the debit and credit totals are equal in amount. This is proof that in recording Transactions (a) to (g) inclusive the total of the debits was equal to the total of the credits.

David Bennett, Engineer
Trial Balance
May 31, 1967

Account	Dr. Balance	Cr. Balance
Cash	2329 00	
Office Supplies	350 00	
Office Equipment	2600 00	
Accounts Payable		1600 00
David Bennett, Capital		3000 00
Professional Fees		900 00
Rent Expense	200 00	
Telephone Expense	21 00	
	5500 00	5500 00

A trial balance is not a formal statement or report. Normally, it is never seen by anyone except the accountant or bookkeeper. It is used to aid in preparing the income statement and the balance sheet. If the above trial balance is studied in conjunction with the income statement and balance sheet shown on pages 9 and 10, it will be seen that those statements could have been prepared quite easily from the information that this trial balance provides.

Report No. 2

Refer to the workbook and complete Report No. 2 in accordance with the instructions given therein. The work involved in completing the assignment requires a knowledge of the principles developed in the preceding discussion. Any difficulty experienced in completing the report will indicate a lack of understanding of these principles. In such event further study should be helpful. After completing the report, you may continue with the textbook discussion in Chapter 2 until the next report is required.

chapter two

accounting procedure

The principles of double-entry bookkeeping were explained and illustrated in the preceding pages. To avoid distraction from the fundamentals, the mechanics of collecting and classifying information about business transactions were ignored. In actual practice the first record of a transaction (sometimes called the "immediate record") is made in the form of a business paper, such as a check stub, receipt, cash register tape, sales ticket, or purchase invoice. The information supplied by business papers is an aid in analyzing transactions to determine their effect upon the accounts.

journalizing transactions

The first formal double-entry record of a transaction is usually made in a record called a *journal* (frequently in book form). The act of recording transactions in a journal is called *journalizing*. It is necessary to analyze each transaction before it can be journalized properly. The purpose of the journal entries is to provide a chronological record of all transactions completed showing the date of each transaction, titles of accounts to be debited and credited, and amounts of the debits and credits. The journal then provides all the information needed to record the debits and credits in the proper accounts. The flow of data concerning transactions can be illustrated in the following manner:

Transactions are evidenced by various
BUSINESS PAPERS————→The business papers provide the information needed to record the transactions in a
JOURNAL————→The journal provides the information needed to record the debits and credits in the accounts which collectively comprise a
LEDGER

Business Papers

The term business papers covers a wide variety of forms and documents. Almost any document that provides information about a business transaction can be called a business paper.

BUSINESS PAPERS

Examples:	Provide Information about:
(a) Check stubs or carbon copies of checks	Cash disbursements
(b) Receipt stubs, or carbon copies of receipts, cash register tapes, or memos of cash register totals	Cash receipts
(c) Copies of sales tickets or sales invoices issued to customers or clients	Sales of goods or services
(d) Purchase invoices received from vendors	Purchases of goods or services

The Journal

While the original record of a transaction usually is a business paper as explained above, the first formal double-entry record of a transaction is made in a journal. For this reason a journal is commonly referred to as a *book of original entry*. The ruling of the pages of a journal varies with the type and size of an enterprise and the nature of its operations. The simplest form of journal is a two-column journal. A standard form of such a journal is illustrated on page 23. It is referred to as a two-column journal because it has only two amount columns, one for debits and one for credits. In the illustration the columns have been numbered as a means of identification in connection with the following discussion.

DATE	DESCRIPTION	POST. REF.	DEBITS	CREDITS
①	②	③	④	⑤

Standard Two-Column Journal

Column No. 1 is a date column. The year should be written in small figures at the top of the column immediately below the column heading and need only be repeated at the top of each new page unless an entry for a new year is made farther down on the page. The date column is a double column, the perpendicular single rule being used to separate the month from the day. Thus in writing June 20, the name of the month should be written to the left of the single line and the number designating the day of the month should be written to the right of this line. The name of the month need only be shown for the first entry on a page unless an entry for a new month is made farther down on the page.

Column No. 2 is generally referred to as a description or an explanation column. It is used to record the titles of the accounts affected by each transaction, together with a description of the transaction. Two or more accounts are affected by each transaction, and the titles of all accounts affected must be recorded. Normally the titles of the accounts debited are written first and then the titles of the accounts credited. A separate line should be used for each account title. The titles of the accounts to be debited are generally written at the extreme left of the column, while the titles of the accounts to be credited are usually indented about one-half inch. The description should be written immediately following the credit entry, and usually is indented an additional one-half inch. Reference to the journal reproduced on pages 29 and 30 will help to visualize the arrangement of the copy in the Description column. An orderly arrangement is desirable.

Column No. 3 is a posting reference column — sometimes referred to as a folio column. No entries are made in this column at the time of journalizing the transactions; such entries are made only at the time of posting (which is the process of entering the debits and credits in the proper accounts in the ledger). This procedure will be explained in detail later in this chapter.

Column No. 4 is an amount column in which the amount that is to be debited to any account should be written on the line on which the title of the account appears. In other words, the name of the account to be debited should be written in the Description column and the amount of the debit entry should be written on the same line in the Debits column.

Column No. 5 is an amount column in which the amount that is to be credited to any account should be written on the line on which the title of the account appears. In other words, the name of the account to be credited should be written in the Description column and the amount of the credit entry should be written on the same line in the Credits column.

Journalizing

Journalizing involves recording the desired information concerning each transaction either (**1**) at the time the transaction occurs or (**2**) subsequently, but in the chronological order in which the transactions occurred. For every transaction the entry should record the date, the title of each account affected, the amount, and a brief description. The only effect a transaction can have on any account is either to increase or to decrease the balance of the account. Before a transaction can be recorded properly, therefore, it must be analyzed in order to determine:

(a) Which accounts are affected by the transaction.
(b) What effect the transaction has upon each of the accounts involved; that is, whether the balance of each affected account is increased or decreased.

The Chart of Accounts

In analyzing a transaction preparatory to journalizing it, the accountant or bookkeeper must know which accounts are being kept. When an accounting system is being established for a new business, the first step is to decide which accounts are required. The accounts used will depend upon the information needed or desired. Ordinarily it will be found desirable to keep a separate account for each type of asset and each type of liability, since it is certain that information will be desired in regard to what is owned and what is owed. A permanent owner's equity or capital account should be kept in order that information may be available as to the owner's interest or equity in the business. Furthermore, it is advisable to keep separate accounts for each type of revenue and each kind of expense. The revenue and expense accounts are the temporary accounts that are used in recording increases and decreases in owner's equity apart from changes caused by the owner's investments and withdrawals. The specific accounts to be kept for recording the increases and the decreases in owner's equity depend

Journalizing Procedure Illustrated

To illustrate journalizing procedure, the transactions completed by The Whitman Advertising Agency through December 31, 1967, will be journalized. A *narrative* of the transactions follows. It provides all of the information that is needed in journalizing the transactions. Some of the transactions are analyzed to explain their effect upon the accounts, with the journal entry immediately following the explanation of the entry. The journal of The Whitman Advertising Agency with all of the entries recorded is reproduced on pages 29 and 30.

THE WHITMAN ADVERTISING AGENCY

NARRATIVE OF TRANSACTIONS

Thursday, November 30, 1967

Mr. Whitman invested $1,500 cash in a business enterprise to be known as The Whitman Advertising Agency.

> As a result of this transaction, the business acquired the asset cash in the amount of $1,500. Since neither a decrease in any other asset nor an increase in any liability was involved, the transaction caused an increase of $1,500 in owner's equity. Accordingly, the entry to record the transaction is a debit to Cash and a credit to C. D. Whitman, Capital, for $1,500.

	JOURNAL			PAGE *1*
DATE	DESCRIPTION	POST. REF.	DEBITS	CREDITS
1967 Nov. 30	Cash		150000	
	C. D. Whitman, Capital			150000
	Original investment in			
	advertising agency.			

Note that the following steps were involved:

(a) Since this was the first entry on the journal page, the year was written at the top of the Date column.

(b) The month and day were written on the first line in the Date column.

(c) The title of the account to be debited, Cash, was written on the first line at the extreme left of the Description column. The amount of the debit, $1,500, was written on the same line in the Debits column.

(d) The title of the account to be credited, C. D. Whitman, Capital, was written on the second line indented one-half inch from the left side of the Description column. The amount of the credit, $1,500, was written on the same line in the Credits column.

(e) The explanation of the entry was started on the next line indented an additional one-half inch. The second line of the explanation was also indented the same distance as the first.

Friday, December 1

Paid office rent for December in advance, $200.

upon the nature and the sources of the revenue and of the expenses incurred in earning the revenue.

A professional man or an individual engaged in operating a small enterprise may need to keep relatively few accounts. On the other hand, a large manufacturing enterprise, a public utility, or any large business may need to keep a great many accounts in order that the information required or desired may be available. Regardless of the number of accounts kept, they can be segregated into the three general classes and should be grouped according to these classes in the ledger. The usual custom is to place the asset accounts first, the liability accounts second, and the owner's equity accounts, including the revenue and the expense accounts, last. It is common practice to prepare a list of the accounts that are to be kept. This list, often in the form of an outline, is called a *chart of accounts.* It has become a general practice to give each account a number and to keep the accounts in numerical order. The numbering usually follows a consistent pattern and becomes a *code*. For example, asset accounts may be assigned numbers that always start with "1," liability accounts with "2," owner's equity accounts with "3," revenue accounts with "4," and expense accounts with "5."

To illustrate: Suppose that on November 30, 1967, C. D. Whitman engages in the advertising business under the name of The Whitman Advertising Agency. He decides to keep his accounts on the calendar year basis; therefore, his first accounting period will be for one month only, that is, the month of December. It is decided that a two-column journal and a ledger with standard form of account will be used. Mr. Whitman realizes that he will not need many accounts at present because the business is new. He also realizes that additional accounts may be added as the need arises. Following is a chart of the accounts to be kept at the start:

THE WHITMAN ADVERTISING AGENCY

CHART OF ACCOUNTS

*Assets**
11 Cash
12 Office Supplies
13 Office Equipment

Liabilities
21 Accounts Payable

Owner's Equity
31 C. D. Whitman, Capital
32 C. D. Whitman, Drawing

Revenue
41 Advertising Fees

Expenses
51 Rent Expense
52 Salary Expense
53 Traveling Expense
54 Telephone Expense
55 Office Supplies Expense
56 Miscellaneous Expense

*Words in italics represent headings and not account titles.

This transaction resulted in a decrease in owner's equity because of expense, with a corresponding decrease in the asset cash. The transaction is recorded by debiting Rent Expense and by crediting Cash for $200.

Dec. 1	Rent Expense		200 00	
	Cash			200 00
	Paid December rent.			

Note: Mr. Whitman ordered several pieces of office equipment. Since the dealer did not have in stock what Mr. Whitman wanted, the articles were ordered from the factory. Delivery is not expected until the latter part of the month. Pending their arrival, the dealer loaned Mr. Whitman some used office equipment. No entry is required until the new equipment is received.

Monday, December 4

Purchased office supplies from the Central Supply Co. on account, $183.14.

In this transaction the business acquired a new asset which represented an increase in the total assets. A liability was also incurred because of the purchase on account. The transaction is recorded by debiting Office Supplies and by crediting Accounts Payable for $183.14. As these supplies are consumed, they will become an expense of the business.

4	Office Supplies		183 14	
	Accounts Payable			183 14
	Central Supply Co.			

Tuesday, December 5

Paid the City Telephone Co. $22.50 covering the cost of installing a telephone in the office, together with the first month's service charges payable in advance.

This transaction caused a decrease in owner's equity because of expense and a corresponding decrease in the asset cash. The transaction is recorded by debiting Telephone Expense and by crediting Cash for $22.50.

5	Telephone Expense		22 50	
	Cash			22 50
	Paid telephone bill.			

Wednesday, December 6

Paid $6 for a subscription to a trade journal.

This transaction resulted in a decrease in owner's equity due to expense and a corresponding decrease in the asset cash. The transaction is recorded by debiting Miscellaneous Expense and by crediting Cash for $6.

6	Miscellaneous Expense		6 00	
	Cash			6 00
	Trade journal subscription.			

Thursday, December 7

Received $125 from the City Hardware Co. for services rendered.

This transaction resulted in an increase in the asset cash with a corresponding increase in owner's equity because of revenue from advertising fees. The transaction is recorded by debiting Cash and by crediting Advertising Fees for $125. In keeping his accounts Mr. Whitman follows the practice of not recording revenue until it is received in cash. This practice is common to professional and personal service enterprises.

7	Cash		125 00		
	Advertising Fees			125 00	
	City Hardware Co.				

Note: The Posting Reference column has been left blank in the six foregoing journal entry illustrations. This is because the column is not used until the amounts are posted to the accounts in the ledger, a process to be described starting on page 31. Account numbers are shown in the Posting Reference column of the journal illustrated on pages 29–30, since the illustration shows how the journal appears *after* the posting has been completed.

The journal entries for the following transactions are illustrated on pages 29–30.

Monday, December 11

Paid the Brown Travel Service $128.30 for a plane ticket to be used the next week for a business trip.

Friday, December 15

Paid Mary Bergstrom $175 covering her salary for the first half of the month.

Miss Bergstrom is employed by Mr. Whitman as his secretary and bookkeeper at a salary of $350 a month. The transaction resulted in a decrease in owner's equity because of salary expense with a corresponding decrease in the asset cash. The transaction is recorded by debiting Salary Expense and by crediting Cash for $175. (The matter of payroll taxes is purposely ignored at this point. These taxes will be discussed in detail in Chapter 4.)

Monday, December 18

Received $365 from The Morton Manufacturing Co. in payment for services rendered.

Wednesday, December 20

Mr. Whitman withdrew $300 for personal use.

Amounts of cash withdrawn for personal use by the owner of a business enterprise represent a decrease in owner's equity. Although amounts withdrawn might be recorded as debits to the owner's capital account, it is better practice to record withdrawals in a separate account. Doing it in this way makes it a little easier to summarize the decreases in owner's equity caused by the owner's withdrawals. This transaction is recorded in the journal by debiting C. D. Whitman, Drawing, and by crediting Cash for $300.

Friday, December 22

Received $520 from Mid-Town Sales Co. for services rendered.

DATE	DESCRIPTION	POST. REF.	DEBITS	CREDITS
1967 Nov. 30	Cash	11	1 50 00	
	C. D. Whitman, Capital	31		1 50 00
	Original investment in			
	advertising agency.			
Dec. 1	Rent Expense	51	200 00	
	Cash	11		200 00
	Paid December rent.			
4	Office Supplies	12	1 83 14	
	Accounts Payable	21		1 83 14
	Central Supply Co.			
5	Telephone Expense	54	22 50	
	Cash	11		22 50
	Paid telephone bill.			
6	Miscellaneous Expense	56	6 00	
	Cash	11		6 00
	Trade journal subscription.			
7	Cash	11	1 25 00	
	Advertising Fees	41		1 25 00
	City Hardware Co.			
11	Traveling Expense	53	1 28 30	
	Cash	11		1 28 30
	Plane fare – business trip.			
15	Salary Expense	52	1 75 00	
	Cash	11		1 75 00
	Paid secretary's salary.			
18	Cash	11	3 65 00	
	Advertising Fees	41		3 65 00
	The Morton Mfg. Co.			
20	C. D. Whitman, Drawing	32	3 00 00	
	Cash	11		3 00 00
	Withdrawn for personal use.			
22	Cash	11	5 20 00	
	Advertising Fees	41		5 20 00
	Mid-Town Sales Co.			
26	Miscellaneous Expense	56	30 00	
	Cash	11		30 00
	N A A A dues.			
27	Office Equipment	13	2 37 2 21	
	Accounts Payable	21		2 37 2 21
	Acme Office Equipment Co.		5 9 27 15	5 9 27 15

The Whitman Advertising Agency Journal

DATE	DESCRIPTION	POST. REF.	DEBITS	CREDITS
1967 Dec. 28	Accounts Payable	21	18314	
	Cash	11		18314
	Central Supply Co.			
28	Cash	11	35000	
	Advertising Fees	41		35000
	Gordon Downey.			
29	Salary Expense	52	17500	
	Cash	11		17500
	Paid secretary's salary.			
29	Office Supplies Expense	55	2000	
	Office Supplies	12		2000
	Cost of supplies used			
	during December.		72814	72814

The Whitman Advertising Agency Journal

Note: Some bookkeepers leave a blank line after the explanation of each entry. This practice is acceptable though not recommended.

Tuesday, December 26

Paid $30 membership dues in the National Association of Advertising Agencies.

Wednesday, December 27

Received the office equipment ordered December 1. These items were purchased on account from the Acme Office Equipment Co. Cost: $2,372.21. The dealer removed the used equipment that had been loaned to Mr. Whitman.

Thursday, December 28

Paid the Central Supply Co. $183.14 for the office supplies purchased on December 4.

This transaction caused a decrease in the liability accounts payable with a corresponding decrease in the asset cash. The transaction was recorded by debiting Accounts Payable and by crediting Cash for $183.14.

Received $350 from Gordon Downey for services rendered.

Friday, December 29

Paid Mary Bergstrom $175 covering her salary for the second half of the month. (Paid this day since it is the last working day of the month.)

Office supplies used during the month, $20.

By referring to the transaction of December 4 it will be noted that office supplies amounting to $183.14 were purchased and were recorded as an asset. By taking an inventory, counting the supplies in stock at the end of the month, Mr. Whitman was able to determine that the cost of supplies used during the month amounted to $20. The expenses for the month of December would not be reflected properly in the accounts if the supplies used during the month were not taken into consideration. Therefore, the cost of supplies used was recorded by debiting the expense account, Office Supplies Expense, and by crediting the asset account, Office Supplies, for $20.

Proving the Journal

Because a double entry is made for each transaction, the equality of debit and credit entries on each page of the journal may be proved merely by totaling the amount columns. The total of each column is usually entered as a footing immediately under the last entry. When a page of the journal is filled, the footings may be entered just under the last single horizontal ruled line at the bottom of the page as shown in the illustration on page 29. When the page is not filled, the footings should be entered immediately under the last entry as shown in the illustration on page 30.

Report No. 3

Refer to the workbook and complete Report No. 3. To complete this assignment correctly, the principles developed in the preceding discussion must be understood. Review the text assignment if necessary. After completing the report, continue with the following study assignment until the next report is required.

posting to the ledger; the trial balance

The purpose of a journal is to provide a chronological record of financial transactions expressed as debits and credits to accounts. These accounts are kept to supply desired information. Collectively the accounts are described as the _general ledger_ or, often, simply as "the ledger." (Frequently, so-called "subsidiary" ledgers are also used. These will be explained and illustrated in Chapter 8.)   The account forms may be on sheets of paper or on cards. When on sheets of paper, the sheets may be bound in book form or they may be kept in a loose-leaf binder. Usually a separate page or card is used for each account. The accounts should be classified properly in the ledger, that is, the asset accounts should be grouped together, the liability accounts together, and the owner's equity accounts together. A proper grouping of the accounts in the ledger is an aid in preparing the various reports desired by the owner. Mr. Whitman decided to keep all of the accounts for The Whitman Advertising Agency in a loose-leaf ledger. The numbers shown in the agency's chart of accounts on page 25 were used as a guide in arranging the accounts in the ledger. The ledger of The Whitman Advertising Agency is reproduced on pages 34 and 35. Note that the accounts are in numerical order.

Since Mr. Whitman makes few purchases on account, he does not keep a separate account for each creditor. When invoices are received for items purchased on account, the invoices are checked and recorded in the journal by debiting the proper accounts and by crediting Accounts Payable. The credit balance of Accounts Payable indicates the total amount owed to creditors. After each invoice is recorded, it is filed in an unpaid invoice file, where it remains until it is paid in full. When an invoice is paid in full, it is removed from the unpaid invoice file and is then filed under the name of the creditor for future reference. The balance of the accounts payable account may be proved at any time by determining the total of the unpaid amounts of the invoices.

Posting

The process of recording information in the ledger is known as *posting*. All amounts entered in the journal should be posted to the accounts kept in the ledger in order to summarize the results. Such posting may be done daily or at frequent intervals. The ledger is not a reliable source of information until all the transactions recorded in the journal have been posted.

Since the accounts provide the information needed in preparing financial statements, a posting procedure that will insure accuracy in maintaining the accounts must necessarily be followed. Posting from the journal to the ledger involves recording the following information in the accounts:

(a) The date of each transaction.
(b) The amount of each transaction.
(c) The page of the journal from which each transaction is posted.

As each amount in the journal is posted to the proper account in the ledger, the number of that account should be entered in the Posting Reference column in the journal so as to provide a cross-reference between the journal and the ledger. The first entry to be posted from the journal (a segment of which is reproduced below) required a debit to Cash of $1,500. This was accomplished by entering the year, "1967," the month, abbreviated "Nov.," and the day, "30," in the Date column of the cash account (reproduced below); the number "1" in the Posting Reference column (since the posting came from Page 1 of the journal); and the amount, "1,500.00," in the Debits column. Inasmuch as the number of the cash account is 11, that number was entered in the Posting Reference column of the journal on the same line as the debit of 1,500.00 that was just posted to Cash. The same pattern was followed in posting the credit part of the entry — $1,500 to C. D. Whitman, Capital, Account No. 31 (reproduced below).

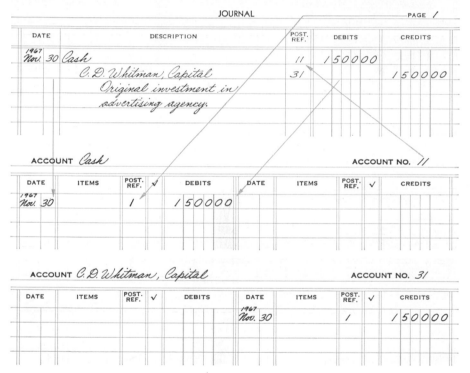

Reference to the journal of The Whitman Advertising Agency (reproduced on pages 29 and 30) and its ledger (reproduced on pages 34 and 35) will indicate that a similar procedure was followed in posting every amount from the journal. Note also that in the ledger, the year "1967" was entered only at the top of each Date column, and that (with the exception of the first posting to Cash and the first posting to C. D. Whitman, Capital, where the month "Nov." was entered) the month "Dec." was entered only with the first posting to an account.

ACCOUNT *Cash*   ACCOUNT NO. 11

DATE	ITEMS	POST. REF.	✓	DEBITS	DATE	ITEMS	POST. REF.	✓	CREDITS
1967 Nov. 30		1		1 5 0 0 0 0	1967 Dec. 1		1		2 0 0 0 0
Dec. 7		1		1 2 5 0 0	5		1		2 2 5 0
18		1		3 6 5 0 0	6		1		6 0 0
22		1		5 2 0 0 0	11		1		1 2 8 3 0
28	1,640.06	2		3 5 0 0 0	15		1		1 7 5 0 0
				2 9 6 0 0 0	20		1		3 0 0 0 0
					26		1		3 0 0 0
					28		2		1 8 3 1 4
					29		2		1 7 5 0 0
									1 2 1 9 9 4

ACCOUNT *Office Supplies*   ACCOUNT NO. 12

DATE	ITEMS	POST. REF.	✓	DEBITS	DATE	ITEMS	POST. REF.	✓	CREDITS
1967 Dec. 4	163.14	1		1 8 3 1 4	1967 Dec. 29		2		2 0 0 0

ACCOUNT *Office Equipment*   ACCOUNT NO. 13

DATE	ITEMS	POST. REF.	✓	DEBITS	DATE	ITEMS	POST. REF.	✓	CREDITS
1967 Dec. 27		1		2 3 7 2 2 1					

ACCOUNT *Accounts Payable*   ACCOUNT NO. 21

DATE	ITEMS	POST. REF.	✓	DEBITS	DATE	ITEMS	POST. REF.	✓	CREDITS
1967 Dec. 28		2		1 8 3 1 4	1967 Dec. 4		1		1 8 3 1 4
					27	2,372.21	1		2 3 7 2 2 1
									2 5 5 5 3 5

ACCOUNT *C. D. Whitman, Capital*   ACCOUNT NO. 31

DATE	ITEMS	POST. REF.	✓	DEBITS	DATE	ITEMS	POST. REF.	✓	CREDITS
					1967 Nov. 30		1		1 5 0 0 0 0

ACCOUNT *C. D. Whitman, Drawing*   ACCOUNT NO. 32

DATE	ITEMS	POST. REF.	✓	DEBITS	DATE	ITEMS	POST. REF.	✓	CREDITS
1967 Dec. 20		1		3 0 0 0 0					

The Whitman Advertising Agency Ledger

ACCOUNT Advertising Fees — ACCOUNT NO. 41

DATE	ITEMS	POST. REF.	✓	DEBITS	DATE	ITEMS	POST. REF.	✓	CREDITS
					1967 Dec. 7		1		1 2 5 0 0
					18		1		3 6 5 0 0
					22		1		5 2 0 0 0
					28		2		3 5 0 0 0
									1 3 6 8 0 0

ACCOUNT Rent Expense — ACCOUNT NO. 51

DATE	ITEMS	POST. REF.	✓	DEBITS	DATE	ITEMS	POST. REF.	✓	CREDITS
1967 Dec. 1		1		2 0 0 0 0					

ACCOUNT Salary Expense — ACCOUNT NO. 52

DATE	ITEMS	POST. REF.	✓	DEBITS	DATE	ITEMS	POST. REF.	✓	CREDITS
1967 Dec. 15		1		1 7 5 0 0					
29		2		1 7 5 0 0					
				3 5 0 0 0					

ACCOUNT Traveling Expense — ACCOUNT NO. 53

DATE	ITEMS	POST. REF.	✓	DEBITS	DATE	ITEMS	POST. REF.	✓	CREDITS
1967 Dec. 11		1		1 2 8 3 0					

ACCOUNT Telephone Expense — ACCOUNT NO. 54

DATE	ITEMS	POST. REF.	✓	DEBITS	DATE	ITEMS	POST. REF.	✓	CREDITS
1967 Dec. 5		1		2 2 5 0					

ACCOUNT Office Supplies Expense — ACCOUNT NO. 55

DATE	ITEMS	POST. REF.	✓	DEBITS	DATE	ITEMS	POST. REF.	✓	CREDITS
1967 Dec. 29		2		2 0 0 0					

ACCOUNT Miscellaneous Expense — ACCOUNT NO. 56

DATE	ITEMS	POST. REF.	✓	DEBITS	DATE	ITEMS	POST. REF.	✓	CREDITS
1967 Dec. 6		1		6 0 0					
26		1		3 0 0 0					
				3 6 0 0					

The Whitman Advertising Agency Ledger

It will be seen from the foregoing discussion that there are four steps involved in posting — three involving information to be recorded in the ledger and one involving information to be recorded in the journal. The date, the amount, and the effect of each transaction are first recorded in the journal. The same information is later posted to the ledger. Posting does not involve an analysis of each transaction to determine its effect upon the accounts. Such an analysis is made at the time of recording the transaction in the journal, and posting is merely transcribing the information in the ledger. In posting, care should be used to record each debit and each credit entry in the proper columns so that the entries will reflect correctly the effects of the transactions on the accounts.

When the posting is completed, the same information is provided in both the journal and the ledger as to the date, the amount, and the effect of each transaction. A cross-reference from each book to the other book is also provided. This cross-reference makes it possible to trace the entry of November 30 on the debit side of the cash account in the ledger to the journal by referring to the page indicated in the Posting Reference column. The entry of November 30 on the credit side of the account for C. D. Whitman, Capital, may also be traced to the journal by referring to the page indicated in the Posting Reference column. Each entry in the journal may be traced to the ledger by referring to the account numbers indicated in the Posting Reference column of the journal. By referring to pages 29 and 30, it will be seen that the account numbers were inserted in the Posting Reference column. This was done as the posting was completed.

The Trial Balance

The purpose of a trial balance is to prove that the totals of the debit and credit balances in the ledger are equal. In double-entry bookkeeping, equality of debit and credit balances in the ledger must be maintained. A trial balance may be taken daily, weekly, monthly, or whenever desired. Before taking a trial balance, all transactions previously completed should be journalized and the posting should be completed in order that the effect of all transactions will be reflected in the ledger accounts.

Footing Accounts. When an account form similar to the one illustrated on page 35 is used, it is necessary to foot or add the amounts recorded in each account preparatory to taking a trial balance. The footings should be recorded immediately below the last item in both the debit and credit amount columns of the account. The footings should be written in small figures close to the preceding line so that they will not interfere with the recording of an item on the next ruled line. At the same time, the balance, the difference between the footings, should be computed and recorded in small figures in the Items column of the account on the side with the larger footing. In other words, if an account has a debit balance, the balance should be written in the Items column on the debit or left side of the account. If the account has a credit balance, the balance should be written in the Items column on the credit or right side of the account. The balance or difference between the footings should be recorded in the Items column just below the line on which the last regular entry appears and in line with the footing.

Reference to the accounts kept in the ledger shown on pages 34 and 35 will reveal that the accounts have been footed and will show how the footings and the balances are recorded. When only one item has been posted to an account, regardless of whether it is a debit or a credit amount, no footing is necessary.

Care should be used in computing the balances of the accounts. If an error is made in adding the columns or in determining the difference between the footings, the error will be carried to the trial balance, and considerable time may be required to locate the mistake. Most accounting errors result from carelessness. For example, a careless bookkeeper may write an account balance on the wrong side of an account or may enter figures so illegibly that they may be misread later. Neatness in writing the amounts is just as important as accuracy in determining the footings and the balances.

Preparing the Trial Balance. It is important that the following procedure be followed in preparing a trial balance:

(a) Head the trial balance, being certain to show the name of the individual, firm, or organization, and the date. (The date shown is the day of the last transaction that is included in the accounts — usually the last day of a month. Actually, the trial balance might be prepared on January 3, but if the accounts reflected only transactions through December 31, this is the date that should be used.)

(b) List the account titles in order, showing each account number.

(c) Record the account balances in parallel columns, entering debit balances in the left amount column and credit balances in the right amount column.

(d) Add the columns and record the totals, ruling a single line across the amount columns above the totals and a double line below the totals in the manner shown in the illustration on page 38.

Even though the trial balance indicates that the ledger is in balance, there may be errors in the ledger. For example, if a journal entry has been made in which the wrong accounts are debited or credited, or if an item has been posted to the wrong account, the ledger will still be in balance. It is important, therefore, that extreme care be used in preparing the journal entries and in posting them to the ledger accounts.

A trial balance is usually prepared on ruled paper (though it can be typewritten on plain paper if desired). An illustration of the trial balance, as of December 31, 1967, of the ledger of The Whitman Advertising Agency is shown below.

The Whitman Advertising Agency
Trial Balance
December 31, 1967

Account	No.	Dr. Balance	Cr. Balance
Cash	11	164006	
Office Supplies	12	16314	
Office Equipment	13	237221	
Accounts Payable	21		237221
C. D. Whitman, Capital	31		150000
C. D. Whitman, Drawing	32	30000	
Advertising Fees	41		136000
Rent Expense	51	20000	
Salary Expense	52	35000	
Traveling Expense	53	12830	
Telephone Expense	54	2250	
Office Supplies Expense	55	2000	
Miscellaneous Expense	56	3600	
		523221	523221

Model Trial Balance

Report No. 4

Refer to the workbook and complete Report No. 4. To complete this assignment correctly, the principles developed in the preceding discussion must be understood. Review the text assignment if necessary. After completing the report, continue with the following study assignment until the next report is required.

the financial statements

The transactions completed by The Whitman Advertising Agency during the month of December were recorded in a two-column journal (see pages 29 and 30). The debits and credits were subsequently posted to the proper accounts in a ledger (see pages 34 and 35). At the end of the month a trial balance was taken as a means of proving that the equality of debits and credits had been maintained throughout the journalizing and posting procedures (see page 38).

Although a trial balance may provide much of the information that the owner of a business may desire, it is primarily a device used by the bookkeeper for the purpose of proving the equality of the debit and credit account balances. Although the trial balance of The Whitman Advertising Agency taken as of December 31 contains a list of all of the accounts showing the amounts of the debit and credit balances, it does not present all of the information that Mr. Whitman may need or desire regarding either the results of operations during the month or the status of his business at the end of the month. To meet these needs it is customary to prepare two types of _financial statements_. One is known as an income statement and the other as a balance sheet or statement of financial position.

The Income Statement

The purpose of an _income statement_ is to provide information regarding the results of operations _during a specified period of time_. It is an itemized statement of the changes in owner's equity resulting from the revenue and expenses of the period. Such changes are recorded in temporary owner's equity accounts known as revenue and expense accounts. Changes in owner's equity resulting from investments or withdrawals of assets by the owner are not included in the income statement as they involve neither revenue nor expense.

A model income statement for The Whitman Advertising Agency showing the results of operations for the month ended December 31, 1967, is reproduced on page 40. The heading of an income statement consists of the following:

(a) The name of the business.
(b) The title of the statement.
(c) The period of time covered by the statement.

The body of an income statement consists of **(1)** an itemized list of the sources and amounts of revenue for the period and **(2)** an itemized list of the various expenses incurred during the period.

The financial statements are usually first prepared on ruled paper. Such handwritten copies may then be typed so that a number of copies will be available for those who are interested in examining the statements. Since the typewritten copies are not on ruled paper, dollar signs are included in the handwritten copy so that the typist will understand just where they are to be inserted. Note that a dollar sign is placed beside the first amount in each column and the first amount below a ruling in each column. The income statement illustrated below is shown on two-column ruled paper; however, the columns do not have any debit-credit significance.

The Whitman Advertising Agency Income Statement For the Month Ended December 31, 1967		
Revenue:		
Advertising fees		$1 360 00
Expenses:		
Rent expense	$2 000 0	
Salary expense	3 500 0	
Traveling expense	1 283 0	
Telephone expense	2 250	
Office supplies expense	2 00 0	
Miscellaneous expense	3 600	
Total expenses		75 68 0
Net income		$ 60 32 0

Model Income Statement

In the case of The Whitman Advertising Agency the only source of revenue was advertising fees that amounted to $1,360. The total expenses for the month amounted to $756.80. The revenue exceeded the expenses by $603.20. This represents the amount of the net income for the month. If the total expenses had exceeded the total revenue, the excess would have represented a net loss for the month.

The trial balance supplied the information needed in preparing the income statement. However, it can be seen readily that the income statement provides more information concerning the results of the month's operations than is supplied by the trial balance.

The Balance Sheet

The purpose of a *balance sheet* is to provide information regarding the financial condition of a business enterprise *as of a specified time or date.* It is an itemized statement of the assets, liabilities, and owner's equity at the close of business on the date indicated in the heading.

A model balance sheet for The Whitman Advertising Agency showing the status of the business as of December 31, 1967, is reproduced on pages 42 and 43. The heading of a balance sheet contains the following:

    (a) The name of the business.
    (b) The title of the statement.
    (c) The date of the statement.

The body of a balance sheet consists of an itemized list of the assets, the liabilities, and the owner's equity, the latter being the difference between the total amount of the assets and the total amount of the liabilities. The balance sheet illustrated is arranged in account form. Note the similarity of this form of balance sheet to the standard account form illustrated on page 12. The assets are listed on the left side and the liabilities and owner's equity are listed on the right side. The information provided by the balance sheet of The Whitman Advertising Agency may be summarized in equation form as follows:

$$\text{ASSETS} = \text{LIABILITIES} + \text{OWNER'S EQUITY}$$
$$\$4{,}175.41 \qquad \$2{,}372.21 \qquad \quad \$1{,}803.20$$

The trial balance was the source of the information needed in listing the assets and the liabilities in the balance sheet. The amount of the owner's equity may be calculated by subtracting the total liabilities from the total assets. Thus, the amount of Mr. Whitman's equity in The Whitman Advertising Agency as of December 31 was computed in the following manner:

Total assets...	$4,175.41
Less total liabilities...	2,372.21
Owner's equity..	$1,803.20

Proof of the amount of the owner's equity as calculated above may be determined by taking into consideration the following factors:

    (a) The amount invested in the enterprise by Mr. Whitman on November 30 as shown by his capital account.
    (b) The amount of the net income of The Whitman Advertising Agency for December as shown by the income statement.
    (c) The total amount withdrawn for personal use during December as shown by Mr. Whitman's drawing account.

Assets												
Cash	$	1	6	4	0	0	6					
Office supplies			1	6	3	1	4					
Office equipment		2	3	7	2	2	1					
Total assets								$	4	1	7	5	4	1

Model Balance Sheet — Account Form (Left Page)

The trial balance on page 38 shows that Mr. Whitman's equity in The Whitman Advertising Agency on November 30 amounted to $1,500. This is indicated by the credit balance of his capital account. The income statement shows that the net income of The Whitman Advertising Agency for December amounted to $603.20. The trial balance on page 38 shows that the amount withdrawn by Mr. Whitman for personal use during the month amounted to $300. This is indicated by the debit balance of his drawing account. On the basis of this information, Mr. Whitman's equity in the Whitman Advertising Agency as of December 31, 1967, may be computed as follows:

Amount of capital November 30		$1,500.00
Net income for December	$603.20	
Less amount withdrawn for personal use during the month.	300.00	303.20
Capital at end of December		$1,803.20

Advertising Agency
Sheet
31, 1967

Liabilities					
Accounts payable	$ 2 3 7 2 2 1				
Total liabilities			$ 2 3 7 2 2 1		
Owner's Equity					
C. D. Whitman, capital					
Capital, Nov. 30, 1967		1 5 0 0 0 0			
Net income	$ 6 0 3. 2 0				
Less withdrawals	3 0 0. 0 0				
Net increase		3 0 3 2 0			
Capital, Dec. 31, 1967			1 8 0 3 2 0		
Total liabilities and owner's equity			$ 4 1 7 5 4 1		

Model Balance Sheet — Account Form (Right Page)

Report No. 5

Refer to the workbook and complete Report No. 5. This assignment provides a test of your ability to apply the principles developed in Chapters 1 and 2 of this textbook. The textbook and the workbook go hand in hand, each serving a definite purpose in the learning process. Inability to solve correctly any problem included in the report indicates that you have failed to master the principles developed in the textbook. After completing the report, you may proceed with the textbook discussion in Chapter 3 until the next report is required.

chapter three

accounting for cash

In the preceding chapters the purpose and nature of business accounting, transaction analysis, and the mechanics of double-entry bookkeeping were introduced. Explanations and illustrations were given of **(1)** *journalizing* (recording transactions in a *general journal* — a "book of original entry"), **(2)** *posting* (transcribing the entries to the accounts that, all together, comprise the *general ledger*), **(3)** taking a *trial balance*, and **(4)** using the latter to aid in preparing an *income statement* and a *balance sheet* (two basic and important *financial statements*). This chapter is devoted to a discussion of the handling of and accounting for cash receipts and disbursements, including various considerations that are involved when cash is kept in a commercial bank. (The use of bank "checking accounts" is a near-universal business practice.)

records of cash receipts and disbursements; petty cash

The term *cash* has different, though not totally dissimilar, meanings. In a very narrow sense, cash means currency and coin. In a broader sense, cash includes checks, drafts, and money orders. All of these, as well as currency and coin, are sometimes called "cash items." Usually any reference to the *cash receipts* of a business relates to the receipt of checks, drafts, and money orders payable to the business, as well as to the receipt of currency and coin. The amount of the balance of the cash account, as well as the amount shown for cash in a balance sheet, normally includes cash and cash items on hand plus the amount on deposit in a checking account in a bank. In some cases the balance sheet figure for cash includes amounts on deposit in more than one bank. In accounting for cash, it is rather rare to make a distinction between "cash on hand" and "cash in bank," but sometimes this is done.

The Cash Account

This account is debited when cash is increased and credited when cash is decreased. This means that the cash account has a debit balance unless the business has no cash. In the latter case, the account will be *in balance* — meaning that the account has no balance since the total of the debits is equal to the total of the credits.

Cash Receipts. It is vital that an accurate and timely record be kept of cash receipts. When the volume of the receipts is large in both number and amount, a practice designed to reduce the danger of mistake and embezzlement may be followed. In order to segregate the functions of **(1)** handling money and cash items and **(2)** keeping the records, some one other than the bookkeeper prepares, in duplicate, a list of all receipts. One copy is kept with the receipts until a deposit ticket has been prepared and checked against the actual receipts. The other copy goes to the bookkeeper for recording purposes. An example of such a list is presented at the top of page 46.

When numerous cash receipts are involved, the amounts received are usually recorded in a cash register. The cash register tape provides a list of the receipts. If a cash register is not used, some form of receipt in duplicate should be used for each cash transaction. The customer should

DATE	FROM WHOM RECEIVED	NATURE OF REMITTANCE	AMOUNT
1967			
Jan. 2	Emerson Colaw	Check	$ 21.40
	Leland Rincker	Postal Money Order	53.07
	Harold Templeton	Currency	30.00
	Mrs. Verne Carroll	Express Money Order	42.16
	James Sargent	Bank Draft	28.75
	Delbert Stoddard	Cashier's Check	19.25
Total Cash Receipts...			$194.63

be given a copy and another copy should be retained for accounting purposes. Under such a plan the bookkeeper does not actually handle any cash; instead he records cash receipts from lists prepared by other persons. The procedure of having transactions involving cash handled by two or more persons reduces the danger of fraud and is one of the important features of a system of internal control.

Cash Disbursements. Disbursements may be made in cash or by bank check. When a disbursement is made in cash, a receipt or a receipted voucher should be obtained as evidence of the payment. When a disbursement is made by bank check, it is not necessary to obtain a receipt since the canceled check that is returned by the bank on which it was drawn serves as a receipt.

Recording Cash Receipts and Disbursements. In the preceding chapter, transactions involving the receipt and disbursement of cash were recorded in a two-column general journal along with other transactions. If the number of cash transactions is relatively small, the manner of recording that was illustrated is quite satisfactory. If, however, the number of such transactions is large, the repetition entailed in making numerous debit postings or credit postings to the cash account is time-consuming, tedious, and burdensome. Reference to the cash account at the top of page 34 discloses that even the brief illustration presented in that chapter involved fourteen postings to Cash (five debits and nine credits) out of a total of thirty-four postings required to record the seventeen transactions. It clearly would be more efficient to reduce the number of postings to the debit side of the cash account by summarizing the cash receipts for the month and posting the total. A similar observation applies to the transactions that involve cash disbursements.

The Four-Column Journal. One means of reducing the number of postings, as well as conserving space and effort in journalizing, is to use a journal that has four amount columns. An illustration of this form is reproduced on page 47. Note that it is the same as the journal used in the preceding chapter except that two additional amount columns have been added. (In this case the additional columns are placed at the left of the date column; however, such placement is not essential.) The two amount columns at the left are used exclusively for debits and credits to Cash; the two amount columns at the right, headed "General," are used for the amounts to be debited or credited to all other accounts. The De-

JOURNAL					PAGE		
CASH		DATE	DESCRIPTION	POST. REF.	GENERAL		
DEBITS	CREDITS				DEBITS	CREDITS

Four-Column Journal

scription column is used primarily to record the titles of the accounts that are to be debited or credited with the amount entered in one of the columns at the right. Sometimes, a brief explanatory note is also included in the Description column.

Journalizing Procedure Illustrated. To illustrate the use of the four-column journal and to contrast it with the two-column type, the transactions of the Whitman Advertising Agency that were given in Chapter 2 (starting on page 26) are recorded in a four-column journal reproduced on page 48. Several features of this journal should be noted:

(a) In the case of each entry that involves either a debit or a credit to Cash, the title of the account to receive the related credit or debit is written starting at the extreme left of the Description column. No indentation is made. However, in the case of any entry that does not involve cash, the title of the account to be debited is written at the extreme left, and the title of the account to be credited is indented about one-half inch. Note the entries of December 4 and 27, and the second entry of December 29. These entries appear just as they did in the two-column journal.

(b) Usually a separate line is not used for an explanation of each entry. While this could be done, it is not customary because it is desirable to save space. Furthermore, in most instances, the entries explain themselves. Consider the first entry: It is evident that Mr. Whitman invested $1,500 in the business. In other cases, an appropriate notation is made following the title of the account. For example, when a debit or a credit to Accounts Payable is involved, the name of the creditor is noted. (See entries of December 4, 27, and 28.) In all entries involving a credit to Advertising Fees, the name of the client is noted. (See entries of December 7, 18, 22, and 28.) A word or two of explanation should be given whenever appropriate. (Note the entries of December 15 and 29 where the word "[Secretary]" was included.) Occasionally an explanation will be of such a length that an additional line will be required. When a cash disbursement is made by check, the check number should be noted. It is quite common to have a narrow column headed "Check Number" placed next to the Cash Credits column to use in noting the number of each check issued. (In Chapter 2, no mention was made of the manner of cash payments; therefore, no check numbers were given and there is no need for a check number column in the illustration below.)

(c) The numbers shown in the Posting Reference column were not entered at the time of journalizing the transactions; they were entered later when the amounts were posted to the accounts in the ledger.

JOURNAL   PAGE 1

| CASH | | DATE | DESCRIPTION | POST. REF. | GENERAL | |
DEBITS	CREDITS				DEBITS	CREDITS
150000		1967 Nov. 30	C. D. Whitman, Capital	31		150000
	20000	Dec. 1	Rent Expense	51	20000	
		4	Office Supplies	12	18314	
			Accounts Payable (Central Supply Co.)	21		18314
	2250	5	Telephone Expense	54	2250	
	600	6	Miscellaneous Expense	56	600	
12500		7	Advertising Fees (City Hardware Co.)	41		12500
	12830	11	Traveling Expense	53	12830	
	17500	15	Salary Expense (Secretary)	52	17500	
36500		18	Advertising Fees (Morton Mfg. Co.)	41		36500
	30000	20	C. D. Whitman, Drawing	32	30000	
52000		22	Advertising Fees (Mid-Town Sales Co.)	41		52000
	3000	26	Miscellaneous Expense	56	3000	
		27	Office Equipment	13	237221	
			Accounts Payable (Acme Office Equip Co.)	21		237221
	18314	28	Accounts Payable (Central Supply Co.)	21	18314	
35000		28	Advertising Fees (Gordon Downey)	41		35000
	17500	29	Salary Expense (Secretary)	52	17500	
		29	Office Supplies Expense	55	2000	
			Office Supplies 1,640.06	12		2000
286000	121994				379529	543535
286000	121994				379529	543535
(11)	(11)				(✓)	(✓)

The Whitman Advertising Agency Four-Column Journal

Proving the Four-Column Journal. In order to be sure that the debits recorded in the journal are equal to the credits, the journal must be *proved.* Each amount column should be footed and the sum of the footings of the debit columns and the sum of the footings of the credit columns compared. The footings should be recorded in small pencil figures immediately below the last regular entry. If these sums are not the same, the journal entries must be checked to discover and correct any errors that are found. The footings should be proved frequently; when the transactions are numerous it may be advisable to prove the footings daily. The footings must be proved when a page of the journal is filled to be sure that no error is carried forward to a new page. Proof of the footings is essential at the end of the month before the journal is ruled or any column totals are posted. The following is a proof of the footings of the four-column journal of The Whitman Advertising Agency at the end of December:

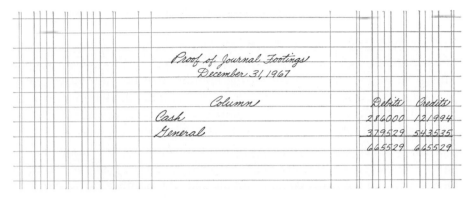

<table>
<tr><td colspan="3" align="center">Proof of Journal Footings
December 31, 1967</td></tr>
<tr><td align="center">Column</td><td align="center">Debits</td><td align="center">Credits</td></tr>
<tr><td>Cash</td><td>286000</td><td>121994</td></tr>
<tr><td>General</td><td>379529</td><td>543535</td></tr>
<tr><td></td><td>665529</td><td>665529</td></tr>
</table>

Four-Column Journal — Proof of Journal Footings

Footing and Ruling the Four-Column Journal. Normally, the journal should be footed and ruled at the end of each month. (In the illustration of The Whitman Advertising Agency, the business was started on November 30, and the single transaction on that date was included with the entries for December.) As previously stated, the footings should be recorded in small pencil figures immediately below the last regular entry. After being proved, the figures should be recorded in ink on the next horizontal line. A single rule should be drawn across all of the amount columns just above the totals and a double rule should be drawn across all of the columns except the Description column just below the totals. A practice often followed when journals of this type are used is to make a notation of the cash balance at the end of the month. This amount should be equal to the balance at the end of the previous month, plus the receipts and minus the disbursements of the month just ended. This balance may be noted in small figures (in pencil, if preferred) in the Description column just below the line on which the last regular entry was made. It is common practice to start the entries for a new month on a fresh page. When this practice is followed, the cash balance at the start of the month (the balance at the end of the month just past) is entered in small figures in the Description column at the top of the new page.

When it is necessary to use more than one journal page for the transactions of a month, no regular entry should be made on the last line of a page. That line is used to show the column totals. These should not be recorded in ink until the equality of the footings has been proven. The words "Carried Forward" should be written in the Description column on the last line. The amount-column totals are entered on the top line of the new page with the words "Amounts Forwarded" written in the Description column.

Posting the Four-Column Journal. Posting from a four-column journal involves both individual posting and summary (column total) posting. The individual amounts in the two General columns are posted. This may be done daily or as often as convenient, but it should be done by the end of each month. The totals of the Cash Debits and Cash Credits columns cannot be posted until the end of the month when the journal has been proved and the column totals recorded. As the individual amounts in the General columns are posted, the numbers of the accounts to which the postings were made are entered in the Posting Reference column of the journal. (Entering the journal page from which an amount has come is a part of the process of posting to the ledger.) When the totals of the Cash Debits and Cash Credits columns are posted, the number of the cash account (No. 11 in the illustration) is shown in parentheses just below the column totals. In order to indicate that the totals of the General Debits and General Credits columns are not to be posted, a check mark is shown in parentheses ($\sqrt{}$) below each of those totals.

The general ledger of The Whitman Advertising Agency after completion of postings from the two-column journal is illustrated on pages 34 and 35. If these postings had come from the four-column journal instead, the ledger accounts would appear exactly the same except for the fact that some of the postings came from page 2 of the two-column journal, whereas all of the postings came from page 1 of the four-column journal. Furthermore, the cash account, instead of containing five debits and nine credits, would contain only one debit and one credit as illustrated below.

ACCOUNT *Cash*　　　　　　　　　　　　　　　　　　　ACCOUNT NO. *11*

DATE	ITEMS	POST. REF.	√	DEBITS	DATE	ITEMS	POST. REF.	√	CREDITS
1967 *Dec. 31*	*1,640.06*		*1*	2 8 6 0 0 0	*1967* *Dec. 31*			*1*	1 2 1 9 9 4

Comparison of the two-column journal illustrated on pages 29 and 30 and the four-column journal shown on page 48 reveals that the former required thirty-four postings, while the latter needed only twenty two. If there had been 100 transactions, of which ninety involved either a debit or a credit to Cash, 200 postings would have been required if the transactions had been recorded in a two-column journal. If the same transactions had been recorded in a four-column journal of the type illustrated, only 112 postings would have been required. These savings in the number of postings roughly reflect comparable savings in space required, words to be written, and time needed.

The four-column journal discussed and illustrated might be called a "junior version" of a book of original entry known as a *combined cash journal*. This designation arises from the fact that such a book combines the features of a two-column general journal and a *cashbook* — the latter being a book in which only transactions involving cash receipts and disbursements are recorded. The fundamental characteristics of a combined cash journal are that it provides columns for debits to cash, credits to cash, debits and credits to be posted individually ("general" columns), and as many other "special" columns as circumstances require. These "special" columns are used to record like debits or credits so that the totals of amounts destined for the same place can be summary posted. Thus, in addition to the four columns whose use has already been explained and illustrated, there may be one, two, three, or even a dozen other "special" columns if needed. The Whitman Advertising Agency example included four transactions requiring a credit to Advertising Fees, Account No. 41. This circumstance suggests that a special column for "Advertising Fees Credit" would have been in order. The use of combined cash journals is explained and illustrated in Chapters 5, 6, and 8.

Other Types of Cash Journals. In many businesses, transactions involving the receipt or the disbursement of cash are so numerous that it is desirable to keep the original journal record of such transactions separate from the record of noncash transactions. When a separate record is kept of cash receipts, it is usually referred to as a *cash receipts journal*. When a separate record is kept of cash payments or disbursements, it is usually referred to as a *cash payments journal* or a *cash disbursements journal*. When all disbursements are made by check, the journal is sometimes called a *check register*. When cash receipts and cash payments are both recorded in the same book of account, the book is usually referred to as a cashbook. This type of record typically has a facing-page arrangement. Receipts are recorded on the left-hand page; disbursements on the right-hand page.

All original entry books (journals) relating to cash have the same characteristics regardless of whether there are separate books for receipts and disbursements or whether they are combined and called a cashbook. For cash receipts, there is one debit column in which the amounts of all receipts are recorded. At the end of a month, the total of this column is posted as a debit to Cash. Some or all of the individual credit amounts are separately posted as credits to the proper accounts. If there are numerous credits to the same account, a column may be provided in which to record the amounts of these credits so that their sum can be posted at the end of the month. Within limits, there may be as many "special" columns as needed. A comparable set of observations relates to the cash disbursements: The major column in this case, of course, is the credit column that assembles all of the decreases in cash so that one summary credit to Cash can be posted each month. The debits may all be posted individually or, if needed, special columns may be used to reduce the number of postings.

In each instance, all of the fundamental qualities of any journal are present: (1) space is provided to show the date of the transaction, (2) provision is made to indicate the titles of the accounts that are affected, (3) space is provided for any needed explanation or description, (4) the amount of each transaction is shown, and (5) space is provided to indicate the number of the account to which each posting was made. If cash disbursements are made by check, the cash disbursements record will probably have a column in which to note the check numbers. It is not uncommon for there to be a memo column in which to note the bank balance after each deposit and each check written. It is possible to "prove" any of these journals at any time by determining whether the total debits recorded are equal to the total credits.

It must be understood that cash journals do not completely eliminate the need for a general journal, unless every transaction of the business involves cash — an unlikely circumstance. At later points in the text, a few other varieties of "special journals" will be introduced. In almost every business, however, there is need for a general journal — either separate or combined with another journal — in which to record unusual, infrequent transactions.

Proving Cash. The process of determining whether the amount of cash (on hand and in the bank) is the amount that should be there according to the records is called *proving cash.* Cash should be proved at least once a week and, perhaps, more often if the volume of cash transactions is large. The first step is to determine from the records what amount of cash should be on hand. The cash balance should be calculated by adding the total of the receipts to the opening balance and subtracting the total of the payments. The result should be equal to the amount of cash on deposit in the bank plus the total of currency, coins, checks, and money orders on hand. Normally, an up-to-date record of cash in bank is maintained — often by using stubs in a checkbook for this purpose. There is space provided on the stubs to show deposits as well as the record of checks drawn, and the resulting balance after each deposit made or check drawn. (See check stubs illustrated on page 67.) The amount of cash and cash items on hand must be determined by actual count.

Cash Short and Over. If the effort to prove cash is not successful, it means that either **(1)** the records of receipts, disbursements, and cash on deposit contain one or more errors, **(2)** the count of cash and cash items was incorrect, or **(3)** a "shortage" or an "overage" exists. If a verification of the records and the cash count does not uncover any error, it is evident that due to some mistake in handling cash, either not enough or too much cash is on hand.

Finding that cash is slightly short or over is not unusual. If there are numerous cash transactions, it is difficult to avoid occasional errors in making change. (There is always the danger of shortages due to dishonesty, but most discrepancies are the result of mistakes.) Many businesses have a ledger account entitled *Cash Short and Over*. If, in the effort to prove cash, it is found that a shortage exists, its amount is treated as a cash disbursement transaction involving a debit to Cash Short and Over. Any overage discovered is regarded as a cash receipt transaction involving a credit to Cash Short and Over. By the end of the fiscal year it is not unlikely that the cash short and over account will have both debits and credits. If the total of the debits exceeds the total of the credits, the balance represents an expense or loss; if the reverse is the case, the balance represents revenue.

The Petty Cash Fund

A good policy for a business enterprise to adopt is one which requires that all cash and cash items which it receives shall be deposited in a bank. When this is done, its total cash receipts will equal its total deposits in the bank. It is also a good policy to make arrangements with the bank so that all checks and other cash items received by the business from customers or others in the usual course of business will be accepted by the bank for deposit only. This will cause the records of cash receipts and disbursements of the business to agree exactly with the bank's record of deposits and withdrawals. Arrangements may also be made with the bank so that no item will be charged to the depositor's account until a check from the depositor for the proper amount is obtained. For example, an arrangement can be made to have dishonored checks (defined on page 62) presented to the depositor for payment instead of having them charged to the depositor's account. Service charges (defined on page 70) also may be paid by check.

When all cash and cash items received are deposited in a bank, an office fund or *petty cash fund* may be established for paying small items. ("Petty" means small or little.) Such a fund eliminates the necessity of writing checks for small amounts.

Operating a Petty Cash Fund. To establish a petty cash fund, a check should be drawn for the amount that is to be set aside in the fund. The amount may be $25, $50, $100, or any amount considered necessary. The check is usually made payable to "Cash," "Petty Cash," or "Office Fund." When the check is cashed by the bank, the money is placed in a cash drawer, a cash register, or a safe at the depositor's place of business, and a designated individual in the office is authorized to make payments from the fund. The one who is responsible for the fund should be able to account for the amount of the fund at any time. Disbursements from the fund should not be made without obtaining a voucher or a receipt. A form of petty cash voucher is shown below. Such a voucher should be used for each expenditure unless a receipt or receipted invoice is obtained.

PETTY CASH VOUCHER

NO. _7_   DATE _December 12, 1967_

PAID TO _R. B. Porter_   AMOUNT

FOR _Red Cross_ | 5 | 00 |

CHARGE TO _Donations Expense_

PAYMENT RECEIVED:
R. B. Porter   APPROVED BY _J. K. Jenkins_

Petty Cash Voucher

The check drawn to establish the petty cash fund may be recorded in the journal by debiting Petty Cash Fund and by crediting Cash. When it is necessary to replenish the fund, the petty cashier usually prepares a statement of the expenditures, properly classified. A check is then drawn for the exact amount of the total expenditures. This check is recorded in the journal by debiting the proper accounts indicated in the statement and by crediting Cash.

The petty cash fund is a revolving fund that does not change in amount unless the fund is increased or decreased. The actual amount of cash in the fund plus the total of the petty cash vouchers or receipts should always be equal to the amount originally charged to the petty cash fund.

Petty Cash Disbursements Record. When a petty cash fund is maintained, it is good practice to keep a formal record of all disbursements from the fund. Various types of records have been designed for this purpose. One of the standard forms is illustrated on pages 56 and 57. The headings of the Distribution columns may vary with each enterprise, depending upon the desired classification of the expenditures. It should be remembered that the headings represent accounts that eventually are to be charged for the expenditures. The desired headings may either be printed on the form or they may be written in. Often the account numbers instead of account titles are used in the headings to indicate the accounts to be charged.

The petty cashier should have a document for each disbursement made from the petty cash fund. Unless a receipt or receipted invoice is obtained, the petty cashier should prepare a voucher. The vouchers should be numbered consecutively.

A model petty cash disbursements record is reproduced on pages 56 and 57. It is a part of the records of J. K. Jenkins, a business consultant. Since Mr. Jenkins is out of the office much of the time, he considers it advisable to provide a petty cash fund from which his secretary is authorized to make petty cash disbursements not to exceed $15 each. A narrative of the petty cash transactions completed by Mr. Jenkins' secretary, during the month of December, follows:

J. K. JENKINS

NARRATIVE OF PETTY CASH TRANSACTIONS

Dec. 1. Issued check for $100 payable to Petty Cash, cashed the check, and placed the proceeds in a petty cash fund.

> This transaction was recorded in the journal by debiting Petty Cash Fund and by crediting Cash. A memorandum entry was also made in the Description column of the petty cash disbursements record reproduced on pages 56 and 57.

During the month of December the following disbursements were made from the petty cash fund:

4. Paid $4 for polishing office furniture. Petty Cash Voucher No. 1.
5. Gave Mr. Jenkins $9 to reimburse him for the amount spent in having his automobile repaired. Petty Cash Voucher No. 2.
6. Gave Mr. Jenkins $7 to reimburse him for the amount spent in entertaining a client at luncheon. Petty Cash Voucher No. 3.
7. Paid $5 for messenger fees. Petty Cash Voucher No. 4.
11. Paid $4 for an ad in local newspaper. Petty Cash Voucher No. 5.
11. Gave Mr. Jenkins $10 for personal use. Petty Cash Voucher No. 6.

> This item was entered in the Amount column provided at the extreme right of the petty cash disbursements record since no special distribution column had been provided for recording amounts withdrawn by the owner for personal use.

12. Gave the Red Cross a $5 donation. Petty Cash Voucher No. 7.
15. Paid $7.50 for typewriter repairs. Petty Cash Voucher No. 8.
18. Gave Mr. Jenkins $3.75 to reimburse him for traveling expenses. Petty Cash Voucher No. 9.
19. Gave Mr. Jenkins $3 to reimburse him for the amount spent in having his automobile washed. Petty Cash Voucher No. 10.
20. Paid $8 for cleaning office. Petty Cash Voucher No. 11.
22. Paid $1.25 for collect telegram. Petty Cash Voucher No. 12.
23. Donated $5 to the Salvation Army. Petty Cash Voucher No. 13.

DAY	DESCRIPTION		VOU. NO.	TOTAL AMOUNT	T.&T. Exp.	Auto Exp.
	AMOUNTS FORWARDED					
1	Received in fund	100.00 ✓				
4	Polishing office furniture		1	4 00		
5	Automobile repairs		2	9 00		9 00
6	Client luncheon		3	7 00		
7	Messenger		4	5 00		
11	Advertising expense		5	4 00		
11	J. K. Jenkins, personal use		6	10 00		
12	Red Cross		7	5 00		
15	Typewriter repairs		8	7 50		
18	Traveling expense		9	3 75		
19	Washing automobile		10	3 00		3 00
20	Cleaning office		11	8 00		
22	Collect telegram		12	1 25	1 25	
23	Salvation Army		13	5 00		
26	Postage stamps		14	5 00		
27	Long distance call		15	3 20	3 20	
28	Polishing office furniture		16	4 00		
				84 70	4 45	12 00
				84 70	4 45	12 00
29	Balance	15.30				
29	Received in fund	84.70				
	Total	100.00				

J. K. Jenkins' Petty Cash Disbursements Record (Left Page)

26. Paid $5 for postage stamps. Petty Cash Voucher No. 14.
27. Gave Mr. Jenkins $3.20 to reimburse him for a long distance telephone call made from a booth. Petty Cash Voucher No. 15.
28. Paid $4 for polishing office furniture. Petty Cash Voucher No. 16.
29. Issued check for $84.70 to replenish the petty cash fund.

    This transaction was recorded in the journal by debiting the proper accounts and by crediting Cash for the total amount of the expenditures.

Proving the Petty Cash Disbursements Record. To prove the petty cash disbursements record, it is first necessary to foot all of the amount columns. The sum of the footings of the Distribution columns should equal the footing of the Total Amount column. After proving the footings, the totals should be recorded and the record should be ruled as shown in the illustration. The illustration shows that a total of $84.70 was paid out during December. Since it was desired to replenish the petty cash fund at this time, the following statement of the disbursements for December was prepared:

		DISTRIBUTION OF CHARGES				
Post. Exp.	Don. Exp.	Adv. Exp.	Travel Exp.	Misc. Exp.	ACCOUNT	AMOUNT
				4 00		
				7 00		
				5 00		
		4 00				
					J. K. Jenkins, Drawing	10 00
	5 00					
				7 50		
			3 75			
				8 00		
	5 00					
5 00						
				4 00		
5 00	10 00	4 00	3 75	35 50		10 00
5 00	10 00	4 00	3 75	35 50		10 00

J. K. Jenkins' Petty Cash Disbursements Record (Right Page)

STATEMENT OF PETTY CASH DISBURSEMENTS
For December

Telephone and telegraph expense..........................	$ 4.45
Automobile expense....................................	12.00
Postage expense.......................................	5.00
Donations expense.....................................	10.00
Advertising expense....................................	4.00
Traveling expense.....................................	3.75
Miscellaneous expense.................................	35.50
J. K. Jenkins, drawing..................................	10.00
Total disbursements.................................	$84.70

The statement of disbursements provides the information for the issuance of a check for $84.70 to replenish the petty cash fund. After footing and ruling the petty cash disbursements record, the balance in the fund and the amount received to replenish the fund may be recorded in the

Description column below the ruling as shown in the illustration. It is customary to carry the balance forward to the top of a new page before recording any of the transactions for the following month.

The petty cash disbursements record reproduced on pages 56 and 57 is an *auxiliary record* that supplements the regular accounting records. No posting is done from this auxiliary record. The total amount of the expenditures from the petty cash fund is entered in the journal at the time of replenishing the fund by debiting the proper accounts and by crediting Cash. A *compound entry* (one that affects more than two accounts, though the sum of the debits is equal to the sum of the credits) is usually required. The statement of petty cash disbursements provides the information needed in recording the check issued to replenish the petty cash fund. The posting is done from the journal.

The method of recording the check issued by J. K. Jenkins on December 29 to replenish the fund is illustrated below. It is assumed that Mr. Jenkins uses a four-column journal similar to the one illustrated on page 47.

JOURNAL   PAGE 15

CASH DEBITS	CASH CREDITS	DATE	DESCRIPTION	POST. REF.	GENERAL DEBITS	GENERAL CREDITS
	8470	1967 Dec. 29	Telephone and Telegraph Expense		445	
			Automobile Expense		1200	
			Postage Expense		500	
			Donations Expense		1000	
			Advertising Expense		400	
			Traveling Expense		375	
			Miscellaneous Expense		3550	
			J. K. Jenkins, Drawing		1000	

J. K. Jenkins' Four-Column Journal

The method of handling a petty cash fund just described is sometimes referred to as the *imprest method*. It is the method most commonly used.

Report No. 6

Refer to the workbook and complete Report No. 6. After completing the report, proceed with the textbook discussion until the next report is required.

banking procedure

A bank is a financial institution that receives deposits, lends money, makes collections, and renders other services, such as providing vaults for the safekeeping of valuables and handling trust funds for its customers. Most banks offer facilities for both checking accounts and savings accounts.

Checking Account

A checking account is sometimes referred to as a commercial account. Important factors in connection with a checking account are (1) opening the account, (2) making deposits, (3) making withdrawals, and (4) reconciling the bank statement.

Opening a Checking Account. To open a checking account with a bank, it is necessary to obtain the approval of an official of the bank and to make an initial deposit. Money, checks, bank drafts, money orders, and other cash items usually will be accepted for deposit. Cash is accepted for deposit subject to verification as to its amount and validity. Cash items are accepted for deposit subject to their being paid by their makers when presented for payment by the bank or its agent.

Signature Card. Banks usually require a new depositor to sign his name on a card or form as an aid in verifying the depositor's signature on checks that he may issue, on cash items that he may endorse for deposit, and on other business papers that he may present to the bank. The form a depositor signs to give the bank a sample of his signature is called a *signature card*. If desired, a depositor may authorize others to sign his name to checks and to other business forms. Each person who is so authorized is required to sign the depositor's name along with his own signature on a signature card. A signature card is one of the safeguards that a bank uses to protect its own interests as well as the interests of its depositors.

Deposit Ticket. Banks provide depositors with a printed form to use for a detailed listing of items being deposited. This form is called a *deposit ticket*. A model filled-in deposit ticket is reproduced on page 60.

In preparing a deposit ticket, the account title, the account number, and the date should be written in the spaces provided for these purposes. Currency (paper money) should be arranged in the order of the denominations, the smaller denominations being placed on top. The bills should all

BELLEVUE TRUST CO.   Cincinnati, Ohio _October 21_ 19_67_

Currency		349	00
Coin		30	94
Checks	*13-1*	217	60
	13-22	500	00
	13-3	150	00
	TOTAL	1,247	54

THE P.G. THOMAS CO.
PLEASE PRINT EXACT TITLE OF ACCOUNT

ACCOUNT NUMBER 3 1 9 — 0 4 5 3 1

Deposit Ticket

be faced up and top up. Coins (pennies, nickels, dimes, quarters, half dollars, and silver dollars) that are to be deposited in considerable quantities should be wrapped in coin wrappers, which the bank will provide. The name of the depositor should be written on the outside of each coin wrapper as a means of identification in the event that a mistake has been made in counting the coins. The amounts of cash represented by currency and by coins should be entered in the amount column of the deposit ticket on the lines provided for these items.

Each additional item to be deposited should be listed on a separate line of the deposit ticket as shown in the illustration above. In listing checks on the deposit ticket, the instructions of the bank should be observed in describing the checks for identification purposes. It was once common practice to list local checks by name of bank and out-of-town checks by name of city. Today the preferred practice is to identify each check by entering the American Bankers Association (ABA) transit number on the deposit ticket.

The ABA numbers usually appear on checks as shown in the illustration on page 61. The numerator of the fraction is the transit number. Such identification numbers are assigned to banks by the American Bankers Association. Numbers 1 to 49 inclusive are assigned to large cities and the numbers 50 to 99 inclusive to the states. The number 13 on the check shown is the number assigned to Cincinnati, Ohio, while 40 is the number assigned to a certain bank in the city of Cincinnati. The digits in the denominator of the fraction are used to aid banks in routing checks from one bank to another.

Endorsements. The signature or stamp of a depositor on the back of a check is called an *endorsement*. Negotiable instruments (checks, notes, and drafts) made payable to the depositor either directly or by prior endorsement, must be endorsed by him before a bank will accept them for deposit. One purpose of such endorsement is to transfer the title of the instrument to the bank. By means of his endorsement the depositor also guarantees the payment of the instrument. Checks and other items submitted for deposit that require endorsements on the back may be endorsed as shown in the illustration below. In endorsing a check, the name of the payee should be written exactly as it appears on the face of the check. Note that the endorsement is written near the left end of the check. An endorsement that limits the holder of the check as to the use to be made of the amount collected is known as a *restrictive endorsement*. The check reproduced below has a restrictive endorsement. This type of endorsement makes it unlikely that the check will be cashed by anyone other than the bank or person to whom it is endorsed. Businesses commonly use a rubber stamp to endorse checks for deposit.

The total of the cash and other items deposited should be entered on the deposit ticket. The deposit ticket, together with the cash and the other items to be deposited, should be delivered to the receiving teller of the bank together with a *passbook* that the bank will have provided for use by receiving tellers in acknowledging the receipt of deposits. The date, amount of deposit, and the initial of the teller are entered in the passbook. Instead of using a passbook, many depositors submit the deposit ticket in duplicate. The teller receipts the duplicate copy and returns it to the depositor.

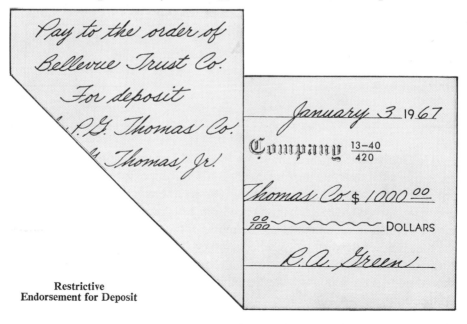

Restrictive
Endorsement for Deposit

Instead of providing the depositor with either a passbook or duplicate deposit tickets, the bank may provide him with a machine-printed receipt for each deposit. Some banks use *automatic teller machines* in preparing the receipts. The use of such machines saves the time required to make manual entries in a passbook and eliminates the need for making duplicate copies of deposit tickets. Such machines are not only timesaving, but they also promote accuracy in the handling of deposits. The deposits handled by each teller during the day may be accumulated so that at the end of the day the total amount of the deposits received by a teller is automatically recorded by the machine. This amount may be proved by counting the cash and cash items accepted by a teller for deposit during the day.

Dishonored Checks. A check that a bank refuses to pay is described as a *dishonored check.* A depositor guarantees all items that he deposits and is liable to the bank for the amount involved if, for any reason, any item is not honored when presented for payment. When a check or other cash item is deposited with a bank and is not honored upon presentation to the bank upon which it is drawn, the depositor's bank may charge the amount of the dishonored item to the depositor's account or may present it to the depositor for reimbursement. It is not uncommon for checks that have been deposited to be returned to the depositor for various reasons, as indicated on the return notice reproduced below. The most common reason for checks being returned unpaid is "not sufficient funds" (NSF).

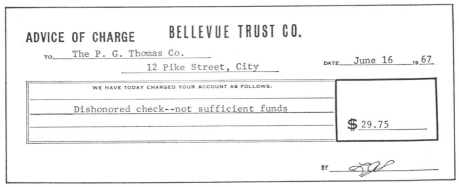

Debit Advice

Under the laws of most states, it is illegal for anyone to issue a check on a bank without having sufficient funds on deposit with that bank to cover the check when it is presented for payment. When a dishonored check is charged to the depositor's account, or is replaced by a check issued by the depositor, an entry should be made in the depositor's records debiting the issuer of the dishonored check and crediting Cash. If the dishonored check is charged to the depositor's account by the bank, the depositor should deduct the amount from the balance shown on his checkbook stub, even though he did not issue a check.

Postdated Checks. Checks dated subsequent to the date of issue are known as *postdated checks*. For example, a check that is issued on March 1 may be dated March 15. The recipient of a postdated check should not deposit it before the date specified on the check. One reason for issuing a postdated check may be that the maker does not have sufficient funds in his bank at the time of issuance to pay it, but he may expect to have a sufficient amount on deposit by the time the check is presented for payment on or after the date of the check. When a postdated check is presented to the bank on which it is drawn and payment is not made, it is handled by the bank in the same manner as any other dishonored check and the payee should treat it as a dishonored check. Generally, it is not considered good practice to issue postdated checks.

Making Deposits by Mail. Bank deposits may be made either over the counter or by mail. The over-the-counter method of making deposits is generally used. It may not always be convenient, however, for a depositor to make his deposits over the counter, especially if he lives at a great distance from the bank. In such a case it may be more convenient for him to make his deposits by mail. When a depositor makes his deposits by mail, the bank may provide him with a special form of deposit ticket.

Night Deposits. A depositor may find it convenient to use the night deposit safe of his bank. The opening to the night deposit safe usually is on the exterior of the bank building. Upon signing a night depository contract, the bank supplies the depositor with a key to the outside door of the safe, together with a bag that has an identifying number and in which valuables may be placed, and two keys to the bag itself. Once the depositor places his bag in the night deposit safe it cannot be retrieved because it moves to a vault in the bank that is accessible to bank employees only. Since only the depositor is provided with keys to his bag, he or his authorized representative must go to the bank to unlock the bag. At that time the depositor may or may not deposit in his account in the bank the funds that he had placed previously in the night deposit safe.

Night deposit banking service is especially valuable to those individuals and concerns that do not have safe facilities in their own places of business and that accumulate cash and other cash items which they cannot take to the bank during banking hours.

Making Withdrawals. The amount deposited in a bank checking account may be withdrawn either by the depositor himself or by any other person who has been properly authorized to make withdrawals from the depositor's account. Such withdrawals are accomplished by the use of checks signed by the depositor or by others having the authority to sign checks drawn on the account.

Checkbook. Banks provide printed forms known as checks for the convenience of their depositors. Such checks are used by depositors to authorize the bank to pay out specified amounts from the funds credited to their accounts. Special forms of checks may be used for payrolls, dividends, or other purposes. It is estimated that roughly 85 percent of all money payments in the United States are made by check.

Blank checks are often bound in a book with one or more checks to a page. Each check usually contains spaces for recording the following information:

(a) The number of the check.
(b) The date of the check.
(c) The name of the payee.
(d) The amount the bank is authorized to pay the payee.
(e) The signature of the drawer — the depositor or his authorized agent.

Very often, each blank check is attached (usually along its left side) to what is called a *check stub*. The stubs usually contain blank spaces for recording the same information as is recorded on the checks so that the completed stubs will provide the depositor with a complete record of all checks issued. Sometimes space is also provided on the stub for recording the title of the account to be debited. In any event, sufficient data should be entered on the stub of each check to provide all information needed for recording purposes.

Checks should be numbered consecutively, and their stubs should bear identical numbers. The numbers may be entered manually or a numbering machine may be used. It is a good plan to number all stubs and checks before any checks are written. This makes it easier to keep track of all blank checks. Frequently businesses have a quantity of blank checks printed with their name and address shown. Usually such checks are prenumbered. Some firms prepare carbon copies of checks instead of using check stubs. The copy itself is not a check; very often it is only a blank sheet except for the carbon-paper imprint of the check number, name of payee, amount, and any notations that were made on the check as to what it pays. Checks with carbon copies usually are prepared on a typewriter.

Writing a Check. If the check has a stub, the latter should be filled in before the check is written. This plan insures that the drawer will retain a record of each check issued.

When a depositor withdraws funds personally, the payee of the check is usually "Cash." If the money is to go into a petty cash fund, the check may be made payable to "Petty Cash."

When a depositor desires the bank to pay the money to a third party, he writes the name of that party, referred to as the payee, on the stub and on the check. When the payee presents the check to the bank for payment, he may be required by the bank to identify himself.

The purpose for which a check is drawn is usually recorded on the stub below the name of the payee. The purpose may also be indicated in some appropriate area of the check itself. Indicating the purpose on the check provides information for the benefit of the payee and provides a specific receipt for the drawer.

The amount of the check is stated on the stub in figures and is stated on the check in both figures and words. If the amount shown on the check in figures does not agree with the amount shown in words, the bank usually will contact the drawer for the correct amount or will return the check unpaid.

Care must be used in writing the amount on the check in order to avoid any possibility that the payee or a subsequent holder may change the amount. If the instructions given below are followed in the preparation of a check, it will be difficult to change the amount.

(a) The amount shown in figures should be written so that there is no space between the dollar sign and the first digit of the amount.

(b) The amount stated in words should be written beginning at the extreme left on the line provided for this information. The cents should be written in the form of a common fraction; if the check is for an even number of dollars, use two ciphers or the word "no" as the numerator of the fraction. If a vacant space remains, a line should be drawn from the amount stated in words to the word "Dollars" on the same line with it, as illustrated on page 67.

A machine frequently used to write the amount of a check in figures and in words is known as a *checkwriter*. The use of a checkwriter is desirable because it practically eliminates the possibility of a change in the amount of a check.

Each check issued by a depositor will be returned to him by the bank on which it is drawn after the check has been paid. Canceled checks are returned to the depositor with the bank statement, which is usually rendered each month. Canceled checks will have been endorsed by the payee and any subsequent holders. They constitute receipts that the depositor should retain for future reference. They may be attached to the stubs from which they were removed originally or they may be filed.

Overdraft. As stated previously, it is illegal in most states for a depositor to issue a check against a bank in excess of the amount on deposit. However, it may happen that through an oversight or an error in calculation a depositor will overdraw his checking account. Should this happen the bank may refuse to honor the check or it may honor the check and notify the depositor by mail that he has overdrawn his account. Sometimes an official of the bank will telephone the depositor instead of notifying him by mail. Overdrawing a bank checking account is considered a serious matter, and the depositor is expected to make the necessary adjustment without delay.

Electronic Processing of Checks. Increasingly, banks are furnishing their depositors with a special type of check that can be processed by MICR (magnetic ink character recognition) equipment. The unique characteristic of such checks is that there is imprinted in magnetic ink along the lower margin of the check a series of numbers or digits in the form of a code that indicates **(1)** the identity of the Federal Reserve District in which the bank is located, **(2)** the identity of the bank, and **(3)** the account number assigned to the depositor. In processing checks with electronic equipment, the first bank that handles a check will imprint its amount in magnetic ink characters to further aid in the processing of the check. The amount will be printed directly below the signature line in the lower right-hand corner of the check.

Checks imprinted with the bank's number and the depositor's number can be fed into MICR machines which will "read" the numbers and cause the checks to be sorted in the desired fashion. If the amounts of the checks are printed thereon in magnetic ink, such amounts can be totaled, and each check can be posted electronically to the customer's account. This process can be carried on at extremely high speed with almost no danger of error.

Shown on the next page is a reproduction of two checks which illustrates the appearance of the magnetic ink characters that have been printed at the bottom. The group of digits at the extreme left indicates the Federal Reserve District and the bank number, and the group that follows is the number that has been assigned to the depositor — The P. G. Thomas Co., in this instance. Some banks are furnishing their depositors with deposit tickets that have similar magnetic characters to assist in the processing of deposits. (For a further discussion of electronic processing of checks, see Appendix, pages A-11 and A-12.)

Recording Bank Transactions. A depositor should keep a record of the transactions he completes with his bank. The usual plan is to keep this record on the checkbook stubs as shown in the illustration on the next page. It will be noted that the record consists of detailed information concerning each check written and an amount column in which should be recorded **(1)** the balance brought forward or carried down, **(2)** the amount of deposits to be added, and **(3)** the amount of checks to be subtracted. The

Checks and Stubs

No. 92 $75.00
DATE *April 3* 19 67
TO *Brandon Bros.*
FOR *Rent*
Rent Expense ✓

	DOLLARS	CENTS
BAL. BRO'T FOR'D	4,198	72
AMT. DEPOSITED		
TOTAL		
AMT. THIS CHECK	75	00
BAL. CAR'D FOR'D	4,123	72

BELLEVUE TRUST CO.
Cincinnati, Ohio
No. 92   13-56/420

April 3 1967

PAY TO THE ORDER OF *Brandon Bros.* $75.00

Seventy-five 00/100 DOLLARS

THE P. G. THOMAS CO.

P. G. Thomas, Jr.

⑅0420⑅0056⑅ 319⑅04⑅531⑅

No. 93 $531.37
DATE *April 5* 19 67
TO *Glenview Mfg. Co.*
FOR *Inv. Mar. 31*
Accounts Pay. ✓

	DOLLARS	CENTS
BAL. BRO'T FOR'D	4,123	72
AMT. DEPOSITED	625	00
TOTAL	4,748	72
AMT. THIS CHECK	531	37
BAL. CAR'D FOR'D	4,217	35

BELLEVUE TRUST CO.
Cincinnati, Ohio
No. 93   13-56/420

April 5 1967

PAY TO THE ORDER OF *Glenview Manufacturing Co.* $531.37

Five hundred thirty-one 37/100 DOLLARS

THE P. G. THOMAS CO.

P. G. Thomas, Jr.

⑅0420⑅0056⑅ 319⑅04⑅531⑅

Checks and Stubs

purpose is to keep a detailed record of deposits made and checks issued and to indicate the balance in the checking account after each check is drawn.

As the amount of each check is recorded in the journal, a check mark may be placed immediately after the account title written on the stub to indicate that it has been recorded. When the canceled check is subsequently received from the bank, the amount shown on the stub may be checked to indicate that the canceled check has been received.

Records Kept by a Bank. The usual transactions completed by a bank with a depositor are:

(a) Accepting deposits made by the depositor.
(b) Paying checks issued by the depositor.
(c) Lending money to the depositor.
(d) Discounting commercial paper for the depositor (another type of lending).
(e) Collecting the amounts of various kinds of commercial paper, such as notes and drafts, for the account of the depositor.

The bank keeps an account for each depositor. Each transaction affecting a depositor's account is recorded by debiting or crediting his account, depending upon the effect of the transaction. When a bank accepts a deposit, the account of the depositor is credited for the amount of the deposit. The deposit increases the bank's liability to the depositor.

When the bank pays a check that has been drawn on the bank, it debits the account of the depositor for the amount of the check. If the bank makes a collection for a depositor, the net amount of the collection is credited to his account. At the same time the bank notifies the depositor on a form similar to the one shown below that the collection has been made.

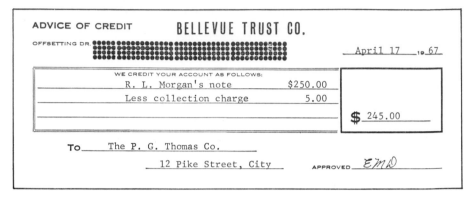

ADVICE OF CREDIT   BELLEVUE TRUST CO.

OFFSETTING DR.

April 17   19 67

WE CREDIT YOUR ACCOUNT AS FOLLOWS:

R. L. Morgan's note $250.00
Less collection charge   5.00

$ 245.00

To   The P. G. Thomas Co.

12 Pike Street, City   APPROVED   EMD

Credit Advice

Bank Statement. Once each month a bank renders a statement of account to each depositor similar to that shown on the next page. This statement is a report showing **(1)** the balance on deposit at the beginning of the period, **(2)** the amounts of deposits made during the period, **(3)** the amounts of checks honored during the period, **(4)** other items charged to the depositor's account during the period, and **(5)** the balance on deposit at the end of the period. With his bank statement, the depositor also receives all checks paid by the bank during the period, together with any other vouchers representing items charged to his account.

Reconciling the Bank Statement. When a bank statement is received, the depositor should check it immediately with the bank balance record kept on his check stubs. This procedure is known as _reconciling the bank statement_. The balance shown on the bank statement may not be the same as the amount shown on the check stubs for one or more of the following reasons:

(a) Some of the checks issued during the period may not have been presented to the bank for payment before the statement was prepared. These are known as *outstanding checks.*

(b) Deposits made by mail may have been in transit, or a deposit placed in the night depository may not have been recorded by the bank until the day following the date of the statement.

(c) Service charges or other charges may appear on the bank statement that the depositor has not recorded on his check stubs.

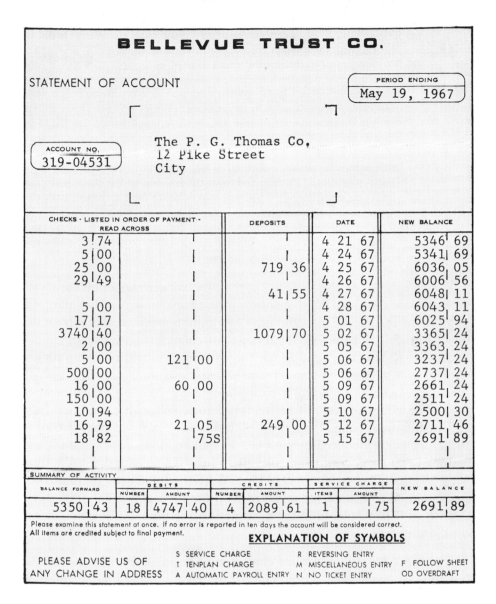

BELLEVUE TRUST CO.

STATEMENT OF ACCOUNT

PERIOD ENDING
May 19, 1967

ACCOUNT NO.
319-04531

The P. G. Thomas Co,
12 Pike Street
City

CHECKS - LISTED IN ORDER OF PAYMENT - READ ACROSS			DEPOSITS	DATE	NEW BALANCE
3 74				4 21 67	5346 69
5 00				4 24 67	5341 69
25 00			719 36	4 25 67	6036 05
29 49				4 26 67	6006 56
			41 55	4 27 67	6048 11
5 00				4 28 67	6043 11
17 17				5 01 67	6025 94
3740 40			1079 70	5 02 67	3365 24
2 00				5 05 67	3363 24
5 00	121 00			5 06 67	3237 24
500 00				5 06 67	2737 24
16 00	60 00			5 09 67	2661 24
150 00				5 09 67	2511 24
10 94				5 10 67	2500 30
16 79	21 05		249 00	5 12 67	2711 46
18 82		75S		5 15 67	2691 89

SUMMARY OF ACTIVITY

BALANCE FORWARD	DEBITS		CREDITS		SERVICE CHARGE		NEW BALANCE
	NUMBER	AMOUNT	NUMBER	AMOUNT	ITEMS	AMOUNT	
5350 43	18	4747 40	4	2089 61	1	75	2691 89

Please examine this statement at once. If no error is reported in ten days the account will be considered correct. All items are credited subject to final payment.

EXPLANATION OF SYMBOLS

PLEASE ADVISE US OF
ANY CHANGE IN ADDRESS

S SERVICE CHARGE
T TENPLAN CHARGE
A AUTOMATIC PAYROLL ENTRY

R REVERSING ENTRY
M MISCELLANEOUS ENTRY
N NO TICKET ENTRY

F FOLLOW SHEET
OD OVERDRAFT

Bank Statement

(d) The depositor may have erred in keeping his bank record.

(e) The bank may have erred in keeping its account with the depositor.

If a depositor is unable to reconcile his bank statement, he should report the matter to his bank immediately.

A suggested procedure in reconciling the bank statement is enumerated on the next page.

(a) The amount of each deposit recorded on the bank statement should be checked with the amount recorded on the check stubs.

(b) The amount of each canceled check should be compared both with the amount recorded on the bank statement and with the amount recorded on the depositor's check stubs. When making this comparison it is a good plan to place a check mark by the amount recorded on each check stub to indicate that the canceled check has been returned by the bank and its amount verified.

(c) The amounts of any items listed on a bank statement that represent charges to a depositor's account which have not been entered on the check stubs should be deducted from the balance on the check stubs and should be recorded in the journal that is being used to record cash disbursements.

(d) A list of the outstanding checks should be prepared. The information needed for this list may be obtained by examining the check stubs and noting the amounts that have not been check marked.

After completing the foregoing steps, the balance shown on the check stubs should equal the balance shown in the bank statement less the total amount of the checks outstanding. A common error on the part of depositors is failure to record the amount of *counter checks* issued. Banks usually provide counter checks for the convenience of their depositors in withdrawing funds for personal use. Such checks are canceled and returned to the depositor with the bank statement so that it is an easy matter for the depositor to detect if he has failed to record such checks.

At the top of page 71 is a reconciliation of the bank balance shown in the statement reproduced on page 69. In making this reconciliation it was assumed that the depositor's check stub indicated a balance of $2,903.51 on May 19, that Checks Nos. 112, 115, and 117 had not been presented for payment and thus were not returned with the bank statement, and that a deposit of $465.92 placed in the night depository on May 19 is not shown on the statement.

Service Charges. A service charge may be made by a bank for the handling of checks and other items. The basis and the amount of such charges vary with different banks in different localities.

When a bank statement indicates that a service charge has been made, the depositor should record the amount of the service charge by debiting an expense account, such as Miscellaneous Expense, and by crediting Cash. He should also deduct the amount of such charges from the check stub balance.

Keeping a Ledger Account with the Bank. As explained previously, a memorandum account with the bank may be kept on the depositor's checkbook stub. The depositor may also keep a ledger account with the bank if desired. The title of such an account usually is the name of the

THE P. G. THOMAS CO.
Reconciliation of Bank Statement
May 19, 1967

Balance, May 19, per bank statement..........		$2,691.89
Add: Deposit, May 19..		465.92
		$3,157.81
Less checks outstanding, May 19:		
No. 112.............................	$ 75.00	
No. 115.............................	19.50	
No. 117.............................	160.55	255.05
Corrected bank balance, May 19.............		$2,902.76
Check stub balance, May 19.................		$2,903.51
Less bank service charge...................		.75
Corrected check stub balance, May 19.........		$2,902.76

bank. Sometimes more than one account is kept with a bank in which case each account should be correctly labeled. Such terms as "commercial," "executive," and "payroll" are used to identify the accounts.

The bank account should be debited for the amount of each deposit and should be credited for the amount of each check written. The account should also be credited for any other items that may be charged to the account by the bank, including service charges.

When both a cash account and a bank account are kept in the ledger, the following procedure should be observed in recording transactions affecting these accounts:

CASH		BELLEVUE TRUST COMPANY	
Debit	Credit	Debit	Credit
For all receipts of cash and cash items.	(a) For all payments in cash. (b) For all bank deposits.	For all deposits.	(a) For all checks written. (b) For all service charges. (c) For all other charges, such as for dishonored checks.

Under this method of accounting for cash and banking transactions, the cash account will be in balance when all cash on hand has been deposited in the bank. To prove the balance of the cash account at any time, it is necessary only to count the cash and cash items on hand and to compare the total with the cash account balance. To prove the bank account balance, it will be necessary to reconcile the bank balance in the same manner in which it is reconciled when only a memorandum record of bank transactions is kept on the check stubs.

The cash account can be dispensed with when a bank account is kept in the ledger and all cash receipts are deposited in the bank. When this is done, all disbursements (except small expenditures made from a petty cash fund) are made by check.

Under this method of accounting, the Cash Debits and the Cash Credits columns of the journal may be headed as follows:

BANK	
DEPOSITS DEBIT	CHECKS CREDIT

When this form of journal is used, all cash receipts should be entered in the Bank Deposits Debit column and all checks issued should be entered in the Bank Checks Credit column. Daily, or at frequent intervals, the receipts are deposited in the bank. If all cash received during the month has been deposited before the books are closed at the end of the month, the total amount of the bank deposits will equal the total cash receipts for the month. If all disbursements during the month are made by check, the total amount of checks issued will be the total disbursements for the month.

Savings Account

When a savings account is opened in a bank, a signature card must be signed by the depositor. He is then given a passbook that he must present at the bank when making deposits or when making withdrawals. By signing the signature card, the depositor agrees to abide by the rules and the regulations of the bank. These rules and regulations vary with different banks and may be altered and amended from time to time. The principal differences between a savings account and a checking account are that interest is paid by the bank on a savings account and withdrawals from a savings account must be made at the bank by the depositor or his authorized agent. Interest usually is computed on a semiannual basis, although it may be computed more often. The passbook must be presented along with a withdrawal slip when money is drawn from the account. Banks do not as a rule pay interest on the balances in checking accounts. Depositors use checking accounts primarily as a convenient means of making payments, while savings accounts are used primarily as a means of accumulating funds with interest.

Savings accounts are not common for businesses. If the assets of a business include money in a bank savings account, there should be a separate account in the ledger with a title and a number that indicate the nature of the deposit. Sometimes the name of the bank is in the title, as, for example, "Bellevue Trust Co. — Savings Account." When the bank credits interest to the account, the depositor should record the amount in his accounts by a debit to the savings account and by a credit to Interest Earned. The interest is revenue whether withdrawn or not.

Report No. 7

Refer to the workbook and complete Report No. 7. This assignment provides a test of your ability to apply the principles developed in the first three chapters of the textbook. After completing the report, you may proceed with the textbook discussion in Chapter 4 until the next report is required.

chapter four

payroll accounting

Employers need to maintain detailed and accurate payroll accounting records. Accurate accounting for employees' earnings preserves the legal and moral right of each employee to be paid according to his employment contract and the laws governing such contracts.

Payroll accounting records also provide information useful in the analysis and classification of labor costs. At the same time, payroll accounting information is invaluable in contract discussions with labor unions, in the settlement of company-union grievances, and in other forms of collective bargaining. Clearly, there is virtually no margin for error in payroll accounting.

earnings and deductions

The first step in determining the amount to be paid to an employee is to calculate the amount of his total or gross earnings for the pay period. The second step is to determine the amounts of any deductions that are required either by law or by agreement. Depending upon a variety of circumstances, either or both of these steps may be relatively simple or quite complicated. An examination of the factors that are involved follows.

Employer-Employee Relationships

Not every individual who performs services for a business is considered to be an employee. A public accountant, lawyer, or management consultant who sells his services to a business does not become its employee. Neither does a plumber nor an electrician who is hired to make specific repairs or installations on business property. These people are told what to do, but not how to do it, and the compensation that they receive for their services is called a *fee*. Any person who agrees to perform a service for a fee and is not subject to the control of those whom he serves is called an *independent contractor*.

In contrast, an employee is one who is under the control and direction of his employer with regard to the performance of services. The difference between an independent contractor and an employee is an important legal distinction. The nature and extent of the responsibilities of a contractor and a client to each other and to third parties are quite different from the mutual obligations of an employer and his employee.

Types of Compensation

Compensation for managerial or administrative services usually is called *salary*. A salary normally is expressed in terms of a month or a year. Compensation either for skilled or for unskilled labor usually is referred to as *wages*. Wages ordinarily are expressed in terms of hours, weeks, or pieces of accomplishment. The terms salary and wages often are used interchangeably in practice.

Supplements to basic salaries or wages of employees include bonuses, commissions, cost-of-living adjustments, pensions, and profit sharing plans. Compensation also may take the form of goods, lodging, meals, or other property, and as such is measured by the fair value of the property or service given in payment for the employee's efforts.

Determination of Total Earnings

An employee's earnings commonly are based on the time worked during the payroll period. Sometimes, earnings are based on units of output or of sales during the period. Compensation based on time requires a record of the time worked by each employee. Where there are only a few employees, a record of times worked kept in a memorandum book may suffice. Where there are many employees, time clocks commonly are used to record time spent on the job each day. With time clocks, a clock card is provided for each employee and the clock is used to record arrival and departure times. Whatever method is used, the total time worked during the payroll period must be computed.

Employees often are entitled to compensation at more than their regular rate of pay for work during certain hours or on certain days. If the employer is engaged in Interstate Commerce, the Federal Fair Labor Standards Act (commonly known as the Wages and Hours Law) provides that all employees covered by the Act must be paid one and one-half times the regular rate for all hours worked in excess of 40 per week. Labor-management agreements often require extra pay for certain hours or days. In such cases, hours worked in excess of eight per day or work on Sundays and specified holidays may be paid for at higher rates.

To illustrate, assume that the company which employs George Hempel pays time and a half for all hours worked in excess of 40 per week and double time for work on Sunday. Hempel's regular rate is $3 per hour, and during the week ended April 15, he worked nine hours each day Monday through Friday, six hours on Saturday, and four on Sunday. Hempel's total earnings for the week ended April 15 would be computed as follows:

40 hours @ $3.00	$120.00
11 hours @ $4.50	49.50
(Hempel worked 9 hours each day Monday through Friday and 6 hours on Saturday — a total of 51 hours. Forty hours would be paid for at the regular rate and 11 hours at time and a half.)	
4 hours (on Sunday) @ $6.00	24.00
Total earnings for the week	$193.50

An employee who is paid a regular salary may be entitled to premium pay for any overtime. If this is the case, it is necessary to compute the regular hourly rate of pay before computing the overtime rate. To illustrate, assume that Robert Virgil receives a regular salary of $500 a month. Virgil is entitled to overtime pay at the rate of one and one-half times his regular hourly rate for any time worked in excess of 40 hours per week. His overtime pay may be computed as follows:

$500 × 12 months = $6,000 annual pay
$6,000 ÷ 52 weeks = $115.38 per week
$115.38 ÷ 40 hours = $2.88 per regular hour
$2.88 × 1½ = $4.32 per overtime hour

Deductions from Total Earnings

With few exceptions, employers are required to withhold portions of each employee's total earnings both for federal income taxes and for social security taxes. Certain states and cities also require tax withholding on the part of employers. Besides these deductions, an agreement between the employer and the employee may call for amounts to be withheld for any one or more of the following reasons.

(a) To purchase United States savings bonds for the employee.
(b) To pay a life, accident, or health insurance premium for the employee.
(c) To pay the employee's union dues.
(d) To add to a pension fund or profit sharing fund.
(e) To pay to some charitable organization.
(f) To repay a loan from the company or from the company credit union.

Social Security and Tax Account Number

Each employee is required to have a social security account and tax account number for payroll accounting purposes. A completed Form SS-5, the official form to be used in applying for an account number, follows:

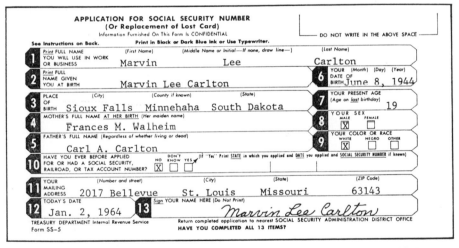

Completed Application for Social Security and Tax Account Number (Form SS-5)

Employees' Income Taxes Withheld

Under federal law, employers are required to withhold certain amounts from the total earnings of each employee to be applied toward the payment of the employee's federal income tax. The amount to be withheld is governed by **(1)** the total earnings of the employee, **(2)** the number of *withholding exemptions* claimed by the employee, **(3)** the marital status of the employee, and **(4)** the length of the employee's pay period.

Each federal income taxpayer is entitled to one exemption for himself or for herself and one each for certain other qualified relatives whom he or she supports. The law specifies the relationship that must exist, the extent of support required, and how much the *dependent* may earn in order that an exemption may be claimed. A taxpayer and spouse each get an extra exemption for age over 65 years and still another exemption for blindness.

An employed taxpayer must furnish his employer with an Employee's Withholding Exemption Certificate (Form W-4) showing the number of exemptions claimed. The exemption certificate completed by Marvin Lee Carlton is shown below.

FORM W-4 (Rev. Jan. 1967) U.S. Treasury Department Internal Revenue Service	**EMPLOYEE'S WITHHOLDING EXEMPTION CERTIFICATE**		

Type or print full name _____ Marvin Lee Carlton _____ Social Security Number __504-38-8340__

Home address _____ 2017 Bellevue _____ City __St. Louis__ State __Missouri__ ZIP code __63143__

EMPLOYEE: File this form with your employer. Otherwise, he must withhold U.S. Income tax from your wages without exemption.

EMPLOYER: Keep this certificate with your records. If the employee is believed to have claimed too many exemptions, the District Director should be so advised.

HOW TO CLAIM YOUR WITHHOLDING EXEMPTIONS

1. If SINGLE (or if married and wish withholding as single person), write "1." If you claim no exemptions, write "0". _____
2. If MARRIED, one exemption each is allowable for husband and wife if not claimed on another certificate.
   (a) If you claim both of these exemptions, write "2"; (b) If you claim one of these exemptions, write "1"; (c) If you claim neither of these exemptions, write "0" _____ **2**
3. Exemptions for age and blindness (applicable only to you and your wife but not to dependents):
   (a) If you or your wife will be 65 years of age or older at the end of the year, and you claim this exemption, write "1"; If both will be 65 or older, and you claim both of these exemptions, write "2" _____
   (b) If you or your wife are blind, and you claim this exemption, write "1"; If both are blind, and you claim both of these exemptions, write "2" _____
4. If you claim exemptions for one or more dependents, write the number of such exemptions. (Do not claim exemption for a dependent unless you are qualified under Instruction 4 on other side.) _____ **1**
5. If you claim additional withholding allowances for itemized deductions fill out and attach Schedule A (Form W-4), and enter the number of allowances claimed (if claimed file new Form W-4 each year) _____
6. Add the exemptions and allowances (if any) which you have claimed above and write total _____ **3**
7. Additional withholding per pay period under agreement with employer. (See Instruction 1.) _____ $

I CERTIFY that the number of withholding exemptions claimed on this certificate does not exceed the number to which I am entitled. 048—16—79061-1

(Date) __January 3__, 19__67__ (Signed) __Marvin Lee Carlton__

Completed Withholding Exemption Certificate (Form W-4)

Employees with large itemized deductions are permitted to claim additional withholding exemptions called *withholding allowances*. Any employee desiring to claim one or more withholding allowances must estimate his expected total earnings and itemized deductions for the coming year. One withholding allowance is granted for each full $700 by which the employee's itemized deductions as estimated exceed the sum of 10 percent of the first $7,500 that he earns and 17 percent of his remaining total earnings. Each withholding allowance will give the taxpayer an additional exemption, but the employed taxpayer will have to file a new Withholding Exemption Certificate (Form W-4) each year to claim one or more such allowances.

Most employers use the *wage-bracket method* of determining the amount of tax to be withheld. This method involves the use of income tax withholding tables provided by the Internal Revenue Service. Such tables cover monthly, semimonthly, biweekly, weekly, and daily or miscellaneous periods. There are two types of tables: **(1)** single persons and unmarried heads of households, and **(2)** married persons. Copies may be obtained from any District Director of Internal Revenue. A portion of a weekly income tax wage-bracket withholding table for married persons is illustrated on page 79. As an example of the use of this table, assume that

Marvin Lee Carlton (who claims 3 exemptions) had gross earnings of $150 for the week ending December 15, 1967. On the line showing the tax on wages of "at least $150, less than $160," in the column headed "3 withholding exemptions," $17 is given as the amount to be withheld.

Married PERSONS *Weekly* PAYROLL PERIOD

WAGES: $76 – $570

Wages are		Number of withholding exemptions claimed										
		0	1	2	3	4	5	6	7	8	9	10 or more
At least	Less than	Amount of income tax to be withheld										
$ 76	$ 78	$10.80	$ 8.80	$ 6.70	$ 4.70	$ 2.70	$ .80					
78	80	11.10	9.10	7.00	5.00	3.00	1.10					
80	82	11.40	9.40	7.30	5.30	3.30	1.40					
82	84	11.70	9.70	7.60	5.60	3.60	1.70					
84	86	12.00	10.00	7.90	5.90	3.90	1.90	$ .10				
86	88	12.30	10.30	8.20	6.20	4.20	2.20	.30				
88	90	12.70	10.60	8.50	6.50	4.50	2.50	.60				
90	92	13.00	10.90	8.80	6.80	4.80	2.80	.90				
92	94	13.30	11.20	9.10	7.10	5.10	3.10	1.20				
94	96	13.70	11.50	9.40	7.40	5.40	3.40	1.50				
96	98	14.00	11.80	9.70	7.70	5.70	3.70	1.70				
98	100	14.40	12.10	10.00	8.00	6.00	4.00	2.00	$ .10			
100	105	15.00	12.70	10.60	8.50	6.50	4.50	2.50	.60			
105	110	15.80	13.50	11.30	9.30	7.30	5.30	3.20	1.30			
110	115	16.70	14.40	12.10	10.00	8.00	6.00	4.00	2.00	$ .10		
115	120	17.50	15.20	12.90	10.80	8.80	6.80	4.70	2.70	.80		
120	125	18.40	16.10	13.80	11.50	9.50	7.50	5.50	3.50	1.50		
125	130	19.20	16.90	14.60	12.30	10.30	8.30	6.20	4.20	2.20	$ .40	
130	135	20.10	17.80	15.50	13.20	11.00	9.00	7.00	5.00	3.00	1.10	
135	140	20.90	18.60	16.30	14.00	11.80	9.80	7.70	5.70	3.70	1.80	
140	145	21.80	19.50	17.20	14.90	12.60	10.50	8.50	6.50	4.50	2.50	$ .60
145	150	22.60	20.30	18.00	15.70	13.50	11.30	9.20	7.20	5.20	3.20	1.30
150	160	23.90	21.60	19.30	17.00	14.70	12.40	10.40	8.30	6.30	4.30	2.30
160	170	25.60	23.30	21.00	18.70	16.40	14.10	11.90	9.80	7.80	5.80	3.80
170	180	27.50	25.00	22.70	20.40	18.10	15.80	13.60	11.30	9.30	7.30	5.30

Portion of Married Persons Weekly Federal Income Tax Withholding Table

Whether the wage-bracket method or some other method is used in computing the amount of tax to be withheld, the employee is given full benefit for all exemptions claimed plus a standard deduction of approximately 10 percent. In any event, the sum of the taxes withheld from an employee's wages only approximates the tax on his actual income derived solely from wages up to $5,000 a year. An employee may be liable for a tax larger than the amount withheld. On the other hand, the amount of the taxes withheld by the employer may be greater than the employee's actual tax liability. In such an event, the employee will be entitled to a refund of the excess taxes withheld, or he may elect to apply the excess to his tax liability for the following year.

Several of the states have adopted state income tax withholding procedures. Some of these states supply employers with withholding exemption certificate forms and income tax withholding tables that are similar in appearance to those used by the federal Internal Revenue Service. Note, however, that each state that has an income tax law uses the specific tax rates and dollar amounts for exemptions as required by its law. Some states determine the amount to be withheld merely by applying a fixed percentage to the federal withholding amount.

Employees' FICA Taxes Withheld

Payroll taxes are imposed on almost all employers and employees for old-age, survivors, and disability insurance (OASDI) benefits and health insurance for the aged (HIP), both under the Federal Insurance Contributions Act (FICA). The base of the tax and the tax rate have been changed several times since the law was first enacted and are subject to change by Congress at any time in the future. For purposes of this chapter, the rate is assumed to be 4 percent of the taxable wages paid during the calendar year for OASDI and 0.5 percent for HIP. Only the first $6,600 of the wages paid to each employee in any calendar year is taxable. Any amount of compensation paid in excess of $6,600 is assumed to be exempt from the tax. The employees' portion of the FICA tax must be withheld from their wages by the employer. Although it is true that the base and rate of the tax may be changed at the pleasure of Congress, the accounting principles or methods of recording payroll transactions are not affected.

A few states require employers to withhold a percentage of the employees' wages for unemployment compensation benefits or for disability benefits. In some states and cities, employers are required to withhold a percentage of the employees' wages for other types of payroll taxes. The withholding of income taxes at the state and city level has already been mentioned. Despite the number of withholdings required, each employer must comply with the proper laws in withholding any taxes based on payrolls and in keeping his payroll accounting records.

Payroll Records

The needs of management and the requirements of various federal and state laws make it necessary for employers to keep records that will provide or make it possible to determine the following information:

PAYROLL REGISTER

NO.	NAME	EXEMP.	MARITAL	EARNINGS			FICA	FEDERAL INC. TAX
				REGULAR	OVERTIME	GROSS		
1	Brown, Harold D.	2	M	120 00		120 00	5 40	13 80
2	Carlton, Marvin L.	3	M	135 00	15 00	150 00		17 00
3	Geckler, Dorene L.	1	S	95 00		95 00	4 28	12 70
4	Heath, William L.	4	M	120 00	15 00	135 00		11 80
5	Johnson, Oscar E.	3	M	125 00	15 00	140 00	6 30	14 90
6	Myers, Kent J.	3	M	105 00		105 00	4 73	9 30
7	Nichols, Joseph E.	2	M	115 00	10 00	125 00	5 63	14 60
8	Roberts, John H.	1	S	100 00		100 00	4 50	14 10
				915 00	55 00	970 00	30 84	108 20
				915 00	55 00	970 00	30 84	108 20

Payroll Register — Manually Prepared (Left Side)

(a) The name, address, and social security number of each employee.

(b) The gross amount of each employee's earnings, the date of payment, and the period of employment covered by each payroll.

(c) The total amount of gross earnings accumulated since the first of the year.

(d) The amount of any taxes or other items withheld from each employee's earnings.

Regardless of the number of employees or type of business, three types of payroll records usually need to be prepared for or by the employer. They are: **(1)** the payroll register or payroll journal; **(2)** the payroll check with earnings statement attached; and **(3)** the earnings record of the individual employee (on a weekly, monthly, quarterly, or annual basis). These records can be prepared either by *manual* or by *automated* methods.

Payroll Register. A manually prepared payroll register used by Central States Paper & Bag Company for the payroll period ended December 15, 1967, is illustrated on pages 80 and 81. The usual source of information for preparing a payroll register is the time memorandum book or the time clock cards. Central States Paper & Bag Company has eight employees, as the illustration shows. Regular deductions are made from the earnings of employees for FICA taxes, federal income taxes, and city earnings tax. In addition, for the pay period ending nearest to the middle of the month, deductions are made for life insurance, private hospital insurance, the company credit union, and (if desired) for the purchase of United States savings bonds. Note that the deduction column labeled "Other" is used for recording bond purchases, and may be used for other infrequent deductions as well.

Marvin L. Carlton and William L. Heath have each authorized Central States Paper & Bag Company to withhold $5 on the payday nearest to the middle of each month for United States savings bonds. When the

FOR PERIOD ENDED *December 15* 19 67

| | | DEDUCTIONS | | | | NET PAY | |
CITY TAX	LIFE INSURANCE	PRIVATE HOSP. INS.	CREDIT UNION	OTHER		CHECK NO.	AMOUNT
1 20	4 00		2 00			203	93 60
1 50	5 00	2 50	2 00	Savings Bond	5 00	204	117 00
95		2 00				205	75 07
1 35				Savings Bond	5 00	206	114 85
1 40	5 00	2 50	2 00			207	107 90
1 05	3 00					208	86 92
1 25			2 00			209	101 52
						210	75 40
9 70	20 00	9 00	10 00		10 00		772 26
9 70	20 00	9 00	10 00		10 00		772 26

Payroll Register — Manually Prepared (Right Side)

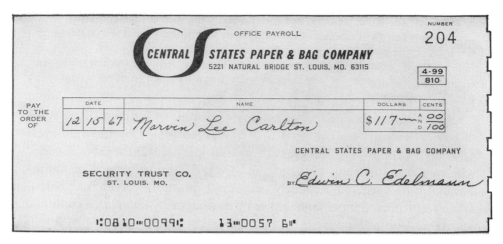

Completed Paycheck — Manually Prepared

amount withheld reaches the sum of $37.50, a $50 Series E, United States savings bond is purchased at the bank for each of the two employees and delivered to them.

Only the first $6,600 of earnings received in any calendar year is subject to FICA taxes. Mr. Carlton's earnings for the week ending December 15 are exempt from the FICA tax because he has already been taxed on earnings totaling $6,600.

After the payroll register has been completed the amount columns should be footed and the footings proved as follows:

Regular earnings..		$915.00
Overtime earnings...		55.00
Gross earnings		$970.00
Deductions:		
FICA taxes...	$ 30.84	
Federal income taxes...................................	108.20	
City earnings taxes	9.70	
Life insurance premiums	20.00	
Private hospital insurance premiums	9.00	
Credit union..	10.00	
United States savings bonds.............................	10.00	197.74
Net amount of payroll.....................................		$772.26

After proving the footings, the totals should be entered in ink and the record should be ruled with single and double lines as shown in the illustration. Employees may be paid in cash or by check. Many businesses prepare a check for the net amount of the payroll and deposit it in a special Payroll Bank Account. Individual paychecks are then drawn on that account for the amount due each employee. The employer usually furnishes a statement of payroll deductions to the employee along with each wage payment. Paychecks with detachable stubs, like the one for Marvin and Deduction Stub

L. Carlton illustrated above, are widely used. The stub should be detached before the check is cashed, and the stub should be retained by the employee as a permanent record of his earnings and payroll deductions.

Employee's Earnings Record. An auxiliary record of each employee's earnings usually is kept in order to provide the information needed in preparing the various federal, state, and local reports required of employers. A manually prepared employee's earnings record used by Central States Paper & Bag Company for Marvin Lee Carlton during the last two quarters of the current calendar year is illustrated on page 84. This record may be kept on separate sheets or on cards, which may be filed alphabetically or numerically for ready reference. The information recorded on this form is taken from the payroll register.

Marvin Carlton's earnings for the last half of the year up to December 15 are shown on this form. The entry for the pay period ended December 15 is posted from the payroll register illustrated on pages 80 and 81. Mr. Carlton's cumulative earnings passed the $6,600 mark during the week ended December 1. Although his total earnings for that week amounted to $135, only $49 of such wages was subject to the combined FICA tax of 4.5 percent, hence only $2.21 was withheld from his wages for that week. For the remainder of the current calendar year, his entire earnings will be exempt from FICA tax withholding.

The payroll register is a summary of the earnings of all employees for each pay period, while the earnings record is a summary of the annual earnings of each employee. The earnings record illustrated on page 84 is designed so that a record of the earnings of the employee for the first half of the year may be kept on one side and a record of the earnings for the

1967 Period Ending	EARNINGS Regular	EARNINGS Overtime	EARNINGS Gross	FICA	Federal Inc. Tax	City Tax	DEDUCTIONS Life Insurance	DEDUCTIONS Private Hosp. Ins.	DEDUCTIONS Credit Union	DEDUCTIONS Other	NET PAY Check No.	NET PAY Amount
1 7/7	135.00		135.00	6.08	14.00	1.35					20	113.57
2 7/14	135.00	10.00	145.00	6.53	15.70	1.45	5.00	2.50	2.00	Earnings Bond 5.00	28	106.82
3 7/21	135.00		135.00	6.08	14.00	1.35					36	113.57
4 7/28	135.00	10.00	145.00	6.53	15.70	1.45					44	121.32
5 8/4	135.00		135.00	6.08	14.00	1.35					52	113.57
6 8/11	135.00		135.00	6.08	14.00	1.35					60	113.57
7 8/18	135.00	7.50	142.50	6.41	14.90	1.43	5.00	2.50	2.00	Earnings Bond 5.00	68	105.26
8 8/25	135.00		135.00	6.08	14.00	1.35					76	113.57
9 9/1	135.00		135.00	6.08	14.00	1.35					84	113.57
10 9/8	135.00	5.00	140.00	6.30	14.90	1.40					92	117.40
11 9/15	135.00		135.00	6.08	14.00	1.35	5.00	2.50	2.00	Earnings Bond 5.00	100	99.01
12 9/22	135.00	10.00	145.00	6.53	15.70	1.45					108	121.32
13 9/29	135.00		135.00	6.08	14.00	1.35					116	113.57
THIRD QUARTER	1,755.00	42.50	1,797.50	80.94	188.90	17.98	15.00	7.50	6.00	15.00		1,466.18
1 10/6	135.00		135.00	6.08	14.00	1.35					124	113.57
2 10/13	135.00	8.00	143.00	6.44	14.90	1.43	5.00	2.50	2.00	Earnings Bond 5.00	132	105.73
3 10/20	135.00	6.00	141.00	6.35	14.90	1.41					140	119.34
4 10/27	135.00		135.00	6.08	14.00	1.35					148	113.57
5 11/3	135.00		135.00	6.08	14.00	1.35					156	113.57
6 11/10	135.00	10.00	145.00	6.53	15.70	1.45					164	121.32
7 11/17	135.00	5.00	140.00	6.30	14.90	1.40	5.00	2.50	2.00	Earnings Bond 5.00	172	102.90
8 11/24	135.00	7.50	142.50	6.41	14.90	1.43					180	119.76
9 12/1	135.00		135.00	2.21	14.00	1.35					188	117.44
10 12/8	135.00		135.00		14.00	1.35					196	119.65
11 12/15	135.00	15.00	150.00		17.00	1.50	5.00	2.50	2.00	Earnings Bond 5.00	204	117.00
12												
13												
FOURTH QUARTER												
YEARLY TOTAL												

SEX M	F	DEPARTMENT	OCCUPATION	SOCIAL SECURITY NO.	NAME – LAST	FIRST	MIDDLE	EMPLOYEE NO.
✓		Maintenance	Service	504-38-8-340	Carlton	Marvin	Lee	2

Employee's Earnings Record — Manually Prepared

last half of the year may be kept on the other side of the form. Thus, at the end of the year, the form provides a complete record of the earnings of the employee for the year. It also provides a record of the earnings for each calendar quarter needed by the employer in the preparation of his quarterly returns. These returns will be discussed later in this chapter.

Automated Payroll Systems

Automated payroll systems may involve the use of small-capacity bookkeeping machines, large-capacity bookkeeping machines, or electronic data processing equipment. Both bookkeeping machine payroll systems and electronic payroll systems make it possible to prepare a payroll check with deduction stub, an earnings record, and a payroll register simultaneously. This is an application of the *write-it-once principle*, which recognizes that each time the same information is recopied there is another chance for an error.

Service Bureaus and Payroll Accounting. The development of automated accounting methods and electronic data processing equipment have led to the establishment of a large number of *service bureaus.* Service bureaus are business organizations engaged in data processing on a contract basis for other businesses of small and medium size. They either are independently operated or are owned and operated by the major business machine manufacturers or by banks. In any case, their employees are trained in accounting and systems work and can set up and operate effective payroll systems for customers.

When payroll accounting is done for a business by a service bureau, the preliminary work that the business needs to do usually is quite limited. One or more cards are punched for each employee with the aid of a keypunch machine for each payroll period, and these cards contain necessary information such as:

(a) Employee name
(b) Employee address
(c) Employee social security number
(d) Regular earnings
(e) Overtime earnings
(f) Federal income tax withheld
(g) FICA (OASDI and HIP) tax withheld
(h) Other deductions

These punched cards are picked up by the service bureau at regular intervals, and the payroll records desired by the business customer are prepared.

In a manual payroll system, the payroll register normally is prepared first and serves as a journal. The employee earnings records, checks, and stubs are then prepared from the payroll register information. However, in an automated payroll system all three records are prepared simultaneously. Because of this, the order of their preparation is not of any concern to the accountant.

Employer-Operated Payroll Systems. A payroll check with deduction stub, earnings record, and payroll register entry prepared simultaneously on a bookkeeping machine are illustrated below and on the following pages. Assume that these records were prepared by the Central States Paper & Bag Company for its employee, Marvin L. Carlton, for the same pay period as the manual records previously illustrated on pages 80 to 84, inclusive. Contrast the two types of payroll systems. The primary advantage of the machine system is the saving of time and labor.

In addition to the *write-it-once* features of modern bookkeeping machines, electronic payroll systems can also provide speed and storage as well as needed adding and multiplying ability. Through the use of electronic equipment, adding and multiplying of payrolls can be speeded up, and information such as wage rates and withholding table amounts can be stored inside the equipment. As one would expect, the cost of electronic payroll equipment is noticeably higher than the cost of more conventional bookkeeping machines. The type of electronic data processing system well suited, among other things, to payroll accounting is described and illustrated in the appendix to this textbook.

Much of the work usually required to figure employees' gross earnings, deductions, and net pay may be eliminated if the equipment provides sufficient automation, storage capacity, and electronic calculation capability. When conventional electric bookkeeping machines are used, gross earnings are often computed separately on a calculator, and withholding and other tax amounts are either read from tables or worked out manually.

An electronic payroll accounting system completes all of the major payroll records at once, just as do modern electric bookkeeping machines. In addition, an electronic payroll accounting system determines automatically:

Completed Paycheck — Machine Prepared

(a) The presence of the proper earnings record.
(b) The next available posting line.
(c) Whether overtime earnings are due.
(d) Whether there are other earnings.
(e) Whether the FICA limit has been reached.
(f) What tax deductions should be made.
(g) Whether insurance premiums should be deducted.
(h) Whether there are any other deductions to be made.
(i) Whether there are any delinquent deductions to be made.
(j) Whether there is anything else to be done.

Once this system is properly set up, the operator is relieved of manual figuring and of looking up amounts in tables. The primary job is one of feeding in blank payroll accounting record forms and getting these forms back as completed payroll accounting records. (For a further discussion of automated accounting systems and procedures, see Appendix, page A-1.)

Withholding Tax Statement

Not later than January 31 of each year the law requires employers to furnish each employee from whom income taxes have been withheld a withholding statement (Form W-2) showing the total amount of wages paid and the amount of such tax withheld during the preceding calendar year. If the employee's wages were subject to FICA taxes as well as income taxes, the employer must report total wages paid and the amounts deducted both for income taxes and for FICA taxes. Information for this purpose should be provided by the employee's earnings record. A completed form W-2 is illustrated on page 90.

CENTRAL STATES PAPER & BAG COMPANY
ST. LOUIS, MO.

STATEMENT OF EARNINGS

MISC.	HOSPITAL	BONDS	INSURANCE	CREDIT UNION	PARKING	CHARITY	EMPLOYEE	DATE
	2 50	5 00	5 00	2 00			2	12 15 67
135 00	15 00		17 00		1 50		33 00	117 00
REGULAR	O'TIME	OTHER	WH. TAX	FICA	CITY	STATE	TOTAL DEDUCTIONS	NET PAY
EARNINGS			TAXES					

NON-NEGOTIABLE

and Deduction Stub

EMPLOYEE'S EARNINGS RECORD

NAME MARVIN LEE CARLTON
ADDRESS 2017 BELLEVUE
CITY ST. LOUIS, MO. 63143

SOC. SEC. NO. 504-38-8340

| EARNINGS | | | DEDUCTIONS | | | | | | | DATE | NET PAY |
REGULAR	OVERTIME	GROSS	FICA	FEDERAL INC. TAX	CITY TAX	LIFE INS.	PRIVATE HOSP. INS.	CREDIT UNION	U.S. SAVINGS BONDS		
135.00		135.00	6.08	14.00	1.35					July 7, '67	113.57
135.00	10.00	145.00	6.53	15.70	1.45	5.00	2.50	2.00	5.00	July 14, '67	106.82
135.00		135.00	6.08	14.00	1.35					July 21, '67	113.67
135.00	10.00	145.00	6.53	15.70	1.45					July 28, '67	121.32
135.00		135.00	6.08	14.00	1.35					Aug. 4, '67	113.57
135.00		135.00	6.08	14.00	1.35					Aug. 11, '67	113.57
135.00	7.50	142.50	6.41	14.90	1.43	5.00	2.50	2.00	5.00	Aug. 18, '67	105.26
135.00		135.00	6.08	14.00	1.35					Aug. 25, '67	113.57
135.00		135.00	6.08	14.00	1.35					Sept. 1, '67	113.57
135.00	5.00	140.00	6.30	14.90	1.40					Sept. 8, '67	117.40
135.00		135.00	6.08	14.00	1.35	5.00	2.50	2.00	5.00	Sept. 15, '67	99.07
135.00	10.00	145.00	6.53	15.70	1.45					Sept. 22, '67	121.32
135.00		135.00	6.08	14.00	1.35					Sept. 29, '67	113.57
THIRD QUARTER		1,797.50	80.94	188.90	17.98	15.00	7.50	6.00	15.00		1,466.18
135.00		135.00	6.08	14.00	1.35					Oct. 6, '67	113.57
135.00	8.00	143.00	6.44	14.90	1.43	5.00	2.50	2.00	5.00	Oct. 13, '67	105.73
135.00	6.00	141.00	6.35	14.90	1.41					Oct. 20, '67	118.34
135.00		135.00	6.08	14.00	1.35					Oct. 27, '67	113.57
135.00		135.00	6.08	14.00	1.35					Nov. 3, '67	113.57
135.00	10.00	145.00	6.53	15.70	1.45					Nov. 10, '67	121.32
135.00	5.00	140.00	6.30	14.90	1.40	5.00	2.50	2.00	5.00	Nov. 17, '67	102.90
135.00	7.50	142.50	6.41	14.90	1.43					Nov. 24, '67	119.76
135.00		135.00	2.21	14.00	1.35					Dec. 1, '67	117.44
135.00		135.00		14.00	1.35					Dec. 8, '67	119.65
135.00	15.00	150.00		17.00	1.50	5.00	2.50	2.00	5.00	Dec. 15, '67	117.00
FOURTH QUARTER											
YEARLY TOTAL											

Employee's Earnings Record — Machine Prepared

PAYROLL REGISTER

NAME	NO. OF EXEMP.	MARI-TAL STATUS	EARNINGS			DEDUCTIONS									DATE	NET PAY	CK. NO.
			REGULAR	OVER-TIME	GROSS	FICA	FEDERAL INC. TAX	CITY TAX	LIFE INS.	PRIVATE HOSP. INS.	CREDIT UNION	U.S. SAVINGS BONDS					
1. BROWN, HAROLD D.	2	M	120.00		120.00	5.40	13.80	1.20	4.00		2.00			Dec. 15, '67	93.60	203
2. CARLTON, MARVIN L.	3	M	135.00	15.00	150.00		17.00	1.50	5.00	2.50	2.00	5.00		Dec. 15, '67	117.00	204
3. GECKLER, DORENE L.	1	S	95.00		95.00	4.28	12.70	.95		2.00				Dec. 15, '67	75.07	205
4. HEATH, WILLIAM L.	4	M	120.00	15.00	135.00	6.30	11.80	1.35			2.00	5.00		Dec. 15, '67	114.85	206
5. JOHNSON, OSCAR E.	3	M	125.00	15.00	140.00	4.73	14.90	1.40	5.00	2.50	2.00			Dec. 15, '67	107.90	207
6. MYERS, KENT J.	3	M	105.00		105.00		9.30	1.05	3.00					Dec. 15, '67	86.92	208
7. NICHOLS, JOSEPH E.	2	M	115.00	10.00	125.00	5.63	14.60	1.25			2.00			Dec. 15, '67	101.52	209
8. ROBERTS, JOHN H.	1	S	100.00		100.00	4.50	14.10	1.00	3.00	2.00				Dec. 15, '67	75.40	210
			915.00	55.00	970.00	30.84	108.20	9.70	20.00	9.00	10.00	10.00			772.26	

Payroll Register — Machine Prepared

Completed Withholding Tax Statement (Form W-2)

The number appearing on the Withholding Tax Statement below the name and address of the employer is an *identification number* assigned to the employer by the Social Security Administration. Every employer of even one person receiving taxable wages must get an identification number within a week of the beginning of such employment. This number must be shown on all reports required of Central States Paper & Bag Company under the Federal Insurance Contributions Act.

Withholding statements must be prepared in quadruplicate (four copies). The first copy goes to the District Director of Internal Revenue with the employer's return of taxes withheld for the fourth quarter of the calendar year. The second and third copies are furnished to the employee, so that he can send one in with his federal income tax return as required and keep one for his files. The fourth copy is kept by the employer for his records. In states which have state income tax withholding laws, a fifth copy is furnished to the employee to be sent in with his state income tax return. In the case of an employee who leaves a job before the end of the year, the employer is expected to furnish the withholding statement within 30 days after the last wage payment is made.

Accounting for Wages and Wage Deductions

In accounting for wages and wage deductions it is desirable to keep separate accounts for (1) wages earned and (2) wage deductions. Various account titles are used in recording wages, such as Wages Expense, Salaries Expense, and Salaries and Commissions Expense. The accounts needed in recording wage deductions depend upon what deductions are involved. A separate account should be kept for recording the liability incurred for each type of deduction, such as FICA taxes, employees' income taxes, and savings bond deductions.

Wages Expense. This is an expense account which should be debited for the total amount of the gross earnings of all employees for each pay period. Sometimes separate

WAGES EXPENSE	
Debit	
to record gross earnings of employees for each pay period.	

wage accounts are kept for the employees of different departments. Thus, separate accounts might be kept for Office Salaries Expense, Sales Salaries Expense, and Factory Wages Expense.

FICA Taxes Payable. This is a liability account which should be credited for **(1)** the FICA taxes withheld from employees' wages and **(2)** the FICA taxes imposed on the employer. The account should be debited for amounts paid to apply on

FICA TAXES PAYABLE	
Debit	**Credit**
to record payment of FICA taxes.	to record FICA taxes (a) withheld from employees' wages and (b) imposed on the employer.

such taxes. When all of the FICA taxes have been paid, the account should be in balance.

Employees' Income Taxes Payable. This is a liability account which should be credited for the total income taxes withheld from employees' wages. The account should be

EMPLOYEES' INCOME TAXES PAYABLE	
Debit	**Credit**
to record payment of income taxes withheld.	to record income taxes withheld from employees' wages.

debited for amounts paid to apply on such taxes. When all of the income taxes withheld have been paid, the account will be in balance. A city or state earnings tax payable account is used in a similar manner.

Life Insurance Premiums Payable. This is a liability account which should be credited with amounts withheld from employees' wages for the future payment of life insurance premiums. The account should be debited for the subsequent payment

LIFE INSURANCE PREMIUMS PAYABLE	
Debit	**Credit**
to record the payment of life insurance premiums withheld.	to record amounts withheld for the future payment of life insurance premiums.

of these premiums to the life insurance company. Accounts for private hospital insurance premiums payable, credit union contributions payable, and savings bond deductions payable are similarly used.

Journalizing Payroll Transactions. The payroll register should provide the information needed in recording wages paid. The payroll register illustrated on page 89 provided the information needed in drafting the following general journal entry to record the wages paid on December 15:

Dec. 15. Wages Expense.................................... 970.00

        FICA Taxes Payable............................   30.84
        Employees' Income Taxes Payable................   108.20
        City Earnings Taxes Payable.....................   9.70
        Life Insurance Premiums Payable.................   20.00
        Private Hospital Insurance Premiums Payable......   9.00
        Credit Union Contributions Payable..............   10.00
        Savings Bond Deductions Payable................   10.00
        Cash..   772.26
           Payroll for week ended December 15.

It will be noted that the above journal entry involves one debit and
eight credits. Regardless of the number of debits and credits needed to
record a transaction, the total amount debited must be equal to the total
amount credited.

Report No. 8

Complete Report No. 8 in the workbook and submit your working
papers to the instructor for approval. After completing the report, continue with the following study assignment until the next report is required.

payroll taxes imposed on the employer

The employer is liable to the government for the taxes which he is required by law to withhold from the wages of his employees. These taxes
include the federal income taxes and the FICA taxes which must be withheld from wages paid to employees. Such taxes are not an expense of the
employer; nevertheless, the employer is required by law to collect the taxes
and he is liable for the taxes until payment is made. Certain taxes are also
imposed on the employer for various purposes, such as old-age, survivors,
and disability insurance benefits; hospital insurance for the aged; and
unemployment, relief, and welfare. Most employers are subject to payroll taxes imposed under the Federal Insurance Contributions Act (FICA)
and the Federal Unemployment Tax Act (FUTA). An employer may

also be subject to the payroll taxes imposed under the unemployment compensation laws of one or more states. These commonly are called "State Unemployment Taxes."

Payroll Tax Expense

All of the payroll taxes imposed on an employer under federal and state social security laws are an expense of the employer. In accounting for such taxes at least one expense account should be maintained. This account may be entitled Payroll Tax Expense. It is an expense account which should be debited for all taxes imposed on the employer under federal and state social security laws. Sometimes separate expense accounts are kept for **(1)** FICA Tax Expense, **(2)** FUTA Tax Expense, and **(3)** State Unemployment Tax Expense. In small business enterprises it is usually considered satisfactory to keep a single expense account for all federal and state social security taxes imposed on the employer.

PAYROLL TAX EXPENSE	
Debit to record FICA, FUTA, and State Unemployment Taxes imposed on the employer.	

Employer's FICA Tax

The taxes imposed under the Federal Insurance Contributions Act apply equally to employers and to employees. As explained on page 80, both the rate and base of the tax may be changed by Congress at any time. In this discussion it is assumed that the combined rate is 4.5 percent which applies both to the employer and to his employees (a total of 9 percent) with respect to taxable wages. Only the first $6,600 of the wages paid to each employee in any calendar year constitutes taxable wages. Any amount of wages paid to an employee during a year in excess of $6,600 is exempt from FICA tax. While the employer is liable to the government both for the taxes withheld from his employees' wages and for the taxes imposed on the business, only the latter constitutes an expense of the business.

Employer's FUTA Tax

Under the Federal Unemployment Tax Act, a payroll tax is levied on employers for the purpose of implementing more uniform administration of the various state unemployment compensation laws. Employers of four or more individuals are subject to this tax. The Federal law imposes a specific rate of tax but allows a substantial credit against this levy if the state in which the employer is located has an unemployment compensation law that meets certain requirements. Since all states have such laws, the rate actually paid by most employers is much less than the maximum legal rate. As in the case of the FICA tax, Congress can and does change the rate from time to time. For the purpose of this discussion, a rate of 3.1 percent with a credit of 2.7 percent available to most employers is used. The difference, 0.4 percent $(3.1 - 2.7)$ is, then, the effective rate. This is applied to the first $3,000 of compensation paid to each employee during the calendar year. It is important to note this limitation in contrast to the $6,600 limit in the case of the FICA tax. It is also important to note that all of the payroll taxes relate to amounts of wages paid — not to amounts earned. Sometimes wages are earned in one quarter or year, but not paid until the following period.

FUTA Taxes Payable

In recording the federal unemployment tax, it is customary to keep a separate liability account entitled FUTA Taxes Payable. This is a liability account which should be

FUTA Taxes Payable	
Debit	Credit
to record payment of FUTA taxes.	to record FUTA taxes imposed on the employer with respect to wages paid.

credited for the taxes imposed on employers under the Federal Unemployment Tax Act. The account should be debited for amounts paid to apply on such taxes. When all of the FUTA taxes have been paid, the account should be in balance.

State Unemployment Taxes

All of the states and the District of Columbia have enacted unemployment compensation laws providing for the payment of benefits to qualified unemployed workers. The cost of administering the state unemployment compensation laws is borne by the federal government. Under the federal law an appropriation is made for each year by the Congress from which grants are made to the states to meet the proper administrative costs of their unemployment compensation laws. As a result of this provision, the entire amount paid into the state funds may be used for the payment of benefits to qualified workers. While in general there is considerable uniformity in the provisions of the state laws, there are many variations in coverage, rates of taxes imposed, and benefits payable to qualified workers. Not all employers covered by the Federal Unemployment Tax Act are covered by the unemployment compensation laws of the states in which they have employees. Only employers of four or more individuals are covered by the federal law.

The number of employees specified under state laws varies from 1 to 8. However, in many of the states an employer who is covered by the federal law and has one or more individuals employed within the state is also covered by the state law. Furthermore, under the laws of most states an employer who is covered by the federal law may elect voluntary coverage in states where he has one or more employees, even though he may have less than the number of employees specified by the law in that particular state. In any event, it is necessary for each employer to be familiar with the unemployment compensation laws of all the states in which he has one or more employees, and if such employees are covered, he must keep such records and pay such taxes for unemployment compensation purposes as are prescribed by those laws.

In most states the unemployment benefit plan is financed entirely by taxes imposed on employers. However, in a few states employees are also required to contribute, and the amount of the tax imposed on the employees must be withheld from their wages.

In most states the maximum tax imposed upon employers is 2.7 percent of the first $3,000 of wages paid to each employee in any calendar year. However, under the laws of most states there is a *merit-rating* system which provides a tax-saving incentive to employers to stabilize employment. Under this system an employer's rate may be considerably less than the maximum rate if he provides steady work for his employees.

There are frequent changes in the state laws with respect to coverage, rates of contributions required, eligibility to receive benefits, and amounts of benefits payable. In the following discussion, it is assumed that the state tax rate is 2.7 percent of the first $3,000 of wages paid each employee each year.

State Unemployment Taxes Payable

STATE UNEMPLOYMENT TAXES PAYABLE

Debit	Credit
to record state unemployment taxes paid.	to record liability for state unemployment taxes required of employers.

In recording the taxes imposed under state unemployment compensation laws, it is customary to keep a separate liability account entitled State Unemployment Taxes Payable. This is a liability account which should be credited for the taxes imposed on employers under the state unemployment compensation laws. The account should be debited for the amount paid to apply on such taxes. When all of the state taxes have been paid, the account should be in balance. Some employers who are subject to taxes imposed under the laws of several states keep a separate liability account for the taxes imposed by each state.

Journalizing Employers' Payroll Taxes

The payroll taxes imposed on employers may be recorded periodically, such as monthly or quarterly. It is more common to record such taxes at the time that wages are paid so that the employer's liability for such taxes and related expenses may be recorded in the same period as the wages on which the taxes are based. The payroll register illustrated on page 89 provides the information needed in recording the FICA tax imposed on Central States Paper & Bag Company with respect to wages paid on December 15. The FICA taxable earnings for the pay period involved amounted to $685.00. Assuming that the combined rate of the tax imposed on the employer was 4.5 percent, which is the same as the rate of the tax imposed on the employees, the tax would amount to $30.84. (This amount will not necessarily be the same as that calculated by multiplying the tax rate times total taxable earnings due to the rounding up of amounts in calculating the tax deduction for each employee.) If only $513.75 of the earnings for the period were subject to unemployment taxes, the federal and state taxes may be computed as follows:

State unemployment taxes, 2.7% of $513.75............................ $13.87
FUTA taxes, 0.4% of $513.75... 2.06

Total unemployment taxes.. $15.93

The following general journal entry may be made to record the payroll taxes imposed on the employer with respect to the wages paid on December 15:

Dec. 15. Payroll Tax Expense............................... 46.77
        FICA Taxes Payable............................. 30.84
        FUTA Taxes Payable............................. 2.06
        State Unemployment Taxes Payable............... 13.87
        Payroll taxes imposed on employer with respect to
        wages paid December 15.

Filing Returns and Paying the Payroll Taxes

If the amount withheld from employees' wages for income tax purposes *plus* the amount of the taxes imposed on both the employer and the employees under the Federal Insurance Contributions Act during any month is more than $100, the total must be paid to the District Federal Reserve Bank or some other United States depositary by the 15th of the following month. However, if desired, the taxes for the last month of a calendar quarter may be remitted to the District Director of Internal Revenue at the time of filing the quarterly return on or before the last day of the following month. If the total amount of the taxes in any month is less than $100, monthly payment is not required and the total taxes for each calendar quarter may be paid at the time of filing the quarterly return. Most employers make monthly payment of the taxes by the 15th of the following month regardless of the amount. If the total amount of income and FICA taxes in any month is more than $2,500, *two* monthly deposits are required. These deposits must be made within three banking days after the 15th and last day of each month, covering taxes withheld and due up to and including the 15th or last day of the month. When paying the taxes, it is necessary to fill in a Federal Depositary Receipt, Form 450, and to send or to take it to the bank with the remittance. A completed copy of this form is shown below. After validating the receipt, the Federal Reserve Bank will return it to the taxpayer.

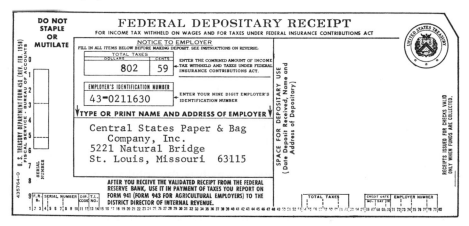

Completed Federal Depositary Receipt (Form 450)

To illustrate the accounting procedure in recording the payment of employees' income taxes and FICA taxes withheld, it will be assumed that on February 15 Central States Paper & Bag Company issued a check in payment of the following taxes imposed with respect to wages paid during the month of January:

Employees' income taxes withheld from wages..............		$478.63
FICA taxes:		
Withheld from employees' wages.......................	$161.98	
Imposed on employer.................................	161.98	323.96
Amount of check......................................		$802.59

A check for this amount accompanied by a Federal Depositary Receipt, Form 450, was sent to a bank that is qualified as a depositary for federal taxes. (All national banks are qualified.) This transaction may be recorded as indicated by the following general journal entry:

Feb. 15. FICA Taxes Payable..........................	323.96	
Employees' Income Taxes Payable...............	478.63	
Cash......................................		802.59
Remitted $802.59 in payment of taxes.		

Further assume that on March 15, $801.38 was deposited. This covered income tax withholdings of $508.17 during February and the employer's and employees' FICA taxes of $293.21 for February. The proper entry was made to record the payment of $801.38. Also assume that during

March, income tax withholdings amounted to $503.28 and FICA taxes (employer's and employees'), $300.39 — a total of $803.67. Finally assume that on April 15, the quarterly return illustrated on page 99 was sent to the nearest office of the District Director of Internal Revenue, accompanied by a check for $803.67 and the two depositary receipts — one for the $802.59 payment made February 15 and the other for the $801.38 payment made March 15. The proper entry was made to record the payment of $803.67.

The amount on lines 1 and 3 of the quarterly tax return illustration, $1,490.08, is the sum of the employees' income taxes withheld in January ($478.63), February ($508.17), and March ($503.28). The amount on line 4a of this return comes from the total of wages reported on line 21 (the total taxable FICA wages reported on Schedule A) times 9 percent (the combined FICA tax rate for employer and employee). The adjusted total FICA taxes on line 7 is added to the adjusted total of income tax withheld, line 3, to give the amount on line 8, which is the total income and FICA taxes due to the federal government.

The amount on line 9 of the quarterly tax return illustration, $1,603.97, is the sum of the depositary receipts for February 15 ($802.59) and March 15 ($801.38). The amount on line 10, $803.67, is the balance due to the Internal Revenue Service for which the check was written and sent to the nearest District Director's office.

The amount of the tax imposed on employers under the state unemployment compensation laws must be remitted to the proper state office during the month following the close of the calendar quarter. Each state provides an official form to be used in making a return of the taxes due. Assuming that a check for $244.89 was issued on April 30 in payment of state unemployment compensation taxes on wages paid during the preceding quarter ended March 31, the transaction may be recorded as indicated by the following journal entry:

```
Apr. 30.  State Unemployment Taxes Payable...............   244.89
              Cash......................................              244.89
              Paid state unemployment taxes.
```

The amount of the tax on employers under the Federal Unemployment Tax Act for the entire year must be paid to the District Director of Internal Revenue during the month following the close of the calendar year. An official form is provided to the employer for use in making a report of the taxes due.

Assuming that a check for $79.10 was issued on January 31 in payment of the taxes imposed under the Federal Unemployment Tax Act with

FORM 941

EMPLOYER'S QUARTERLY FEDERAL TAX RETURN
U.S. Treasury Department—Internal Revenue Service

FEDERAL INCOME TAX WITHHELD FROM WAGES	1. AMOUNT OF INCOME TAX WITHHELD (If not required write "None")......................	1,490.08
	2. ADJUSTMENT FOR PRECEDING QUARTERS OF CALENDAR YEAR...................................	- - -
	3. ADJUSTED TOTAL OF INCOME TAX WITHHELD...→	1,490.08
FEDERAL INSURANCE CONTRI-BUTIONS ACT TAXES	4a. TAXABLE WAGES PAID (From Item 21)...$ 10,195.10	917.56
	4b. TAXABLE TIPS REPORTED (Item 22).....$	- - -
	5. TOTAL F.I.C.A. TAXES (Item 4a plus Item 4b)...............................→	917.56
	6. ADJUSTMENT (See instructions)...	- - -
	7. ADJUSTED TOTAL OF F.I.C.A. TAXES...→	917.56
TOTALS	8. TOTAL TAXES (Item 3 plus Item 7)...	2,407.64
	9. TOTAL OF ENCLOSED DEPOSITARY RECEIPTS (From Schedule B, other side)...........	1,603.97
	10. BALANCE DUE (Item 8 minus Item 9) PAY TO "INTERNAL REVENUE SERVICE"..........	803.67

Under penalties of perjury, I declare that I have examined this return, including accompanying schedules and statements, and to the best of my knowledge and belief it is true, correct, and complete.

Date 4-15-67 Signature *Edwin C. Edelmann* Title Treasurer
(Owner, President, Partner, Member, etc.)

If not liable for returns in succeeding quarters write "FINAL" here .... Complete items 11—13 on reverse.

BE SURE TO ENCLOSE REMITTANCE, DEPOSITARY RECEIPTS, AND SCHEDULE A WITH THIS RETURN.

Employer's name, address, identification number, and calendar quarter. (If not correctly printed please change)

Name (as distinguished from trade name)
Central States Paper & Bag Company, Inc.
Trade name, if any
Central States
Address and Postal ZIP code
5221 Natural Bridge, St. Louis, Mo. 63115

Date quarter ended 3-31-67
Identification No. 43-0211630

If form is not preaddressed, check type of employer—
☐ Sole owner ☐ Partnership
☐ Corporation ☐ Other (specify)

------ Entries must be made both above and below this line ------

Name (as distinguished from trade name)
Central States Paper & Bag Company, Inc.
Trade name, if any
Central States
Address and Postal ZIP code
5221 Natural Bridge, St. Louis, Mo. 63115

Date quarter ended
Identification No.

U.S. TREASURY DEPARTMENT
District Director of Internal Revenue

OFFICIAL BUSINESS
POSTAGE AND FEES PAID

POSTMASTER: If undeliverable treat in accordance with Section 355.56 of Postal Manual.

SCHEDULE A—QUARTERLY REPORT OF WAGES TAXABLE UNDER THE FEDERAL INSURANCE CONTRIBUTIONS ACT (FOR SOCIAL SECURITY)
IF WAGES WERE NOT TAXABLE UNDER THE F.I.C.A. MAKE NO ENTRIES BELOW

14. (First quarter only) Number of employees (except household) employed in the pay period including March 12th.	15. Total pages of this return, including this page and any pages of Form 941a.	16. Total number of employees listed.
8	2	8

List for each employee, except agricultural employees, the WAGES taxable under the Federal Insurance Contributions Act (for Social Security) which were paid during the quarter. If you pay an employee more than $6,600 in a calendar year, report ONLY THE FIRST $6,600 of such wages. In the case of "Tip Income" see instructions.

SAVE TIME AND MONEY—If your report shows each employee's name and number *exactly* as they appear on his Social Security card it will not be necessary to write back to you to ask for the correct information

17. EMPLOYEE'S SOCIAL SECURITY ACCOUNT NUMBER (If number is unknown, see Circular E) 000 00 0000	18. NAME OF EMPLOYEE (Please type or print)	19. TAXABLE F.I.C.A. WAGES Paid to Employee in Quarter (Before deductions) Dollars Cents	20. TAXABLE TIPS REPORTED (See instructions on page 4) Dollars Cents
258-05-3753	Harold D. Brown	1,251.40	
504-38-8340	Marvin L. Carlton	1,625.00	
810-04-1629	Dorene L. Geckler	968.00	
411-02-9708	William L. Heath	1,438.10	
258-08-8221	Oscar E. Johnson	1,508.00	
472-04-2335	Kent J. Myers	1,052.00	
521-08-6503	Joseph E. Nichols	1,344.60	
269-07-1132	John H. Roberts	1,008.00	

If you need more space for listing employees, use Schedule A continuation sheets, Form 941a. Totals of wages and tips reported in columns 19 and 20 on this page →		10,195.10

21. TOTAL WAGES TAXABLE UNDER F.I.C.A. PAID DURING QUARTER
(Total of column 19 on this page and continuation sheets.) Enter here and in Item 4a above.......... $ 10,195.10

22. TOTAL TIPS REPORTED UNDER F.I.C.A. DURING QUARTER
(Total of column 20 on this page and continuation sheets.) Enter here and in Item 4b above ....→ $

FILE THIS RETURN WITH YOUR DISTRICT DIRECTOR OF INTERNAL REVENUE. (Form 941) Page 1

Employer's Quarterly Federal Tax Return and Quarterly Report, Schedule A (Form 941)

respect to wages paid during the preceding year ended December 31, the transaction may be recorded as indicated by the following journal entry:

Jan. 31. FUTA Taxes Payable............................. 79.10
       Cash..   79.10
           Paid federal unemployment taxes.

Report No. 9

Complete Report No. 9 in the workbook and submit your working papers to the instructor for approval. After completing the report, you may continue with the textbook discussion in Chapter 5 until the next report is required.

chapter five

accounting for a personal service enterprise

A personal service enterprise is one in which the principal source of revenue is compensation for personal services rendered. There are two types of personal service enterprises:

(a) Business enterprises
(b) Professional enterprises

Business enterprises of the personal service type include real estate, insurance, advertising, transportation, storage, entertainment, brokerage, and many other enterprises in which the revenue is derived chiefly from personal services rendered. Mercantile enterprises are not classified as personal service enterprises for the reason that their principal source of revenue is from the sale of merchandise rather than from compensation received for services rendered.

Professional enterprises include law, medicine, dentistry, public accounting, engineering, architecture, art, and education. The principal source of revenue for individuals engaged in such professions is usually the compensation received for the personal services rendered.

The Cash Basis of Accounting for a Personal Service Enterprise

Accounting for revenue on a cash basis means that, in most cases, no record of revenue is made in the accounts until cash is received for the services performed. This may mean that the services are rendered in one period with the revenue being accounted for in the succeeding period. The business or professional man may well take the view that, in most cases, he has had no revenue until it is received in such form that it can be spent. He cannot "spend" the promise of a customer or client to pay him some money.

The cash basis of accounting for the revenue of a personal service enterprise is widely used. It is acceptable for federal and state income tax purposes. Not only is the receipt of cash accounted for as revenue under this basis; many other types of transactions are accounted for similarly. Any property or service that is accepted in place of cash for services is treated as revenue to the extent of its fair market value at the time received. Revenue is said to be *constructively received* if it is credited to a person's account or set apart so that he can draw upon it. For example, when interest on a savings account is credited to the depositor's account, such interest is considered to be revenue to the depositor even though it is not actually received in cash or is not immediately withdrawn.

Accounting for expenses on the cash basis generally means that expenses are not recorded in the accounts until paid in cash. An expense may be incurred in one period and recorded in the accounts in the succeeding period. In the case of many expenses of a recurring nature, however, this set of circumstances is regarded as a minor objection. If, for example, twelve monthly telephone bills of about the same amount must be paid during each year, little importance is attached to the fact that the bill that is paid and recorded as an expense in January was really for service received in December.

An exception to the cash basis of accounting for expenses is made in connection with most long-lived assets. For example, it would be unreasonable to consider the entire cost of a building or of most equipment to be an expense of the period in which such assets were purchased. If it is expected that an asset will serve for a number of years, its cost (less expected scrap or salvage value, if any) is prorated over its estimated life. The share of cost assigned to each period is described as *depreciation expense*. Such expense cannot be calculated with great accuracy. Still, an allocation that eventually turns out to have been somewhat in error results in a far more equitable periodic net income (profit) or loss measurement than simply considering the cost of such assets to be entirely an expense of the period in which they were purchased.

Another exception to the cash basis of accounting for expenses is sometimes made in connection with supplies purchased and used. If the amount of money involved is substantial and the end of the accounting period finds a considerable quantity of expensive supplies still on hand, an effort is made to determine the cost of those items which are on hand, so that only the cost of the supplies used will be treated as an expense of the period. If both the quantity and the cost of the items on hand at the end of a period are small, the usual practice is to ignore them and to consider the total cost of all items purchased during that period to be an expense of that accounting period.

accounting procedure

As an aid in applying the principles involved in keeping the accounts of a personal service enterprise on the cash basis, a system of accounts for Howard C. Miller, an architect, will be described. While certain distinctive problems may arise in keeping the accounts of any specific enterprise, it will be found that the principles are generally the same; hence, the system of accounts used by Mr. Miller may readily be adapted to the needs of any personal service enterprise regardless of whether it is of a professional or a business nature.

Chart of Accounts

Mr. Miller's chart of accounts is reproduced on page 104. Note that all account numbers beginning with 1 relate to assets; 2, liabilities; 3, owner's equity; 4, revenue; and 5, expenses. Account numbers beginning with 0 represent *contra accounts* (meaning "opposite" or "offsetting" accounts) used to show the decrease in the related element. This system of account numbering permits the addition of new accounts as they may be needed without disturbing the numerical order of the existing accounts.

*Assets**
- 11 First National Bank
- 12 Petty Cash Fund
- 13 Office Equipment
- 013 Accumulated Depreciation—
  Office Equipment

Liabilities
- 21 Employees' Income Taxes Payable
- 22 FICA Taxes Payable

Owner's Equity
- 31 Howard C. Miller, Capital
- 031 Howard C. Miller, Drawing
- 32 Expense and Revenue Summary

Revenue
- 41 Professional Fees

Expenses
- 511 Salary Expense
- 512 Payroll Tax Expense
- 513 Rent Expense
- 514 Telephone and Telegraph Expense
- 515 Blueprints and Supplies Expense
- 516 Automobile Expense
- 517 Depreciation Expense
- 518 Insurance Expense
- 519 Travel and Entertainment Expense
- 520 Charitable Contributions Expense
- 521 Miscellaneous Expense

*Words in italics represent headings and not account titles.

Most of the accounts in the foregoing list have been discussed and their use illustrated in the preceding chapters. Three notable exceptions are: Accumulated Depreciation — Office Equipment (No. 013), Depreciation Expense (No. 517), and Expense and Revenue Summary (No. 32). Each of these will be explained and its use illustrated as the need for the account arises in the narrative of transactions later in the chapter. Except for Depreciation Expense (No. 517), every debit to an expense account arises in connection with a cash disbursement. The cost of all blueprints and supplies purchased is debited (charged) to Account No. 515. The amount of any unused supplies that may be on hand at the end of the year is ignored because such quantities normally are very small. (Note that there is no asset account for supplies.) The car that Mr. Miller uses for business purposes is leased. The monthly car rental and the cost of gasoline, oil, lubrication, washing, and automobile insurance are charged to Automobile Expense, Account No. 516. The cost of all other types of insurance that relate to the enterprise, such as workmen's compensation, "errors and omissions" insurance (normally carried by architects), and fire insurance on the office equipment and contents, is charged to Insurance Expense, Account No. 518, when the premiums on the policies are paid.

Books of Account

Mr. Miller uses the following books of account:

(a) General books
  (1) Combined cash journal
  (2) General ledger
(b) Auxiliary records
  (1) Petty cash disbursements record
  (2) Employees' earnings records
  (3) Copies of statements rendered to clients (billings for fees) with collections noted thereon

Combined Cash Journal. Mr. Miller uses only one book of original entry — a combined cash journal. This journal, reproduced on pages 110–113, has eight amount columns, two at the left and six at the right of the Description column. The headings of the amount columns (as they read from left to right on the journal page) are as follows:

First National Bank
    Deposits 11 Dr.
    Checks 11 Cr.

General
    Debits
    Credits

Professional Fees 41 Cr.

Salary Expense 511 Dr.

Wage Deductions
    Employees' Income Taxes Payable 21 Cr.
    FICA Taxes Payable 22 Cr.

The account numbers in the headings are an aid in completing the summary posting at the end of each month. Comparison of this combined cash journal and the four-column journal illustrated in Chapter 3 (page 47) will reveal two differences: **(1)** the presence of a Check Number column just to the right of the Checks 11 Cr. column, and **(2)** the four special columns to the right of the pair of General columns. Each of these four special columns is justified because there are enough transactions requiring entries in the accounts indicated by the column headings to warrant this arrangement which will save time and labor in the bookkeeping process. A narrative of transactions completed by Mr. Miller during the month of December, 19--, is given on pages 106–111. These transactions are recorded in the combined cash journal on pages 110–113. Attention is called to the fact that before any transactions were recorded in this journal, the bank balance at the start of the month, $2,647.45, was entered in the Description column just above the words "Amounts Forwarded."

General Ledger. The standard form of account is used in the general ledger of Mr. Miller's enterprise. The ledger is reproduced on pages 114–116. In each instance, the balance of the account as of December 1 has been entered. Two accounts are omitted: Expense and Revenue Summary (No. 32) and Depreciation Expense (No. 517). They are not included because neither had a balance on December 1, and neither received any debits or credits as a result of the cash receipt and disbursement transactions in December. These accounts are not used until the end-of-year process of adjusting and closing the accounts takes place. This procedure will be explained and illustrated on pages 121–122.

Auxiliary Records. The auxiliary records included in Mr. Miller's system of accounts are not reproduced in this chapter. The petty cash dis-

bursements record that is used is almost identical in form to the one illustrated in Chapter 3 on pages 56 and 57. However, the combined cash
journal entry to record the reimbursement of the petty cash fund at the end
of December is shown (see the first entry of December 29 on pages 112 and
113). Mr. Miller has two employees: Mr. Robert Cox, a full-time drafts-
man, and Miss Susan Dunn, a half-time secretary. An employee's earnings
record, similar to the one illustrated in Chapter 4 on page 84, is maintained
for each employee. Mr. Miller keeps a file for each client which includes,
among other things, a copy of the contract or agreement with the client.
This agreement stipulates the fee for the assignment and the time of payment (or payments, if the fee is to be paid in installments — which is the
usual case). A carbon copy of each statement or billing for fees earned is
placed in each client's file. When money is received from a client, the date
and amount are noted on the copy of the billing in addition to the formal
record made in the combined cash journal.

HOWARD C. MILLER, ARCHITECT
NARRATIVE OF TRANSACTIONS

Friday, December 1

Issued Check No. 231 for $157.90 to Robert Cox, draftsman, in pay-
ment of his salary for week: $180 less income tax withholding, $22.10.
(Note: Mr. Cox has been employed since the start of the year. His gross
earnings reached $6,600 during the week of September 10. Since that
time, no FICA tax has been withheld.)

> Since individual posting of this entry was not required, a check mark was placed in
> the Posting Reference column of the combined cash journal at the time the transaction
> was recorded.

Issued Check No. 232 for $34.70 to Susan Dunn, secretary (half-time),
in payment of her salary for week: $40 less income tax withholding, $3.50,
and FICA tax withholding, $1.80.

Issued Check No. 233 for $225 to W. J. Johnson for December office
rent.

Monday, December 4

Received a check for $600 from L. H. Maxwell, a client.

> Note that the client's name was written in the Description column and that a check
> mark was placed in the Posting Reference column.

Wednesday, December 6

Issued Check No. 234 for $29.50 to C. A. Stern, an insurance agent, in
payment of the one-year premium on a fire insurance policy covering
Mr. Miller's office equipment and contents.

Friday, December 8

Issued Check No. 235 for $157.90 to Robert Cox and Check No. 236 for $34.70 to Susan Dunn in payment of salaries for the week. (See explanation relating to Checks Nos. 231 and 232 issued on December 1.)

END-OF-THE-WEEK WORK

(1) Proved the footings of the combined cash journal as follows:

Column	Dr.	Cr.
First National Bank	$ 600.00	$ 639.70
General	254.50	
Professional Fees		600.00
Salary Expense	440.00	
Employees' Income Taxes Payable		51.20
FICA Taxes Payable		3.60
	$1,294.50	$1,294.50

(2) Deposited the $600 check from L. H. Maxwell in the bank, proved the bank balance ($2,607.75), and entered the new balance in the Description column following the second transaction of December 8. **(3)** Posted each entry individually from the General Debits column of the combined cash journal to the proper general ledger accounts.

Monday, December 11

Issued Check No. 237 for $52.78 to Quality Blue Print Co. in payment for prints.

Received a check for $3.60 from C. A. Stern, the insurance agent to whom Mr. Miller had sent a check (No. 234) a few days earlier in the amount of $29.50 in payment of the premium on a fire insurance policy on his office equipment and contents. The check for $3.60 was accompanied by a letter from Mr. Stern explaining that a clerk in his office had made an error in preparing the invoice for the policy. The correct amount was $25.90 — not $29.50. Mr. Miller's check for $29.50 had been deposited before the mistake was discovered. Accordingly, Mr. Stern sent his check for $3.60 as a refund of the excess premium.

> This insurance premium refund check was recorded in the combined cash journal by a debit to First National Bank, Account No. 11, and a credit to Insurance Expense, Account No. 518, in the amount of $3.60. Since the entry to record Check No. 234 had already been posted as a debit to Insurance Expense, this manner of handling was required. (The trouble resulted from the fact that the clerk in Mr. Stern's office had made a *transposition* error — a mistake well known to bookkeepers and accountants. The intention was to write or type "$25.90," but "$29.50" was written instead. The "5" and the "9" were placed in the wrong order — they were *transposed*.)

Tuesday, December 12

Received a check for $725 from M. F. Brownell, a client.

Chapter 5 / Accounting for a Personal Service Enterprise   107

Issued Check No. 238 for $116.80 to the First National Bank, a United States depositary, in payment of the following taxes:

Employees' income taxes withheld during November...........		$102.40
FICA taxes imposed —		
On employees (withheld during November).................	$ 7.20	
On the employer......................................	7.20	14.40
Total..		$116.80

This disbursement involved three factors (in addition to the decrease in the bank balance): (1) payment of the recorded liability, Employees' Income Taxes Payable, Account No. 21, of $102.40; (2) payment of the recorded liability, FICA Taxes Payable, Account No. 22, of $7.20; and (3) payment of the unrecorded liability of $7.20, the employer's FICA tax relating to the taxable earnings paid in November. To record the transaction correctly, the first two amounts were debited to the proper liability accounts, and the third amount was debited to Payroll Tax Expense, Account No. 512. Note that three lines were needed in the combined cash journal.

(The checks from Mr. Brownell and Mr. Stern were deposited in the bank, and the check for $116.80, together with a Federal Depositary Receipt, was presented at the bank in payment of the taxes. The Federal Depositary Receipt was validated and returned.)

Wednesday, December 13

Issued Check No. 239 for $1,000 to Mr. Miller for personal use.

Thursday, December 14

Issued Check No. 240 for $65.90 to the Central Car Leasing Co. in payment of one month's rent of the leased automobile used by Mr. Miller for business purposes.

This disbursement was recorded by a debit to Automobile Expense, Account No. 516.

Friday, December 15

Issued Check No. 241 for $157.90 to Robert Cox and Check No. 242 for $34.70 to Susan Dunn in payment of salaries for week. (See explanation relating to Checks Nos. 231 and 232 issued on December 1.)

Issued Check No. 243 for $50 to American Red Cross.

END-OF-THE-WEEK WORK

(1) Proved the footings of the combined cash journal. (2) Proved the bank balance ($1,858.27). (3) Posted each entry individually from the General Debits and General Credits columns of the combined cash journal to the proper general ledger accounts. When the entry of December 12 relating to Check No. 238 was posted, debits were made to Employees' Income Taxes Payable, Account No. 21, and FICA Taxes Payable, Account No. 22, which caused those accounts to be in balance. Each of those two accounts was ruled with a double line as illustrated on page 114.

Monday, December 18

Issued Check No. 244 for $23.11 to Bill Nix's Service Station in payment of charges for gasoline, oil, and lubrication purchased on credit during the past month. (All of these purchases related to the leased car used for business purposes.)

Issued Check No. 245 for $7.95 to Park Typewriter Service in payment of charges for cleaning and repairing office typewriter.

The amount of this check was charged to Miscellaneous Expense, Account No. 521.

Tuesday, December 19

Issued Check No. 246 for $31.15 to General Telephone Co. in payment of statement just received showing charges for local service, long distance calls, and telegrams during the past month. (This telephone bill related exclusively to the phone in Mr. Miller's office.)

Wednesday, December 20

Received a check for $890 from Mrs. Charles Winfield, a client.

Thursday, December 21

Issued Check No. 247 for $64.17 to Architects Supply Co. in payment for supplies purchased.

Friday, December 22

Issued Check No. 248 for $157.90 to Robert Cox and Check No. 249 for $34.70 to Susan Dunn in payment of salaries for week. (See explanation relating to Checks Nos. 231 and 232 issued on December 1.)

END-OF-THE-WEEK WORK

(1) Proved the footings of the combined cash journal. (2) Deposited the $890 check from Mrs. Winfield and proved the bank balance ($2,429.29). (3) Posted each entry individually from the General Debits column of the combined cash journal.

Because a page of the combined cash journal was filled after Check No. 249 was recorded, the footings of the columns were proved, these footings were recorded as totals on the last line of the page, and the words "Carried Forward" were written in the Description column. The totals were entered in the appropriate columns on the top line of the next page.

Wednesday, December 27

Issued Check No. 250 for $76.48 to Norwood Hills Country Club in payment of food and beverage charges for one month.

The amount of this check was charged to Travel and Entertainment Expense, Account No. 519. Mr. Miller uses the facilities of the club to entertain prospective clients.

Thursday, December 28

Received a check for $500 from Thurman Osborne, a client.

| FIRST NATIONAL BANK | | CK. NO. | DATE | | DESCRIPTION | POST. REF. |
DEPOSITS 11 DR.	CHECKS 11 CR.		MO.	DAY		
					AMOUNTS FORWARDED *Balance 2,647.45*	
	1 5 7 90	231	Dec	1	Robert Cox	✓
	3 4 70	232		1	Susan Dunn	✓
	2 2 5 00	233		1	Rent Expense	513
6 0 0 00				4	L. H. Maxwell	✓
	2 9 50	234		6	Insurance Expense	518
	1 5 7 90	235		8	Robert Cox	✓
6 0 0 00	6 3 4 70	236		8	Susan Dunn *2,607.75*	✓
	5 2 78	237		11	Blueprints and Supplies Expense	515
3 60				11	Insurance Expense	518
7 2 5 00				12	M. F. Brownell	✓
	1 1 6 80	238		12	Employees' Income Taxes Payable	21
					FICA Taxes Payable	22
					Payroll Tax Expense	512
	1 0 0 0 00	239		13	Howard C. Miller, Drawing	031
	6 5 90	240		14	Automobile Expense	516
	1 5 7 90	241		15	Robert Cox	✓
	3 4 70	242		15	Susan Dunn	✓
1 3 2 8 60	2 1 7 7 78 5 0 00	243		15	Charitable Contributions Expense *1858.27*	520
	2 3 11	244		18	Automobile Expense	516
	7 95	245		18	Miscellaneous Expense	521
	3 1 15	246		19	Telephone and Telegraph Expense	514
8 9 0 00				20	Mrs. Charles Winfield	✓
	6 4 17	247		21	Blueprints and Supplies Expense	515
	1 5 7 90	248		22	Robert Cox	✓
	3 4 70	249		22	Susan Dunn	✓
2 2 1 8 60	2 4 3 6 76			22	Carried Forward *2,429.29*	

Howard C. Miller, Architect — Combined Cash Journal (Left Page

Friday, December 29

Issued Check No. 251 for $46.45 to replenish the petty cash fund. Following is a summary of the petty cash disbursements for the month of December prepared from the Petty Cash Disbursements Record:

Howard C. Miller, drawing	$10.00
Telephone and telegraph expense	.90
Blueprints and supplies expense	6.18
Automobile expense	2.70
Travel and entertainment expense	18.65
Charitable contributions expense	5.00
Miscellaneous expense	3.02
Total disbursements	$46.45

GENERAL DEBITS	GENERAL CREDITS	PROFESSIONAL FEES 41 CR.	SALARY EXPENSE 511 DR.	EMPLOYEES' INC. TAXES PAY. 21 CR.	FICA TAXES PAY. 22 CR.
			1 8 0 0 0	2 2 1 0	
			4 0 0 0	3 5 0	1 8 0
7 2 6 0 0					
		6 0 0 0 0			
2 9 5 0					
			1 8 0 0 0	2 2 1 0	
2 5 4 5 0		6 0 0 0 0	4 4 0 0 0	3 5 0	1 8 0
5 2 7 8				5 1 2 0	3 6 0
		3 6 0			
			7 2 5 0 0		
1 0 2 4 0					
7 2 0					
7 2 0					
1 0 0 0 0 0					
6 5 9 0					
			1 8 0 0 0	2 2 1 0	
			4 0 0 0	3 5 0	1 8 0
1 5 3 9 9 5		3 6 0	1 3 2 5 0 0	6 6 0 0 0	7 6 8 0	5 4 0
2 3 1 1					
7 9 5					
3 1 1 5					
			8 9 0 0 0		
6 4 1 7					
			1 8 0 0 0	2 2 1 0	
			4 0 0 0	3 5 0	1 8 0
1 6 6 6 3 6		3 6 0	2 2 1 5 0 0	7 7 0 0 0	1 0 2 4 0	7 2 0
1 6 6 6 3 6		3 6 0	2 2 1 5 0 0	8 8 0 0 0	1 0 2 4 0	7 2 0

Howard C. Miller, Architect — Combined Cash Journal (Right Page)

Issued Check No. 252 for $157.90 to Robert Cox and Check No. 253 for $34.70 to Susan Dunn in payment of salaries for week. (See explanation relating to Checks Nos. 231 and 232 issued on December 1.)

ROUTINE END-OF-THE-MONTH WORK

(1) Proved the footings and entered the totals in the combined cash journal. (2) Deposited the $500 check from Mr. Osborne and proved the bank balance ($2,613.76). (3) Completed the individual posting from the General Debits column of the combined cash journal. (4) Completed the summary posting of the column totals of the combined cash journal and ruled as illustrated on pages 112 and 113. (Note that the number of the

Chapter 5 / Accounting for a Personal Service Enterprise 111

COMBINED CASH JOURNAL

| FIRST NATIONAL BANK | | CK. | DATE | | DESCRIPTION | POST. |
DEPOSITS 11 DR.	CHECKS 11 CR.	NO.	MO.	DAY		REF.
2 2 1 8 6 0	2 4 3 6 7 6		Dec.	22	AMOUNTS FORWARDED *Balance* 2,429.29	✓
	7 6 4 8	250		27	*Travel and Entertainment Expense*	519
5 0 0 0 0				28	*Thurman Osborne*	✓
	4 6 4 5	251		29	*Howard C. Miller, Drawing*	031
					Telephone and Telegraph Expense	514
					Blueprints and Supplies Expense	515
					Automobile Expense	516
					Travel and Entertainment Expense	519
					Charitable Contributions Expense	520
					Miscellaneous Expense	521
	1 5 7 9 0	252		29	*Robert Cox*	✓
	3 4 7 0	253		29	*Susan Dunn* 2,613.76	✓
2 7 1 8 6 0	2 7 5 2 2 9					
2 7 1 8 6 0	2 7 5 2 2 9					
(11)	(11)					

Howard C. Miller, Architect — Combined Cash Journal — Concluded (Left Page)

account to which the total was posted was written in parentheses just below the total, and that check marks were placed below the General Debits and General Credits column totals in parentheses to indicate that these amounts were not posted.) **(5)** Footed the ledger accounts and noted the account balances where necessary, as illustrated on pages 114–116. **(6)** Prepared a trial balance of the ledger accounts.

> Usually a trial balance at the end of a month is prepared using two-column paper. However, because Mr. Miller has chosen the calendar year for his fiscal year (a common, but by no means universal, practice), the trial balance at the end of December is put in the first two amount columns of a page known as a *work sheet*. The purpose and manner of preparation of a work sheet is explained and illustrated starting on page 113.

Work at Close of the Fiscal Period

As soon as possible after the end of the fiscal period, the owner (or owners) of an enterprise wants to be provided with **(1)** an income statement covering the period just ended, and **(2)** a balance sheet as of the last day of the period. In order to provide these statements, the accountant must consider certain matters that will not have been recorded in routine fashion. (Depreciation of Office Equipment for the past year is the one such matter in the case of Mr. Miller's enterprise.) Furthermore, the revenue accounts, the expense accounts, and the account showing the owner's withdrawals will have performed their function for the period just ended (in this case, the year) and need to be made ready to receive the entries of the new period.

| GENERAL | | PROFESSIONAL FEES 41 CR. | SALARY EXPENSE 511 DR. | WAGE DEDUCTIONS | |
DEBITS	CREDITS			EMPLOYEES' INC. TAXES PAY. 21 CR.	FICA TAXES PAY. 22 CR.
1666 36		3 60	2215 00	102 40	7 20
76 48					
		500 00			
10 00					
90					
6 18					
2 70					
18 65					
5 00					
3 02					
			180 00	22 10	
			40 00	3 50	1 80
1779 29	3 60	2715 00	1100 00	127 00	9 00
1789 29	3 60	2715 00	1100 00	128 00	9 00
(✓)	(✓)	(41)	(511)	(21)	(22)

Howard C. Miller, Architect — Combined Cash Journal — Concluded (Right Page)

In the language of accountants and bookkeepers, "the books must be adjusted and closed." Actually, it is only the temporary owner's equity accounts — those for revenue, expense, and the owner's drawings — that are closed, but the remark quoted is widely used to describe what takes place at this time.

The End-of-Period Work Sheet. To facilitate (1) the preparing of the financial statements, (2) the making of needed adjustments in the accounts, and (3) the closing of the temporary owner's equity accounts, it is common practice to prepare what is known as a *work sheet*. Because that term is used to describe a variety of schedules and computations that accountants may prepare, the specific type to be discussed here is commonly called an *end-of-period work sheet*. Various forms of this device are used. Because of the nature of Mr. Miller's enterprise, an eight-column work sheet is adequate. This form is illustrated on page 117. Note that the heading states that it is for the year ended December 31, 19--. The fact that December 29 was the last working day is not important. The income statement will relate to the full year, and the balance sheet will show the financial position as of the last day of the fiscal period.

The first pair of columns of the work sheet was used to show the trial balance taken after the routine posting for the month of December had been completed. Note that the account, Depreciation Expense, No. 517, was included in the list of accounts and account numbers even though that

ACCOUNT *First National Bank*   ACCOUNT NO. *11*

DATE	ITEMS	POST. REF.	✓	DEBITS	DATE	ITEMS	POST. REF.	✓	CREDITS
19— Dec. 1	Balance	✓		2 6 4 7 4 5	19— Dec. 29			CJ37		2 7 5 2 2 9
29	2,613.76	CJ37		2 7 1 8 6 0						
				5 3 6 6 0 5						

ACCOUNT *Petty Cash Fund*   ACCOUNT NO. *12*

DATE	ITEMS	POST. REF.	✓	DEBITS	DATE	ITEMS	POST. REF.	✓	CREDITS
19— Dec. 1	Balance	✓		5 0 0 0						

ACCOUNT *Office Equipment*   ACCOUNT NO. *13*

DATE	ITEMS	POST. REF.	✓	DEBITS	DATE	ITEMS	POST. REF.	✓	CREDITS
19— Dec. 1	Balance	✓		3 9 2 6 9 5						

ACCOUNT *Accumulated Depreciation—Office Equipment*   ACCOUNT NO. *013*

DATE	ITEMS	POST. REF.	✓	DEBITS	DATE	ITEMS	POST. REF.	✓	CREDITS
					19— Dec. 1	Balance	✓		1 2 6 7 1 2

ACCOUNT *Employees' Income Taxes Payable*   ACCOUNT NO. *21*

DATE	ITEMS	POST. REF.	✓	DEBITS	DATE	ITEMS	POST. REF.	✓	CREDITS
19— Dec. 12		CJ36		1 0 2 4 0	19— Dec. 1	Balance	✓		1 0 2 4 0
					Dec. 29		CJ37		1 2 8 0 0

ACCOUNT *FICA Taxes Payable*   ACCOUNT NO. *22*

DATE	ITEMS	POST. REF.	✓	DEBITS	DATE	ITEMS	POST. REF.	✓	CREDITS
19— Dec. 12		CJ36		7 2 0	19— Dec. 1	Balance	✓		7 2 0
					Dec. 29		CJ37		9 0 0

ACCOUNT *Howard C. Miller, Capital*   ACCOUNT NO. *31*

DATE	ITEMS	POST. REF.	✓	DEBITS	DATE	ITEMS	POST. REF.	✓	CREDITS
					19— Dec. 1	Balance	✓		3 7 1 5 4 6

Howard C. Miller, Architect — General Ledger

ACCOUNT Howard C. Miller, Drawing — ACCOUNT NO. 031

DATE	ITEMS	POST. REF.	✓	DEBITS	DATE	ITEMS	POST. REF.	✓	CREDITS
19— Dec. 1	Balance	✓		1591740					
13		CJ36		100000					
29		CJ37		1000 1692740					

ACCOUNT Professional Fees — ACCOUNT NO. 41

DATE	ITEMS	POST. REF.	✓	DEBITS	DATE	ITEMS	POST. REF.	✓	CREDITS
					19— Dec. 1	Balance	✓		3513000
					29		CJ37		271500 3774500

ACCOUNT Salary Expense — ACCOUNT NO. 511

DATE	ITEMS	POST. REF.	✓	DEBITS	DATE	ITEMS	POST. REF.	✓	CREDITS
19— Dec. 1	Balance	✓		1034000					
29		CJ37		110000 1144000					

ACCOUNT Payroll Tax Expense — ACCOUNT NO. 512

DATE	ITEMS	POST. REF.	✓	DEBITS	DATE	ITEMS	POST. REF.	✓	CREDITS
19— Dec. 1	Balance	✓		38340					
12		CJ36		720 39060					

ACCOUNT Rent Expense — ACCOUNT NO. 513

DATE	ITEMS	POST. REF.	✓	DEBITS	DATE	ITEMS	POST. REF.	✓	CREDITS
19— Dec. 1	Balance	✓		247500					
1		CJ36		22500 270000					

ACCOUNT Telephone and Telegraph Expense — ACCOUNT NO. 514

DATE	ITEMS	POST. REF.	✓	DEBITS	DATE	ITEMS	POST. REF.	✓	CREDITS
19— Dec. 1	Balance	✓		32560					
19		CJ36		3115					
29		CJ37		90 35765					

Howard C. Miller, Architect — General Ledger (Continued)

ACCOUNT Blueprints and Supplies Expense   ACCOUNT NO. 515

DATE		ITEMS	POST. REF.	✓	DEBITS	DATE	ITEMS	POST. REF.	✓	CREDITS
19– Dec.	1	Balance	✓		1445 18					
	11		CJ36		52 78					
	21		CJ36		64 17					
	29		CJ37		1568 13					

ACCOUNT Automobile Expense   ACCOUNT NO. 516

DATE		ITEMS	POST. REF.	✓	DEBITS	DATE	ITEMS	POST. REF.	✓	CREDITS
19– Dec.	1	Balance	✓		1042 32					
	14		CJ36		65 90					
	18		CJ36		23 11					
	29		CJ37		1134 03					

ACCOUNT Insurance Expense   ACCOUNT NO. 518

DATE		ITEMS	POST. REF.	✓	DEBITS	DATE		ITEMS	POST. REF.	✓	CREDITS
19– Dec.	1	Balance	✓		127 56	19– Dec.	11		CJ36		3 60
	6		CJ36	153.46	29 50						
					157 06						

ACCOUNT Travel and Entertainment Expense   ACCOUNT NO. 519

DATE		ITEMS	POST. REF.	✓	DEBITS	DATE	ITEMS	POST. REF.	✓	CREDITS
19– Dec.	1	Balance	✓		1153 43					
	27		CJ37		76 48					
	29		CJ37		1248 56					

ACCOUNT Charitable Contributions Expense   ACCOUNT NO. 520

DATE		ITEMS	POST. REF.	✓	DEBITS	DATE	ITEMS	POST. REF.	✓	CREDITS
19– Dec.	1	Balance	✓		264 00					
	15		CJ36		50 00					
	29		CJ37		319 00					

ACCOUNT Miscellaneous Expense   ACCOUNT NO. 521

DATE		ITEMS	POST. REF.	✓	DEBITS	DATE	ITEMS	POST. REF.	✓	CREDITS
19– Dec.	1	Balance	✓		123 89					
	18		CJ36		7 95					
	29		CJ37		134 86					

Howard C. Miller, Architect — General Ledger (Concluded)

Howard C. Miller, Architect
Work Sheet
For the Year Ended December 31, 19—

Account	Acct. No.	Trial Balance Debits	Trial Balance Credits	Adjustments Debits	Adjustments Credits	Income Statement Debits	Income Statement Credits	Balance Sheet Debits	Balance Sheet Credits
First National Bank	11	261376						261376	
Petty Cash Fund	12	5000						5000	
Office Equipment	13	392695						392695	
Accumulated Deprec.—Office Equip.	013		126712		39270				165982
Employees' Income Taxes Payable	21		12800						12800
FICA Taxes Payable	22		900						900
Howard C. Miller, Capital	31		371546						371546
Howard C. Miller, Drawing	031	1692740						1692740	
Professional Fees	41		3784500				3784500		
Salary Expense	511	1144000				1144000			
Payroll Tax Expense	512	39060				39060			
Rent Expense	513	270000				270000			
Telephone and Telegraph Expense	514	35765				35765			
Blueprints and Supplies Expense	515	156831				156831			
Automobile Expense	516	113403				113403			
Depreciation Expense	517			39270		39270			
Insurance Expense	518	15346				15346			
Travel and Entertainment Exp.	519	124856				124856			
Charitable Contributions Expense	520	31900				31900			
Miscellaneous Expense	521	13456				13456			
		4294458	4294458	39270	39270	1983917	3784500	2351811	551311
Net Income						1800513			1800513
						3784500	3784500	2351811	2351811

Howard C. Miller, Architect — End-of-Period Work Sheet

account had no balance at this point. The second pair of columns, headed "Adjustments," was used to show the manner in which the expense of depreciation of office equipment for the year affects the accounts. The trial balance shows that the account, Office Equipment (No. 13) had a balance of $3,926.95, and that the balance of the account, Accumulated Depreciation — Office Equipment (No. 013) was $1,267.12. No new equipment was purchased during the year and there were no sales or retirements of such property during the year. Accordingly, the balances of these two accounts had not changed during the year. The two accounts are closely related: the debit balance of the office equipment account indicates the cost of such assets, and the credit balance of the accumulated depreciation account indicates the amount of such cost that has been charged off as depreciation in past years — that is, to January 1 of the current year. The amount of the difference between the two balances, $2,659.83, is described as the *book value* of the office equipment. Book value means simply "value per books," but the amount, in this instance, can more accurately be described as "cost yet to be charged off."

Since the year had just ended, it was necessary to record as an expense the depreciation for that year. Mr. Miller estimates that the various items of office equipment have average useful lives of ten years and that any scrap or salvage value at the end of that time is likely to be so small that it can be ignored. Accordingly, depreciation expense for the year was calculated to be $392.70 (10 percent of $3,926.95). This expense was due to be recorded in the ledger accounts, but that had to wait. The immediate need was to get the expense entered on the work sheet so that it would be considered when the financial statements were prepared. The record was made on the work sheet as follows: $392.70 was written in the Adjustments Debits column on the line for Depreciation Expense, and the same amount was written in the Adjustments Credits column on the line for Accumulated Depreciation — Office Equipment. The Adjustments Debits and Credits columns were totaled.

The next step was to combine each amount in the Trial Balance columns with the amount, if any, in the Adjustments columns and to extend the total into the Income Statement or Balance Sheet columns. Income and expense account balances are extended to the Income Statement columns and balance sheet account balances to the Balance Sheet columns. Note that the new amount for Accumulated Depreciation — Office Equipment, $1,659.82 ($1,267.12 + $392.70), appears in the Balance Sheet Credits column, and that the depreciation expense of $392.70 appears, along with all other expenses, in the Income Statement Debits column. The last four columns were totaled. The total of the Income Statement Credits column exceeded the total of the Income Statement Debits column by $18,005.83 —

the calculated net income for the year. That amount, so designated, was placed in the Income Statement Debits column to bring the pair of Income Statement columns into balance. When the same amount ($18,005.83) was placed in the Balance Sheet Credits column, the last pair of columns was brought into balance. The final totals of the last four columns were recorded at the bottom of the work sheet.

The fact that adding the net income for the year, $18,005.83, to the Balance Sheet Credits column caused its total to equal the total of the Balance Sheet Debits column is explained as follows. The amounts for the assets and liabilities in the last pair of columns were up-to-date. The difference between total assets and total liabilities, $4,793.89, was Mr. Miller's equity in the enterprise at the year's end. The balance of his capital account was $3,715.46 — the amount of his equity at the start of the year (since he had made no additional investments during the year). His withdrawals during the year, according to the balance in the account Howard C. Miller, Drawing, were $16,927.40. How could he start the year with an owner's equity of $3,715.46, make no additional investments, withdraw $16,927.40, and end the year with an owner's equity of $4,793.89? The explanation is that there had been profitable operations during the year that caused the owner's equity element to increase $18,005.83. This can be expressed in the form of the following equation:

OWNER'S EQUITY AT START OF PERIOD	+	NET INCOME FOR THE PERIOD	+	INVESTMENTS	−	WITHDRAWALS	=	OWNER'S EQUITY AT END OF PERIOD
$3,715.46	+	$18,005.83	+	0	−	$16,927.40	=	$4,793.89

Since the correct amounts for assets and liabilities and two of the three factors (owner's equity at start of period and withdrawals) needed to determine the correct amount of the owner's equity as of December 31 were already in the Balance Sheet columns, only the amount of the third factor — the net income for the year — had to be included in order that those columns would reflect the basic equation: Assets = Liabilities + Owner's Equity.

The Financial Statements. The work sheet supplied all of the information needed to prepare an income statement and a balance sheet. These statements for Mr. Miller's enterprise are reproduced on page 120.

Three features of the following balance sheet should be noted: **(1)** It is in so-called "report form" — the liabilities and the owner's equity sections are shown below the assets section. An alternative is the so-called "account form" — the assets are at the left, and the liabilities and the owner's equity sections are at the right. (See the balance sheet of The Whitman Advertising Agency on pages 42 and 43.) **(2)** The assets are classified on the basis of whether they are *current* or *long-lived*. Current assets include cash and any

HOWARD C. MILLER, ARCHITECT
Income Statement
For the Year Ended December 31, 19--

Professional fees...........................		$37,845.00
Professional expenses:		
Salary expense.........................	$11,440.00	
Payroll tax expense.....................	390.60	
Rent expense..........................	2,700.00	
Telephone and telegraph expense...............	357.65	
Blueprints and supplies expense...............	1,568.31	
Automobile expense.....................	1,134.03	
Depreciation expense....................	392.70	
Insurance expense......................	153.46	
Travel and entertainment expense.............	1,248.56	
Charitable contributions expense...............	319.00	
Miscellaneous expense.....................	134.86	
Total professional expenses................		19,839.17
Net income..................................		$18,005.83

HOWARD C. MILLER, ARCHITECT
Balance Sheet
December 31, 19--

Assets

Current assets:		
Cash.......................................		$2,663.76
Long-lived assets:		
Office equipment	$3,926.95	
Less accumulated depreciation.................	1,659.82	2,267.13
Total assets..................................		$4,930.89

Liabilities

Current liabilities:		
Employees' income taxes payable.................	$ 128.00	
FICA taxes payable..........................	9.00	
Total current liabilities........................		$ 137.00

Owner's Equity

Howard C. Miller:		
Capital, January 1, 19--.....................	$3,715.46	
Net income for year............... $18,005.83		
Less withdrawals................ 16,927.40	1,078.43	
Capital, December 31, 19--.....................		4,793.89
Total liabilities and owner's equity.................		$4,930.89

Howard C. Miller, Architect — Financial Statements

DATE		DESCRIPTION	POST. REF.	GENERAL	
MO.	DAY			DEBITS	CREDITS
		AMOUNTS FORWARDED			
Dec.	31	Adjusting Entry			
		Depreciation Expense	517	39270	
		Accumulated Deprec. —Office Equip.	013		39270
	31	Closing Entries			
		Professional Fees	41	3784500	
		Expense and Revenue Summary	32		3784500
		Expense and Revenue Summary	32	1983917	
		Salary Expense	511		1144000
		Payroll Tax Expense	512		39060
		Rent Expense	513		270000
		Telephone and Telegraph Expense	514		35765
		Blueprints and Supplies Expense	515		156831
		Automobile Expense	516		113403
		Depreciation Expense	517		39270
		Insurance Expense	518		15346
		Travel and Entertainment Exp.	519		124856
		Charitable Contributions Expense	520		31900
		Miscellaneous Expense	521		13486
		Expense and Revenue Summary	32	1800583	
		Howard C. Miller, Capital	31		1800583
		Howard C. Miller, Capital	31	1692740	
		Howard C. Miller, Drawing	031		1692740
				9301010	9301010

Adjusting and Closing Entries

other assets that will be converted into cash within the *normal operating cycle* of the business. This cycle is often a year in length. Mr. Miller's enterprise does not take into account any current assets other than cash. (The amount shown includes both cash in bank and petty cash.) The long-lived assets are those which are expected to serve for many years. **(3)** All of the liabilities are classified as current, since they must be paid in the near future. Certain types of obligations are classified as long-term, but Mr. Miller had no debts of this type.

Adjusting Entries for a Personal Service Enterprise. The financial statements must agree with the ledger accounts. To speed up the preparation of the statements, a work sheet was used with the one needed adjustment included. Subsequently this adjustment had to be formally recorded in the accounts. This was accomplished by posting the first journal entry in the illustration above. The two accounts affected by the entry, Depreciation Expense, No. 517 and Accumulated Depreciation — Office Equipment, No. 013, are reproduced below as they appeared after the entry was posted. After this posting was completed, the balances of all asset and liability accounts agreed exactly with the amounts shown in the balance sheet.

ACCOUNT *Depreciation Expense* ACCOUNT NO. *517*

DATE	ITEMS	POST. REF.	✓	DEBITS	DATE	ITEMS	POST. REF.	✓	CREDITS
19— Dec. 31		CJ38		3 9 2 7 0					

ACCOUNT *Accumulated Depreciation - Office Equipment* ACCOUNT NO. *013*

DATE	ITEMS	POST. REF.	✓	DEBITS	DATE	ITEMS	POST. REF.	✓	CREDITS
					19— Dec. 1	Balance	✓		1 2 6 7 1 2
					31		CJ38		3 9 2 7 0

Closing Entries for a Personal Service Enterprise. The revenue and expense accounts and the account for Howard C. Miller, Drawing (No. 031) had served their purpose for the year 19-- and the balance of each of these accounts needed to be reduced to zero in order to make the accounts ready for entries in the following year. Since the means of closing a ledger account under the double-entry procedure is to add the amount of the account's balance to the side of the account having the smaller total (so that the account will have no balance), each of the temporary owner's equity accounts was closed in this way. The net effect was an increase in the credit balance of the account for Howard C. Miller, Capital (No. 31) of $1,078.43 — the excess of his net income for the year, $18,005.83, over his withdrawals for the year, $16,927.40. However, this result was accomplished by means of four entries illustrated in the combined cash journal shown on page 121:

(a) The $37,845 credit balance of Professional Fees, Account No. 41, was closed (transferred) to the credit side of Expense and Revenue Summary, Account No. 32.

(b) The debit balances of all eleven expense accounts (Nos. 511 through 521) which, in total, amounted to $19,839.17, were closed to the debit side of Expense and Revenue Summary (No. 32). Some accountants favor showing and identifying each amount that is being closed to the summary account. This procedure, called *posting in detail*, is followed in the illustration on page 123.

(c) The result of entries (a) and (b) was a credit balance of $18,005.83 — the net income for the year — in Expense and Revenue Summary (No. 32). This was closed to Howard C. Miller, Capital, Account No. 31.

ACCOUNT Howard C. Miller, Drawing — ACCOUNT NO. 031

DATE	ITEMS	POST. REF.	✓	DEBITS	DATE	ITEMS	POST. REF.	✓	CREDITS
19— Dec. 1	Balance	✓		1591740	19— Dec. 31		CJ38		1692740
13		CJ36		100000					
29		CJ37		1000					
				1692740					
				1692740					1692740

ACCOUNT Expense and Revenue Summary — ACCOUNT NO. 32

DATE	ITEMS	POST. REF.	✓	DEBITS	DATE	ITEMS	POST. REF.	✓	CREDITS
19— Dec. 31	Salary Exp.	CJ38		1144000	19— Dec. 31	Prof. Fees	CJ38		3784500
	Pay. Tax Exp.	CJ38		39060					
	Rent Exp.	CJ38		270000					
	Tel. + Tel. Exp.	CJ38		35765					
	Blprts + Sup. Exp.	CJ38		156831					
	Auto Exp.	CJ38		113403					
	Deprec. Exp.	CJ38		39270					
	Ins. Exp.	CJ38		15346					
	Trav. + Ent. Exp.	CJ38		124856					
	Char. Cont. Exp.	CJ38		31900					
	Misc. Exp.	CJ38		13486					
	H. C. Miller, Cap.	CJ38		1800583					
				3784500					
				3784500					3784500

ACCOUNT Professional Fees — ACCOUNT NO. 41

DATE	ITEMS	POST. REF.	✓	DEBITS	DATE	ITEMS	POST. REF.	✓	CREDITS
19— Dec. 31		CJ38		3784500	19— Dec. 1	Balance	✓		3513000
					29		CJ37		271500
									3784500
				3784500					3784500

ACCOUNT Salary Expense — ACCOUNT NO. 511

DATE	ITEMS	POST. REF.	✓	DEBITS	DATE	ITEMS	POST. REF.	✓	CREDITS
19— Dec. 1	Balance	✓		1034000	19— Dec. 31		CJ38		1144000
29		CJ37		110000					
				1144000					1144000

Howard C. Miller, Architect — Partial General Ledger

DATE	ITEMS	POST. REF.	✓	DEBITS	DATE	ITEMS	POST. REF.	✓	CREDITS
19— Dec. 1	Balance	✓		383 40	19— Dec. 31		CJ38		390 60
12		CJ36		7 20					
				390 60					390 60
				390 60					390 60

ACCOUNT Rent Expense   ACCOUNT NO. 513

DATE	ITEMS	POST. REF.	✓	DEBITS	DATE	ITEMS	POST. REF.	✓	CREDITS
19— Dec. 1	Balance	✓		2475 00	19— Dec. 31		CJ38		2700 00
1		CJ36		225 00					
				2700 00					
				2700 00					2700 00

ACCOUNT Telephone and Telegraph Expense   ACCOUNT NO. 514

DATE	ITEMS	POST. REF.	✓	DEBITS	DATE	ITEMS	POST. REF.	✓	CREDITS
19— Dec. 1	Balance	✓		325 60	19— Dec. 31		CJ38		357 65
19		CJ36		31 15					
29		CJ37		90					
				357 65					
				357 65					357 65

ACCOUNT Blueprints and Supplies Expense   ACCOUNT NO. 515

DATE	ITEMS	POST. REF.	✓	DEBITS	DATE	ITEMS	POST. REF.	✓	CREDITS
19— Dec. 1	Balance	✓		1445 18	19— Dec. 31		CJ38		1568 31
11		CJ36		52 78					
21		CJ36		64 17					
29		CJ37		6 18					
				1568 31					1568 31

ACCOUNT Automobile Expense   ACCOUNT NO. 516

DATE	ITEMS	POST. REF.	✓	DEBITS	DATE	ITEMS	POST. REF.	✓	CREDITS
19— Dec. 1	Balance	✓		1042 32	19— Dec. 31		CJ38		1134 03
14		CJ36		65 90					
18		CJ36		23 11					
29		CJ37		2 70					
				1134 03					
				1134 03					1134 03

Howard C. Miller, Architect — Partial General Ledger (Continued)

ACCOUNT *Depreciation Expense*

DATE	ITEMS	POST. REF.	✓	DEBITS	DATE	ITEMS	POST. REF.	✓	CREDITS
19— Dec. 31		CJ38		3 9 2 7 0	19— Dec. 31		CJ38		3 9 2 7 0

ACCOUNT *Insurance Expense*   ACCOUNT No. 518

DATE	ITEMS	POST. REF.	✓	DEBITS	DATE	ITEMS	POST. REF.	✓	CREDITS
19— Dec. 1	Balance	✓		1 2 7 5 6	19— Dec. 11		CJ36		3 6 0
6	153.46	CJ36		2 9 5 0	31		CJ38		1 5 3 4 6
				1 5 7 0 6					1 5 7 0 6
				1 5 7 0 6					

ACCOUNT *Travel and Entertainment Expense*   ACCOUNT No. 519

DATE	ITEMS	POST. REF.	✓	DEBITS	DATE	ITEMS	POST. REF.	✓	CREDITS
19— Dec. 1	Balance	✓		1 1 5 3 4 3	19— Dec. 31		CJ38		1 2 4 8 5 6
27		CJ37		7 6 4 8					
29		CJ37		1 8 6 5					
				1 2 4 8 5 6					1 2 4 8 5 6
				1 2 4 8 5 6					

ACCOUNT *Charitable Contributions Expense*   ACCOUNT No. 520

DATE	ITEMS	POST. REF.	✓	DEBITS	DATE	ITEMS	POST. REF.	✓	CREDITS
19— Dec. 1	Balance	✓		2 6 4 0 0	19— Dec. 31		CJ38		3 1 9 0 0
15		CJ36		5 0 0 0					
29		CJ37		5 0 0					
				3 1 9 0 0					3 1 9 0 0
				3 1 9 0 0					

ACCOUNT *Miscellaneous Expense*   ACCOUNT No. 521

DATE	ITEMS	POST. REF.	✓	DEBITS	DATE	ITEMS	POST. REF.	✓	CREDITS
19— Dec. 1	Balance	✓		1 2 3 8 9	19— Dec. 31		CJ38		1 3 4 8 6
18		CJ36		7 9 5					
29		CJ37		3 0 2					
				1 3 4 8 6					1 3 4 8 6
				1 3 4 8 6					

Howard C. Miller, Architect — Partial General Ledger (Concluded)

(d) The $16,927.40 debit balance of Howard C. Miller, Drawing, Account No. 031, was closed to Howard C. Miller, Capital (No. 31).

As in the case of the adjusting entry, these closing entries were made as of December 31. It should be noted that the work sheet provided all of the data needed to prepare the adjusting and closing entries. The purpose and use of Expense and Revenue Summary, Account No. 32, should be apparent from this illustration. As its name indicates, the account is used to summarize the amounts of expense and revenue which are *reasons* for changes in owner's equity that were *not* the result of investments and withdrawals by the owner.

Ruling the Closed Accounts. After posting the closing entries, all of the temporary owner's equity accounts were in balance (closed), and they were ruled in the manner illustrated on pages 123–125.

The following procedures were used:

    (a) Where two or more amounts had been posted to either side of an account, the amount columns were footed to be sure that the total debits were equal to the total credits.

    (b) A single line was ruled across the debit and credit amount columns immediately below the last amount on the side with the most entries.

    (c) The totals of the debit and credit amount columns were entered on the next line in ink.

    (d) Double lines were ruled just below the totals. These rulings extended through all but the Items columns.

If an account had only one item on each side, only the double ruling was made. (Note the ruling for Depreciation Expense, Account No. 517.) If an account page is not filled, it may be used for recording the transactions of the following period.

Balancing and Ruling Open Accounts. After the temporary owner's equity accounts were closed, the open accounts (those for assets, liabilities, and Howard C. Miller, Capital) were balanced and ruled, where necessary, to prepare them to receive entries in the next fiscal period. Only two of

ACCOUNT First National Bank   ACCOUNT NO. 11

DATE	ITEMS	POST. REF.	✓	DEBITS	DATE	ITEMS	POST. REF.	✓	CREDITS
19— Dec. 1	Balance	✓		2 6 4 7 45	19— Dec. 29		CJ37		2 7 5 2 29
29		CJ37	2,613.76	2 7 1 8 60	31	Balance	✓		2 6 1 3 76
				5 3 6 6 05					5 3 6 6 05
				5 3 6 6 05					5 3 6 6 05
19— Jan. 1	Balance			2 6 1 3 76					

ACCOUNT Howard C. Miller, Capital   ACCOUNT NO. 31

DATE	ITEMS	POST. REF.	✓	DEBITS	DATE	ITEMS	POST. REF.	✓	CREDITS
19— Dec. 31		CJ38		1 6 9 2 7 40	19— Dec. 1	Balance	✓		3 7 1 5 46
31	Balance	✓		4 7 9 3 89	31		CJ38		1 8 0 0 5 83
				2 1 7 2 1 29					2 1 7 2 1 29
				2 1 7 2 1 29					2 1 7 2 1 29
					19— Jan. 1	Balance	✓		4 7 9 3 89

Mr. Miller's ledger accounts needed to be balanced and ruled: First National Bank, Account No. 11, and Howard C. Miller, Capital, Account No. 31. These two accounts are shown at the bottom of page 126. The procedure in each case was as follows:

(a) The amount of the balance of the account was entered on the side having the smaller total to equalize total debits and total credits. The word "Balance" was written in the Items column.

(b) The columns were footed to prove the equality of the debits and credits.

(c) A single line was ruled across the debit and credit amount columns immediately below the line with the last amount. (This line would have been below the last amount on the side with the most entries, if the number of entries on each side had not been the same.)

(d) The totals of the debit and credit amount columns were entered on the next line in ink.

(e) Double lines were ruled just below the totals extending through all but the Items column.

(f) An entry was made on the next line under date of January 1, with the amount of the balance — so labeled in the Items column — entered in the amount column on the proper side (the debit side for the asset account and the credit side for the owner's equity account). If the account page had been filled, the balance would have been entered at the top of a new account page.

No balancing and ruling was needed in the cases of Petty Cash Fund, Account No. 12, or Office Equipment, Account No. 13, since each of these accounts had only one entry. (These two accounts remained just as illustrated on page 114.) Accumulated Depreciation — Office Equipment, Account No. 013, needed no further attention since it had entries on one side only. (This account remains as illustrated on page 122.) The two liability accounts, Employees' Income Taxes Payable (No. 21) and FICA Taxes Payable (No. 22) remain as illustrated on page 114, inasmuch as each has had only one entry since previously ruled.

Post-Closing Trial Balance. After posting the closing entries, it is advisable to take a *post-closing trial balance* to prove the equality of the debit and credit balances. The post-closing trial balance of Mr. Miller's ledger is shown at the top of page 128.

The Accounting Cycle

The steps involved in handling all of the transactions and events completed during an accounting period, beginning with recording in a book of original entry and ending with a post-closing trial balance, are referred to collectively as the *accounting cycle*. This chapter has illustrated a complete accounting cycle. A brief summary of the various steps follows:

Howard C. Miller, Architect
Post-Closing Trial Balance
December 31, 19—

Account	Acct. No.	Dr. Balance	Cr. Balance
First National Bank	11	2 6 1 3 7 6	
Petty Cash Fund	12	5 0 0 0	
Office Equipment	13	3 9 2 6 9 5	
Accumulated Depreciation – Office Equipment	013		1 6 5 9 8 2
Employees' Income Taxes Payable	21		1 2 8 0 0
FICA Taxes Payable	22		9 0 0
Howard C. Miller, Capital	31		4 7 9 3 8 9
		6 5 9 0 7 1	6 5 9 0 7 1

Howard C. Miller, Architect — Post-Closing Trial Balance

(a) Journalizing the transactions.
(b) Posting to the ledger accounts.
(c) Taking a trial balance.
(d) Determining the needed adjustments.
(e) Completing an end-of-period work sheet.
(f) Preparing an income statement and a balance sheet.
(g) Journalizing and posting the adjusting and closing entries.
(h) Ruling the closed accounts and balancing and ruling the open accounts.
(i) Taking a post-closing trial balance.

In visualizing the accounting cycle, it is important to realize that steps **(c)** through **(i)** in the foregoing list are performed *as of the last day of the accounting period*. This does not mean that they necessarily are done *on* the last day. The accountant or bookkeeper may not be able to do any of these things until the first few days (sometimes weeks) of the next period. Nevertheless, the work sheet, statements, and entries are prepared or recorded as of the closing date. While the journalizing of transactions in the new period proceeds in regular fashion, it is not usual to post to the general ledger any entries relating to the new period until the steps relating to the period just ended have been completed.

Report No. 10

Complete Report No. 10 in the workbook and submit your working papers to the instructor for approval. After completing the report you will then be given instructions as to the work to be done next.

chapters 1-5

practical accounting problems

The following problems supplement those in Reports 1 through 10 of the Part 1 Workbook. These problems are numbered to indicate the chapter of the textbook with which they correlate. For example, Problem 1-A and Problem 1-B correlate with Chapter 1. Loose-leaf stationery should be used in solving these problems. The paper required includes plain ruled paper, two-column, three-column, and four-column journal paper, cash journal paper, ledger paper, and work sheet paper.

Problem 1-A

W. S. Dickey is a practicing attorney. As of December 31 he owned the following property that related to his business: Cash, $961; office equipment, $1,500; and an automobile, $2,560. At the same time he owed business creditors $630.

REQUIRED: (1) On the basis of the above information, compute the amounts of the accounting elements and show them in equation form. (2) Assume that during the following year there is an increase in Mr. Dickey's business assets of $1,800 and a decrease in his business liabilities of $75. Indicate the changes in the accounting elements by showing them in equation form after the changes have occurred.

Problem 1-B

H. L. Scholl, a CPA who has been employed by a large national firm of certified public accountants, decides to go into business for himself. His business transactions for the first month of operations were as follows:

(a) Mr. Scholl invested $5,000 cash in the business.
(b) Paid office rent for one month, $100.
(c) Purchased office equipment from the Office Supply Co., $1,840, on account.
(d) Paid telephone bill, $17.
(e) Received $500 for services rendered to James J. Hughes & Co.
(f) Paid $600 to the Office Supply Co. on account.
(g) Received $325 for services rendered to the Barford Garage.
(h) Paid $300 salary to office secretary.

REQUIRED: (1) On a plain sheet of paper rule eight "T" accounts and enter the following titles: Cash, Office Equipment, Accounts Payable, H. L. Scholl, Capital, Professional Fees, Rent Expense, Telephone Expense, and Salary Expense. (2) Record the foregoing transactions directly in the accounts. (3) Foot the accounts and enter the balances where necessary. (4) Prepare a trial balance of the accounts, using a sheet of two-column journal paper.

Problem 2-A

Following is a narrative of the transactions completed by R. H. Blinn, a management consultant, during the first month of his business operations:

Oct. 1. Mr. Blinn invested $3,000 cash in the business.
1. Paid office rent, $125.
2. Purchased office furniture for $975 cash.
3. Paid $16.85 for installation of telephone and for one month's service.
4. Received $225 from The Munger Linen Service for consulting services rendered.
5. Purchased stationery and supplies on account from American Lithofold Co., $189.64.
6. Paid $6 for subscription to a professional management magazine. (Charge Miscellaneous Expense.)
8. Paid $35 to Dr. Leo Shanley, a dentist, for dental service performed for Mrs. Blinn.
(Note: This is equivalent to a withdrawal of $35 by Mr. Blinn for personal use. Charge to his drawing account.)
9. Received $80 from Midwest Pool and Court Co. for professional services rendered.
12. Paid $48.72 for a plane ticket for a business trip.
14. Paid other traveling expenses, $38.70.
19. Paid account of American Lithofold Co. in full, $189.64.
20. Received $265 from Moloney Electric Co. for professional services rendered.
31. Paid $290 monthly salary to secretary.

REQUIRED: Journalize the foregoing transactions, using a sheet of two-column journal paper. Number the pages and use both sides of the sheet, if necessary. Select the account titles from the following chart of accounts:

CHART OF ACCOUNTS

Assets
11 Cash
12 Stationery and Supplies
13 Office Furniture

Liabllities
21 Accounts Payable

Owner's Equity
31 R. H. Blinn, Capital
32 R. H. Blinn, Drawing

Revenue
41 Professional Fees

Expenses
51 Rent Expense
52 Telephone Expense
53 Traveling Expense
54 Salary Expense
55 Miscellaneous Expense

After journalizing the transactions, prove the equality of the debits and credits by footing the amount columns. Enter the footings in pencil immediately under the line on which the last entry appears.

Problem 2-B

L. S. LEES, CERTIFIED PUBLIC ACCOUNTANT
Trial Balance
June 30, 19--

Cash	11	$ 942.31	
Office Equipment	12	525.00	
Automobile	13	2,200.00	
Accounts Payable	21		$ 312.36
L. S. Lees, Capital	31		2,512.00
L. S. Lees, Drawing	32	1,800.00	
Professional Fees	41		4,000.00
Rent Expense	51	750.00	
Telephone Expense	52	87.75	
Electric Expense	53	60.00	
Automobile Expense	54	217.90	
Charitable Contributions Expense	55	160.00	
Miscellaneous Expense	56	81.40	
		$6,824.36	$6,824.36

L. S. Lees is a certified public accountant engaged in practice on his own account.

NARRATIVE OF TRANSACTIONS FOR JULY

July 1. (Thursday) Paid one month's rent, $125.
2. Paid telephone bill, $14.20.
2. Paid electric bill, $10.25.
5. Received $325 from Sealtest Foods for services rendered.
7. Paid a garage bill, $27.60.

July 9. Received $100 from the Mayfair-Lennox Hotels for services rendered.
    12. Paid Scruggs Department Store, $32.40. (Charge to Mr. Lees' drawing account.)
    15. Mr. Lees withdrew $275 for personal use.
    16. Paid Smith-Corona Marchant, Inc., $90 on account.
    19. Received $120 from Tri-City Food Stores for services rendered.
    23. Gave the American Red Cross $15.
    26. Paid the American Institute of Certified Public Accountants $50 for annual membership dues.
    29. Received $52.50 from Goddard Motor Sales Co. for professional services.
    30. Mr. Lees withdrew $25 for personal use.

REQUIRED: (1) Journalize the July transactions, using a sheet of two-column journal paper. Number the pages and use both sides of the sheet, if necessary. Foot the amount columns. (2) Open the necessary accounts, using the standard account form of ledger paper. Allow one page for each account. Record the July 1 balances as shown in the June 30 trial balance and post the journal entries for July. (3) Foot the ledger accounts, enter the balances, and prove the balances by taking a trial balance as of July 31. Use a sheet of two-column journal paper for the trial balance.

Problem 2-C

THE G. C. HETLAGE AGENCY
Trial Balance
January 31, 19 - -

Cash.....................................	11	$2,896.41	
Stationery and Supplies......................	12	562.76	
Office Furniture	13	1,842.00	
Notes Payable.............................	21		$ 900.00
Accounts Payable...........................	22		643.29
G. C. Hetlage, Capital......................	31		3,516.88
G. C. Hetlage, Drawing.....................	32	630.40	
Professional Fees...........................	41		1,687.20
Rent Expense..............................	51	150.00	
Telephone Expense..........................	52	21.60	
Salary Expense............................	53	280.00	
Traveling Expense.........................	54	316.52	
Stationery and Supplies Expense..............	55	18.43	
Miscellaneous Expense......................	56	29.25	
		$6,747.37	$6,747.37

REQUIRED: (1) Prepare an income statement for The G. C. Hetlage Agency showing the results of operations for the month of January. (2) Prepare a balance sheet in account form showing the financial condition of the agency as of January 31. Use a sheet of two-column journal paper for the income statement. Two sheets of two-column journal paper may be used for the balance sheet. List the assets on one sheet and the liabilities and owner's equity on the other sheet.

Problem 3-A

S. V. Smith is an advertising counselor. The only book of original entry for his business is a four-column journal. He uses the standard account form of general ledger Following is the trial balance of his business taken as of November 30:

S. V. SMITH, ADVERTISING COUNSELOR
Trial Balance
November 30, 19 - -

Cash.	11	$1,673.41	
Office Equipment.	13	350.00	
Accounts Payable.	21		$ 75.97
S. V. Smith, Capital.	31		3,125.00
S. V. Smith, Drawing	32	2,375.00	
Advertising Fees.	41		4,240.00
Rent Expense	51	880.00	
Telephone Expense.	52	105.20	
Electric Expense	53	67.45	
Salary Expense.	54	1,786.50	
Charitable Contributions Expense	55	151.00	
Miscellaneous Expense.	56	52.41	
		$7,440.97	$7,440.97

NARRATIVE OF TRANSACTIONS FOR DECEMBER

Dec. 1. (Friday) Paid December office rent in advance, $80.
1. Paid electric bill, $6.52.
4. Paid telephone bill, $10.75.
4. Received a check from Moloney Electric Co. for $200 for services rendered.
4. Received $225 from Drew Foods Co. for services rendered.
7. Donated $10 to the American Red Cross.
7. Paid $5.25 for cleaning office.
8. Received check for $225 from Eden Publishing House for advertising counsel.
11. Mr. Smith withdrew $200 for personal use.
15. Paid secretary's salary for the half month, $150.
18. Purchased office furniture on credit from Lammert Furniture Co., $400.
19. Paid $3 for having the office windows washed.
20. Received $150 from Wetterau Grocery Co. for services rendered.
22. Paid traveling expenses while on business, $22.50.
25. Donated $20 to the United Fund.
26. Paid Lammert Furniture Co. $75 on account.
28. Mr. Smith withdrew $100 for personal use.
29. Paid secretary's salary for the half month, $150.

REQUIRED: **(1)** Journalize the December transactions. For the journal use one sheet of four-column journal paper and number the page. **(2)** Open the necessary ledger accounts. Allow one page for each account and number the accounts. Record the December 1 balances and post the four-column journal entries. Foot and rule the four-column journal and enter the new cash balance. **(3)** Take a trial balance.

Problem 3-B

Oscar Sutter, a plumber, completed the following transactions with the Delmar Trust and Savings Bank during the month of October:

Oct.	2. (Monday) Balance in bank per record kept on check stubs..........	$2,500.00	Oct.	11. Check No. 118....	$ 80.00
				11. Check No. 119....	45.90
				13. Check No. 120....	447.75
				14. Check No. 121....	41.80
				14. Check No. 122....	247.32
	2. Deposit.........	1,500.00		14. Deposit..........	381.43
	2. Check No. 108...	288.20		16. Check No. 123....	125.00
	3. Check No. 109...	30.00		18. Check No. 124....	265.01
	4. Check No. 110...	475.00		21. Check No. 125....	97.45
	4. Check No. 111...	110.00		21. Deposit..........	971.00
	5. Check No. 112...	125.00		24. Check No. 126....	131.42
	6. Check No. 113...	90.00		25. Check No. 127....	108.38
	7. Check No. 114...	155.60		27. Check No. 128....	277.97
	7. Check No. 115...	50.00		28. Check No. 129....	83.00
	7. Check No. 116...	46.00		30. Check No. 130....	547.63
	7. Deposit.........	268.45		30. Deposit..........	825.14
	10. Check No. 117...	454.32			

REQUIRED: **(1)** A record of the bank account as it would appear on the check stubs. **(2)** A reconciliation of the bank statement for October which indicated a balance of $2,930.87 on October 31, with Checks Nos. 116, 126, 129, and 130 outstanding, and a service charge of 45 cents.

Problem 3-C

Alan Taylor, a general contractor, had a balance of $60 in his petty cash fund as of June 1. During June the following petty cash transactions were completed:

June 2. (Friday) Paid $1.50 for typewriter repairs. Petty Cash Voucher No. 22.
    6. Paid for telegram, $3.25. Petty Cash Voucher No. 23.
    8. Gave $10 to the United Fund. Petty Cash Voucher No. 24.
    9. Paid garage for washing car, $1.75. Petty Cash Voucher No. 25.
    12. Gave Mr. Taylor's son $3. (Charge Alan Taylor, Drawing.) Petty Cash Voucher No. 26.
    14. Paid for postage stamps, $4. Petty Cash Voucher No. 27.
    19. Paid for newspaper for month, $1.65. Petty Cash Voucher No. 28.

June 22. Paid for window washing, $2.50. Petty Cash Voucher No. 29.
27. Paid $2.00 to the Parent-Teachers Association for dues. (Charge Alan Taylor, Drawing.) Petty Cash Voucher No. 30.
28. Paid for car lubrication, $2.00. Petty Cash Voucher No. 31.
29. Donated $15 to the American Red Cross. Petty Cash Voucher No. 32.
30. Rendered report of petty cash expenditures for month and received the amount needed to replenish the petty cash fund.

REQUIRED: (1) Record the foregoing transactions in a petty cash disbursements record, distributing the expenditures as follows:

Alan Taylor, Drawing   Charitable Contributions Expense
Automobile Expense   Miscellaneous Expense
Telephone and Telegraph Expense

(2) Prove the petty cash disbursements record by footing the amount columns and proving the totals. Enter the totals and rule the amount columns with single and double lines. (3) Prepare a statement of the petty cash disbursements for June. (4) Bring down the balance in the petty cash fund below the ruling in the Description column. Enter the amount received to replenish the fund and record the total.

Problem 4-A

Following is a summary of the hours worked, rates of pay, and other relevant information concerning the employees of The Winston Machine Tool Co., R. J. Winston, Owner, for the week ended Saturday, November 3. Employees are paid at the rate of time and one half for all hours worked in excess of 8 in any day or 40 in any week.

No.	NAME	EXEMPTIONS CLAIMED	HOURS WORKED M T W T F S						REGULAR HOURLY RATE	CUMULATIVE EARNINGS JAN. 1–OCT. 28
1	Blake, Allen H............	3	8	8	8	8	8	6	$2.00	$4,805
2	Harter, Thomas R.........	4	8	9	8	8	8	4	2.20	5,564
3	Markland, Robert E.......	3	8	8	8	8	8	0	2.10	5,460
4	Reardon, John H..........	1	8	8	8	9	8	4	1.90	3,217
5	Stevens, James R.........	2	8	8	8	8	0	4	2.15	3,815
6	Willey, James L...........	1	8	8	8	8	0	0	2.40	4,464

Blake and Reardon each have $3 withheld this payday for group life insurance. Harter and Willey each have $2 withheld this payday for private hospital insurance. Stevens has $5 withheld this payday as a contribution to the United Fund.

REQUIRED: (1) Using plain ruled paper size 8½" by 11", rule a payroll register form similar to that reproduced on pages 80 and 81 and insert the necessary columnar headings. Enter on this form the payroll for the week ended Saturday, November 3. Refer to the Weekly Income Tax Table on page 79 to determine the amounts to be withheld from the wages of each worker for income tax purposes. All of Winston's employees are married. Four and one-half percent of the taxable wages of each employee should be withheld for FICA taxes. Checks Nos. 511 through 516 were issued to the employees. Complete the payroll record by footing the amount columns, proving the footings, entering the totals, and ruling. (2) Assuming that the wages were paid on November 7, record the payment on a sheet of two-column general journal paper.

Problem 4-B

The Clayton Store employs twelve people. They are paid by checks on the 15th and last day of each month. The entry to record each payroll includes the liabilities for the amounts withheld. The expense and liabilities arising from the employer's payroll taxes are recorded on each payday.

Following is a narrative of the transactions completed during the month of January that relate to payrolls and payroll taxes:

Jan. 15. Payroll for first half of month:

Total salaries..............................		$2,240.00
Less amounts withheld:		
FICA taxes............................	$100.80	
Employees' income taxes................	182.20	283.00
Net amount paid.......................		$1,957.00

15. Social security taxes imposed on employer:
FICA taxes, 4.5%
State unemployment taxes, 2%
FUTA taxes, 0.4%

28. Paid $710.13 for December's payroll taxes:
FICA taxes, $256.73.
Employees' income taxes withheld, $453.40.

28. Paid State unemployment taxes for quarter ended December 31, $68.80.

28. Paid FUTA taxes for year ended December 31, $572.55.

31. Payroll for last half of month:

Total salaries............................		$2,360.00
Less amounts withheld:		
FICA taxes............................	$106.20	
Employees' income taxes................	196.80	303.00
Net amount paid.......................		$2,057.00

31. Social security taxes imposed on employer:
All salaries taxable; rates same as on January 15.

REQUIRED: (1) Journalize the foregoing transactions, using two-column general journal paper. (2) Foot the debit and credit amount columns as a means of proof.

Problem 5-A

Robert Murphy is an architect engaged in professional practice on his own account. Since his revenue consists entirely of compensation for personal services rendered, he keeps his accounts on the cash basis. His trial balance for the current year ending December 31 appears below.

REQUIRED: (1) Prepare an eight-column work sheet making the necessary entries in the Adjustments columns to record the depreciation of the following assets:

Office equipment, 10%, $192
Automobile, 25%, $910

(2) Prepare the following financial statements:

(a) An income statement for the year ended December 31.
(b) A balance sheet in report form as of December 31.

ROBERT MURPHY, ARCHITECT
Trial Balance
December 31, 19 - -

Cash..	$ 3,835.06	
Office Equipment............................	1,920.00	
Accumulated Depreciation — Office Equipment......		$ 192.00
Automobile..................................	3,640.00	
Accumulated Depreciation — Automobile...........		455.00
Accounts Payable............................		757.02
Employees' Income Taxes Payable...............		85.20
FICA Taxes Payable..........................		87.50
Robert Murphy, Capital.......................		5,728.40
Robert Murphy, Drawing.......................	8,500.00	
Professional Fees............................		19,918.98
Rent Expense...............................	2,400.00	
Salary Expense..............................	5,600.00	
Automobile Expense..........................	406.00	
Depreciation Expense.........................		
Payroll Tax Expense.........................	175.00	
Charitable Contributions Expense................	240.00	
Miscellaneous Expense........................	508.04	
	$27,224.10	$27,224.10

Problem 5-B

Earl McMillan operates an airline charter service, specializing in all weather passenger and freight service. A trial balance of his general ledger accounts is reproduced at the top of page 138.

EARL McMILLAN AIR SERVICE
Trial Balance
December 31, 19--

Cash..	$ 11,964.46	
Office Equipment................................	2,500.00	
Accumulated Depreciation — Office Equipment...		$ 500.00
Air Service Equipment..........................	119,200.00	
Accumulated Depreciation — Air Service Equipment		47,680.00
Accounts Payable...............................		5,341.00
Employees' Income Taxes Payable................		270.00
FICA Taxes Payable.............................		250.00
Earl McMillan, Capital.........................		43,000.00
Earl McMillan, Drawing.........................	8,400.00	
Traffic Revenue................................		85,562.52
Rent Expense...................................	5,600.00	
Salary Expense.................................	16,000.00	
Office Expense.................................	1,240.00	
Air Service Expense............................	16,910.26	
Depreciation Expense...........................		
Payroll Tax Expense............................	500.00	
Charitable Contributions Expense...............	200.00	
Miscellaneous Expense..........................	88.80	
	$182,603.52	$182,603.52

REQUIRED: **(1)** Prepare an eight-column work sheet making the necessary adjustments to record the depreciation of long-lived assets as shown below.

PROPERTY	RATE OF DEPRECIATION	AMOUNT OF DEPRECIATION
Office equipment...............................	10%	$ 250
Air service equipment..........................	20	23,840

(2) Prepare an income statement for the year ended December 31. **(3)** Prepare a balance sheet in report form as of December 31. **(4)** Using two-column journal paper, prepare the entries required:

> **(a)** To adjust the general ledger accounts so that they will be in agreement with the financial statements.
>
> **(b)** To close the temporary owner's equity accounts on December 31.

Foot the amount columns as a means of proof.

Problem 5-C

Edith Walden is the sole proprietor of a dry cleaning establishment called Walden Cleaners. Since revenue consists of compensation for services rendered, she keeps her accounts on the cash basis. She does not extend credit to customers but operates on a cash-on-delivery basis. The Trial Balance columns of her work sheet for the current year ended December 31 are reproduced on page 139.

WALDEN CLEANERS
Work Sheet
For the Year Ended December 31, 19--

Account	Trial Balance Debits	Trial Balance Credits
Security National Bank......................	6,312.80	
Office Equipment	1,000.00	
Accumulated Depreciation — Office Equipment....		100.00
Cleaning Equipment.........................	3,600.00	
Accumulated Depreciation — Cleaning Equipment..		288.00
Delivery Truck..............................	1,840.00	
Accumulated Depreciation — Delivery Truck.......		552.00
Accounts Payable...........................		323.08
Employees' Income Taxes Payable...............		214.12
FICA Taxes Payable..........................		128.52
Edith Walden, Capital.......................		7,616.44
Edith Walden, Drawing.......................	6,324.90	
Dry Cleaning Revenue........................		18,617.70
Pressing Revenue............................		7,979.02
Rent Expense...............................	4,160.00	
Heat, Light, and Power Expense...............	2,607.34	
Salary Expense..............................	8,225.00	
Delivery Expense............................	828.86	
Depreciation Expense........................		
Payroll Tax Expense.........................	257.04	
Miscellaneous Expense.......................	662.94	
	35,818.88	35,818.88

REQUIRED: **(1)** Complete the work sheet making the necessary adjusting entries to record the depreciation of long-lived assets as follows:

> Office equipment, 10% a year, $100
> Cleaning equipment, 8% a year, $288
> Delivery truck, 30% a year, $552

(2) Prepare an income statement for the year ended December 31. **(3)** Prepare a balance sheet as of December 31 in report form. **(4)** Using two-column general journal paper, prepare the entries required to adjust and close the ledger. Foot the amount columns as a means of proof.

chapter six

accounting for merchandise

In the preceding chapter, accounting and bookkeeping practices suitable for a personal service enterprise were discussed and illustrated. The calculation of net income for the year was made on the so-called "cash basis" except for the matter of depreciation expense. Revenue was not recorded until money was received for the service performed, even though the service may have been performed in a prior period. Similarly, most expenses were not recorded until cash was disbursed for them, even though many of the payments were for things of value received and consumed in a prior period or for things to be received in a later period. An exception to this practice was made in the matter of depreciation since it would be unrealistic to consider the entire cost of assets such as office equipment (expected to be used for many years) to be an expense of the month or year of purchase. The cost of such long-lived assets is spread over their expected useful lives.

The cash basis, even when slightly modified, is not technically perfect, but it has the virtues of simplicity and ease of understanding. This basis has proved to be quite satisfactory for most personal service enterprises. In the case of business enterprises whose major activity is the purchase and sale of merchandise, however, the cash basis of periodic income calculation usually does not give a meaningful or useful measure of net income or net loss. There are two reasons why this is true: **(1)** Merchandising businesses commonly purchase and often sell merchandise "on account" or "on credit" — meaning that payment is postponed a few days or weeks. The amount of cash paid or collected in any accounting period is almost never the same as the amount of purchases and sales of that period. **(2)** Merchandising businesses normally start and end each period with some goods on hand (commonly called *merchandise inventory*), but the dollar amount is not likely to be the same at both points of time. To illustrate, consider the following circumstances:

Cost of merchandise (goods) on hand, beginning of period.............	$ 8,000
Cost of merchandise purchased during the period......................	60,000
Cost of goods returned to the supplier for some reason (not ordered, unsatisfactory for some reason, etc.).......................................	2,000
Cash disbursements during the period for goods purchased both in prior periods and the current period......................................	55,000
Sales price of all goods sold and delivered to customers during the current period...	80,000
Sales price of goods returned by customers............................	3,000
Cash received from customers during the period in payment for sales both of prior periods and the current period.................................	70,000
Cost of merchandise (goods) on hand, end of period...................	12,000

The first step in calculating the net income or net loss of an accounting period is to determine the *gross profit* or *gross margin* for the period. Gross profit (margin) is the difference between **(1)** the amount of *net sales* of the period, and **(2)** the amount of the *cost of goods sold* during the period. Net sales is the amount received or promised in exchange for merchandise transferred to customers, less the amount of any returns or adjustments allowed to customers for some reason. Cost of goods sold is determined by the formula:

$$\text{COST OF GOODS SOLD} = \text{MERCHANDISE INVENTORY, BEGINNING OF PERIOD} + \text{NET PURCHASES} - \text{MERCHANDISE INVENTORY, END OF PERIOD}$$

Net purchases is the difference between the cost of goods purchased and the total of **(1)** the cost of goods returned to suppliers and **(2)** the amount of any allowances made by suppliers. Applying these definitions and formulas to the above data gives the following result:

Sales..			$80,000
Less sales returns and allowances...................			3,000
Net sales..			$77,000
Cost of goods sold:			
Merchandise inventory, beginning of period........		$ 8,000	
Add: Purchases................................	$60,000		
Less purchases returns and allowances............	2,000		
Net purchases..................................		58,000	
Cost of goods available for sale...................		$66,000	
Less merchandise inventory, end of period.........		12,000	
Cost of goods sold.............................			54,000
Gross profit on sales.............................			$23,000

The foregoing is an important application of what is known as the *accrual basis* of accounting. On this basis, revenue is recognized in the period in which it is earned, and expense (cost of goods sold, in this instance) is recognized in the period in which it is incurred. The movement of cash in either direction is a relatively unimportant consideration. In the foregoing calculation of gross profit for the period, the cash collections from customers ($70,000) and the cash payments to suppliers ($55,000) did not enter into the computation. (It should be mentioned that the manner of accounting for depreciation illustrated in the last chapter was in accordance with the accrual basis of accounting.) Because accrual accounting is widely used, and because one of its major applications relates to the accounting for merchandise transactions, this subject will be examined in some detail.

In recording transactions concerned with merchandising, it is desirable to keep at least the following accounts:

(a) Purchases
(b) Purchases Returns and Allowances
(c) Sales
(d) Sales Returns and Allowances
(e) Merchandise Inventory

purchases and the purchases journal

The word *purchase* can refer to the act of buying almost anything or, if used as a noun, to the thing that is bought. In connection with the accounting for a merchandising business, however, the term usually refers to merchandise. A reference to "purchases for the year," unless qualified in some way, would relate to the merchandise (*stock in trade*) that had been bought.

Purchases Account

The purchases account is a temporary owner's equity account in which the cost of merchandise purchased is recorded. The account should be debited for the cost of all merchandise purchased during the accounting period. If the purchase was for cash, the cash account should be credited; if on account, Accounts Payable should be credited. The purchases account may also be debited for any transportation charges, such as freight, express, and parcel post charges, that increase the cost of the merchandise purchased.

PURCHASES	
Debit to record the cost of merchandise purchased.	

Purchases Returns and Allowances Account

This account is a temporary owner's equity account in which purchases returns and allowances are recorded. The account should be credited for the cost of any merchandise returned to creditors or suppliers and for any allowances received from creditors that decrease the cost of the merchandise purchased. The offsetting debit is to Accounts Payable if the goods were purchased on account, or to Cash if a refund is received because the purchase was originally for cash. Allowances may be received from creditors

PURCHASES RETURNS AND ALLOWANCES	
	Credit to record returns and allowances.

for merchandise delivered in poor condition or for merchandise that does not meet specifications as to quality, weight, size, color, grade, or style.

Although purchases returns and allowances might be credited directly to Purchases, it is better to credit Purchases Returns and Allowances. The accounts will then show both the amount of gross purchases and the amount of returns and allowances. If returns and allowances are large in proportion to gross purchases, a weakness in the purchasing operations is indicated. It may be that better sources of supply should be sought or that purchase specifications should be stated more clearly.

Purchase Invoice

A document received by the buyer from the seller that provides information for recording a purchase transaction is known as a *purchase invoice*. An invoice includes the supplier's invoice number, the purchaser's order number, the dates of shipment and billing, the terms of sale, a description of the goods, the quantities shipped, the unit prices, and the total amount of the purchase. A variety of forms and sizes of purchase invoices is in common use.

When both the goods and the invoice have been received, it is customary for the purchaser to assign the incoming invoice a number. (Note that the invoice on page 144 was marked "#23.") Someone must check to see that the invoice is correct as to quantities and unit prices, and that the extensions and total are correct. ("Extensions" are the amounts resulting from multiplying the quantity times the price of each item purchased.) It is common practice for the purchaser to imprint a form on the face of the invoice by means of a rubber stamp. This form provides spaces for the initials of the persons who have verified that the goods were received, and that the prices, extensions, and total are correct. Sometimes there is space to show the number of the account to be debited — Purchases, if the invoice relates to merchandise bought for resale. If everything is found to be in order, the invoice will be paid at the proper time.

Below is a reproduction of a purchase invoice as it would appear after the various aspects of the transaction have been verified and approved.

Merchandise may be bought for cash or on account. When merchandise is bought for cash, the transaction results in an increase in purchases and a decrease in the asset cash; hence, it should be recorded by debiting Purchases and by crediting Cash. When merchandise is bought on account, the transaction results in an increase in purchases with a corresponding increase in the liability accounts payable; hence, it should be recorded by debiting Purchases and by crediting Accounts Payable.

Empire Furniture Company
Grand Rapids, Michigan 49501

#23
INVOICE

Sold To

B. C. SMYTHE
5401 MADISON ROAD
CINCINNATI, OHIO 45227

Date	May 2, 1967
Invoice No.	8712
Cust. Order No.	196
Shipped Via	C. & O. R.R.
Date Shipped	May 2, 1967

Terms   30 days

QUANTITY		DESCRIPTION		UNIT PRICE	AMOUNT
ORDERED	SHIPPED				
2	2	4119	Tier Table	21.50	43.00
1	1	662	Mhg. Table	82.00	82.00
2	2	635	Mhg. Table	51.00	102.00
4	4	2630	Night Stand	22.50	90.00
2	2	2317	Coffee Table	34.75	69.50
					386.50

Date received...... 5/5 R.B.
Received by .... R.B.
Items o.k. .... W.H.
Prices o.k. .... W.H.
Ex. and tot. o.k. .. 51
Acct. no. .... B.R.
Appr. for pymt. ....

Purchase Invoice

Accounts Payable

In order that the owner or manager may know the total amount owed to his creditors, it is advisable to keep a summary ledger account for Accounts Payable. This is a liability account. The credit balance of the account at the beginning of the period represents the total amount owed to creditors. During the period, the account should be credited for the amount of any transactions involving increases and should be debited for the amount of any transactions involving decreases in the amount owed to creditors. At the end of the period, the credit balance of the account again represents the total amount owed to creditors.

It is also necessary to keep some record of the transactions completed with each creditor in order that information may be readily available at all times as to the amount owed to each creditor and as to when each invoice should be paid. The following methods of accounting for purchases on account are widely used:

The Invoice Method. Under this method it is customary to keep a chronological record of the purchase invoices received and to file them systematically. All other vouchers or documents representing transactions completed with creditors should be filed with the purchase invoices. Special filing equipment facilitates the use of this method.

The Ledger Account Method. Under this method it is customary to keep a chronological record of the purchase invoices received. An individual ledger account with each creditor is also kept. Special equipment may be used in maintaining a permanent file of the invoices and other vouchers or documents supporting the records.

Purchases Journal

All of the transactions of a merchandising business can be recorded in an ordinary two-column general journal or in a combined cash journal. However, in many such enterprises purchase transactions occur frequently. If most of the purchases are made on account, such transactions may be recorded advantageously in a special journal called a *purchases journal*. One form of a purchases journal is illustrated on page 146.

It will be noted that in recording each purchase, the following information is entered in the purchases journal:

- (a) Date on which the invoice is received.
- (b) Number of the invoice (i.e., the number assigned by the buyer).
- (c) From whom purchased (the creditor).
- (d) Amount of the invoice.

When the invoice method of accounting is used for purchases on account, it is not necessary to record the address of the creditor in the pur-

DATE	NO. OF INVOICE	FROM WHOM PURCHASED	POST. REF.	AMOUNT
1967 May 5	23	Empire Furniture Company	✓	386 50
6	24	A. L. Foster Company	✓	758 92
12	25	Marsh Manufacturing Company	✓	1223 60
29	26	Jackson Brothers	✓	1398 60
31		Purchases Dr. - Accounts Payable Cr.	51/23	3767 62

Model Purchases Journal

chases journal; neither is it necessary to record the terms in the purchases journal. With this form of purchases journal, each transaction can be recorded on one horizontal line.

If an individual ledger account is not kept with each creditor, the purchase invoices should be filed immediately after they have been recorded in the purchases journal. It is preferable that they be filed according to due date in an unpaid invoice file.

If a partial payment is made on an invoice, a notation of the payment should be made on the invoice, and it should be retained in the unpaid invoice file until it is paid in full. It is generally considered a better policy to pay each invoice in full. Paying specific invoices in full simplifies record keeping for both the buyer and the seller. If credit is received because of returns or allowances, a notation of the amount of the credit should also be made on the invoice so that the balance due will be indicated.

When an invoice is paid in full, the payment should be noted on the invoice, which should be transferred from the unpaid invoice file to a paid invoice file.

The unpaid invoice file is usually arranged with a division for each month with folders numbered 1 to 31 in each division. This makes it possible to file the unpaid invoices according to the date they will become due, which facilitates payment of the invoices on or before their due dates. Since certain invoices may be subject to discounts if paid within a specified time, it is important that they be handled in such a manner that payment in time to get the benefit of the discounts will not be overlooked.

The folders in the paid invoice file are usually arranged in alphabetic order, according to the names of creditors. This facilitates the filing of all paid invoices, and all other vouchers or documents representing transactions with creditors, in such a manner that a complete history of the business done with each creditor is maintained.

Posting from the Purchases Journal. Under the invoice method of accounting for purchases on account, individual posting from the purchases journal is not required. When this plan is followed, it is customary to place a check mark in the Posting Reference column of the purchases journal at the time of entering each invoice.

At the end of the month the Amount column of the purchases journal should be totaled and the ruling completed as illustrated. The total of the purchases on account for the month should then be posted as a debit to Purchases and as a credit to Accounts Payable. A proper cross-reference should be provided by entering the page of the purchases journal preceded by the initial "P" in the Posting Reference column of the ledger and by entering the account number in the Posting Reference column of the purchases journal. The titles of both accounts and the posting references may be entered on one horizontal line of the purchases journal as shown in the illustration. Posting the total in this manner usually is referred to as *summary posting*.

The proper method of completing the summary posting from B. C. Smythe's purchases journal on May 31 is shown in the following illustration of the accounts affected.

ACCOUNT *Accounts Payable*   ACCOUNT NO. *23*

DATE	ITEMS	POST. REF.	✓	DEBITS	DATE	ITEMS	POST. REF.	✓	CREDITS
					1967 *May 31*		*P9*		3 7 6 7 6 2

ACCOUNT *Purchases*   ACCOUNT NO. *51*

DATE	ITEMS	POST. REF.	✓	DEBITS	DATE	ITEMS	POST. REF.	✓	CREDITS
1967 *May 31*		*P9*		3 7 6 7 6 2					

The Ledger Account Method. If an individual ledger account is kept for each creditor, all transactions representing either increases or decreases in the amount owed to each creditor should be posted individually to the proper account. The posting may be done by hand or posting machines may be used. If the posting is done by hand, it may be completed either directly from the purchase invoices and other vouchers or documents representing the transactions, or it may be completed from the books of original entry. If the posting is done with the aid of posting machines, it will usually be completed directly from the purchase invoices and other vouchers or documents. The ledger account method of accounting for accounts payable is explained in detail in Chapter 8.

Report No. 11

Refer to the workbook and complete Report No. 11. After completing the report, continue with the following study assignment until the next report is required.

sales and the sales journal

On page 142 reference was made to the fact that in recording transactions arising from merchandising activities it is desirable to keep certain accounts, including accounts for sales and for sales returns and allowances. A discussion of these accounts, together with a discussion of the sales journal, follows.

Sales Account

The sales account is a temporary owner's equity account in which the revenue resulting from sales of merchandise is recorded. The account should be credited for the selling price of all merchandise sold during the accounting period. If sales are for cash, the credit to Sales is offset by a debit to Cash; if the sales are on account, the debit is made to an asset account, Accounts Receivable.

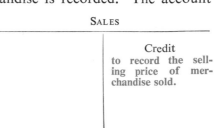

SALES

	Credit
	to record the selling price of merchandise sold.

Sales Returns and Allowances Account

This account is a temporary owner's equity account in which sales returns and allowances are recorded. The account should be debited for the selling price of any merchandise returned by customers or for any allowances made to customers that decrease the selling price of the merchandise sold. The offsetting credit is to Accounts Receivable if the goods were sold on account, or to Cash if a refund was made because the sale was originally for cash. Such allowances may be granted to customers for merchandise delivered in poor condition or for merchandise that does not meet specifications as to quality, weight, size, color, grade, or style.

SALES RETURNS AND ALLOWANCES

| Debit |
| to record returns and allowances. |

While sales returns and allowances could be debited directly to Sales, it is better to debit Sales Returns and Allowances. The accounts will then show both the amount of gross sales and the amount of returns and allowances. If returns and allowances are large in proportion to gross sales, a weakness in the merchandising operations is indicated and the trouble should be determined and corrected.

Retail Sales Tax

A tax imposed upon the sale of tangible personal property at retail is known as a *retail sales tax*. The tax is usually measured by the gross sales price or the gross receipts from sales. Retail sales taxes are imposed by most states and by many cities. Retail sales taxes may also include taxes imposed upon persons engaged in furnishing services at retail, in which case they are measured by the gross receipts for furnishing such services. The rates of the tax vary considerably but usually range from 1 percent to 4 percent. In most states the tax is a general sales tax. However, in some states the tax is imposed only on specific items, such as automobiles, cosmetics, radios, and playing cards.

To avoid fractions of cents and to simplify the determination of the tax, it is customary to use a sales tax table or schedule. For example, where the rate is 4 percent the tax may be calculated as shown in the following schedule:

AMOUNT OF SALE	AMOUNT OF TAX
1¢ to 12¢	None
13¢ to 34¢	1¢
35¢ to 59¢	2¢
60¢ to 87¢	3¢
88¢ to $1.12	4¢
$1.13 to $1.37	5¢

and so on

The amount of the tax imposed under the schedule approximates the legal rate. Retail sales tax reports accompanied by remittances for the amounts due must be filed periodically, usually monthly or quarterly, depending upon the law of the state or city in which the business is located.

In the case of a retail store operated in a city or state where a sales tax is imposed on merchandise sold for cash or on account, it is advisable to keep an account with Sales Tax Payable. This is a liability account which should be credited for the amount of the tax collected or imposed on sales. The account should be debited for the amount of the tax paid to the proper taxing authority. A credit balance in the account at any time indicates the amount of the merchant's liability for taxes collected or imposed.

SALES TAX PAYABLE

Debit	Credit
to record payment of tax to the proper taxing authority or for tax on merchandise returned by customers.	to record tax imposed on sales.

Sales tax accounting may be complicated by such factors as (1) sales returns and allowances and (2) exempt sales. If the tax is recorded at the time the sale is recorded, it will be necessary to adjust for the tax when recording sales returns and allowances. If some sales are exempt from the tax, it will be necessary to distinguish between taxable and nontaxable sales. A common example of nontaxable sales is sales to out-of-state customers.

Sales Ticket

The first written record of a sales transaction is called a *sales ticket*. Whether merchandise is sold for cash or on account, a sales ticket should be prepared. When the sale is for cash, the ticket may be printed by the cash register at the time that the sale is rung up. However, some stores prefer to use handwritten sales tickets no matter whether the sale is for cash or on account. Regardless of the method used

B. C. SMYTHE
CINCINNATI, OHIO
RETURN POSTAGE GUARANTEED
2049- 23

SOLD TO	16 6 1
	W L MELVIN
STREET	7251 BERWOOD DR
CITY-STATE	CINCINNATI O 45243

SEND TO	*same*
STREET	
CITY-STATE	

HOW SOLD	DATE	SALES NUMBER	DEPT. NO.	IF C. O. D. COLLECT
Chg.	5/5/67	240	12	

. B. C. SMYTHE	DATE	SALES NO.	DEPT.
2049- 23	5/5/67	240	12

NO. ENCL.	HOW SOLD	AMT. SOLD	AMT. RECD.	DEPOSIT
	Chg.	211.15		

BOUGHT BY *self* | CUSTOMER'S SIGNATURE *W. L. Melvin*

QUAN.	ARTICLES	AMOUNT
1	Buffet	165 00
1	Coffee table	26 60
1	Table lamp	13 40
		205 00
	Sales Tax	6 15
		211 15

Entered 5/5 RJ
Posted 5/5 RJ

OFFICE RECORD

Sales Ticket

in recording cash sales, it is necessary to prepare a handwritten sales ticket or charge slip for every sale on account. Such sales tickets are usually prepared in duplicate or in triplicate. The original copy is for the bookkeeping department. A carbon copy is given to the customer. Where more than one salesperson is employed, each is usually provided with his own pad of sales tickets. Each pad bears a different number that identifies the clerk. The individual sales tickets are also numbered consecutively. This facilitates sorting the tickets by clerks if it is desired to compute the amount of goods sold by each clerk. Reference to the sales ticket reproduced on page 150 will show the type of information usually recorded.

When merchandise is sold for cash in a state or a city which has a retail sales tax, the transaction results in an increase in the asset cash offset by an increase in sales revenue and an increase in the liability sales tax payable. Such transactions should be recorded by debiting Cash for the amount received and by crediting Sales for the sales price of the merchandise and crediting Sales Tax Payable for the amount of the tax collected. When merchandise is sold on account in such a state or city, the transaction results in an increase in the asset accounts receivable offset by an increase in sales revenue and an increase in the liability sales tax payable. Such transactions should be recorded by debiting Accounts Receivable for the total amount charged to the customer and by crediting Sales for the amount of the sale and crediting Sales Tax Payable for the amount of the tax imposed.

An alternative procedure that is permissible under some sales tax laws is to credit the total of both the sales and the tax to the sales account in the first place. Periodically — usually at the end of each month — a calculation is made to determine how much of the balance of the sales account is presumed to be tax, and an entry is made to remove this amount from the sales account and to transfer it to the sales tax payable account. Suppose, for example, that the tax rate is 3 percent, and that the sales account includes the tax collected or charged, along with the amount of the sales. In this event, 100/103 of the balance of the account is presumed to be the amount of the sales, and 3/103 of the balance is the amount of the tax. If the sales account had a balance of $10,300, the tax portion would be $300 (3/103 of $10,300). A debit to Sales of $300 would remove this tax portion; the credit would be to Sales Tax Payable.

Accounts Receivable

In order that the owner or manager may know the total amount due from charge customers at any time, it is advisable to keep a summary ledger account with Accounts Receivable. This is an asset account. The debit balance of the account at the beginning of the period represents the total amount due from customers. During the period, the account should be debited for the amount of any transactions involving increases and should be credited for the amount of any transactions involving decreases in the amount due from customers. At the end of the period, the debit balance of the account again represents the total amount due from charge customers.

It is also necessary to keep some record of the transactions completed with each customer in order that information may be readily available at all times as to the amount due from each customer. The following methods of accounting for charge sales are widely used:

The Sales Ticket Method. Under this method it is customary to file the charge sales tickets systematically. All other vouchers or documents representing transactions with customers should be filed with the sales tickets. Special filing equipment facilitates the use of this method. In some cases a chronological record of the charge sales tickets is kept as a means of control.

The Ledger Account Method. Under this method it is customary to keep a chronological record of the charge sales tickets. An individual ledger account with each customer is also kept. Special equipment may be used in maintaining a permanent file of the charge sales tickets and other vouchers or documents supporting the records.

Under either of these methods of accounting for transactions with charge customers, it is necessary that a sales ticket or charge slip be made for each sale on account. In making a charge sales ticket the date, the name and address of the customer, the quantity, a description of the items sold, the unit prices, the total amount of the sale, and the amount of the sales tax should be recorded.

Sales Journal

Transactions involving the sale of merchandise on account can be recorded in an ordinary two-column general journal or in a combined cash journal. However, in many merchandising businesses sales transactions occur frequently, and if it is the policy to sell merchandise on account, such transactions may be recorded advantageously in a special journal. If the business is operated in an area where no sales taxes are imposed, all sales on account can be recorded in a *sales journal* with only one amount column as illustrated at the top of page 153.

At the end of the month, the total of the amount column should be posted as a debit to Accounts Receivable and as a credit to Sales.

The second model sales journal illustrated on page 153 provides three amount columns. This format is most appropriate for use in an area where

DATE	NO. OF SALE	TO WHOM SOLD	POST. REF.	AMOUNT

Sales Journal Without Sales Taxes

a sales tax is imposed. The transactions recorded in the journal were completed by B. C. Smythe, a retail merchant, during the month of May. His store is located in a state that imposes a tax of 3 percent on the retail sale of all merchandise whether sold for cash or on account.

It will be noted that the following information regarding each charge sales ticket is recorded in the sales journal:

(a) Date.

(b) Number of the sales ticket.

(c) To whom sold (the customer).

(d) Amount charged to customer.

(e) Amount of sale.

(f) Amount of sales tax.

SALES JOURNAL — PAGE 14

DATE	NO. OF SALE	TO WHOM SOLD	POST. REF.	ACCOUNTS REC. DR.	SALES CR.	SALES TAX PAY. CR.
1967 May 5	61	W. L. Melvin	✓	2 1 1 1 5	2 0 5 0 0	6 1 5
5	62	L. B. Howard	✓	1 2 1 0 2 5	1 1 7 5 0 0	3 5 2 5
11	63	E. H. Pratt	✓	4 3 8 2 7	4 2 5 5 0	1 2 7 7
15	64	R. A. Ball	✓	1 3 0 0 6 3	1 2 6 2 7 5	3 7 8 8
22	65	S. L. Dunn	✓	7 4 6 7 5	7 2 5 0 0	2 1 7 5
26	66	J. L. Herbert	✓	1 2 0 0 1 6	1 1 6 5 2 0	3 4 9 6
				5 1 0 7 2 1	4 9 5 8 4 5	1 4 8 7 6
				(12)	(41)	(24)

Sales Journal With Sales Taxes

With this form of sales journal, each transaction can be recorded on one horizontal line. The sales ticket should provide all the information needed in recording each sale.

If an individual ledger account is not kept with each customer, the charge sales tickets should be filed immediately after they have been recorded in the sales journal. They are usually filed under the name of the customer. There are numerous types of trays, cabinets, and files on the market that are designed to facilitate the filing of charge sales tickets by customers. Such devices are designed to save time, to promote accuracy, and to provide a safe means of keeping a record of the transactions with each charge customer.

When a customer makes a partial payment on his account, the amount of the payment should be noted on the most recent charge sales ticket and the new balance should be indicated. Sales tickets paid in full should be receipted and may either be given to the customer or may be transferred to another file for future reference. If a customer is given credit for merchandise returned or because of allowances, a notation of the amount of credit should be made on the most recent charge sales ticket and the new balance should be indicated. If a credit memorandum is issued to a customer, it should be prepared in duplicate and the carbon copy should be attached to the sales ticket on which the amount is noted.

Posting from the Sales Journal. Under the sales ticket method of accounting for sales on account, individual posting from the sales journal is not required. When this plan is followed, it is customary to place a check mark in the Posting Reference column of the sales journal at the time of entering each sale.

At the end of the month the amount columns of the sales journal should be footed in small figures. On a separate sheet of paper the total of the credit columns should then be added. The sum of the totals of the credit columns should equal the total of the debit column. If it does, the totals should be entered in ink and the ruling completed as illustrated. The totals should be posted to the general ledger accounts indicated in the column headings. This summary posting should be completed in the following order:

    (a) Post the total of the Accounts Receivable Dr. column to the debit of Accounts Receivable.

    (b) Post the total of the Sales Cr. column to the credit of Sales.

    (c) Post the total of the Sales Tax Payable Cr. column to the credit of Sales Tax Payable.

A proper cross-reference should be provided by entering the page of the sales journal preceded by the initial "S" in the Posting Reference column of the ledger and by entering the account number immediately below the column total of the sales journal. The proper method of completing the summary posting from B. C. Smythe's sales journal on May 31 is shown in the accounts affected as illustrated on page 155.

The Ledger Account Method. If an individual ledger account is kept for each customer, all transactions representing either increases or decreases in the amount due from each customer should be posted individually to the proper account. The posting may be done by hand or posting machines may be used. If the posting is done by hand, it may be completed either directly from the charge sales tickets and other vouchers or documents representing the transactions, or it may be completed from the books of original entry. If the posting is done with posting machines, it will usually be completed directly from the charge sales tickets and other vouchers or documents.

ACCOUNT *Accounts Receivable*   ACCOUNT NO. 12

DATE	ITEMS	POST. REF.	✓	DEBITS	DATE	ITEMS	POST. REF.	✓	CREDITS
1967 May 31		S14		5 1 0 7 2 1					

ACCOUNT *Sales Tax Payable*   ACCOUNT NO. 24

DATE	ITEMS	POST. REF.	✓	DEBITS	DATE	ITEMS	POST. REF.	✓	CREDITS
					1967 May 31		S14		1 4 8 7 6

ACCOUNT *Sales*   ACCOUNT NO. 41

DATE	ITEMS	POST. REF.	✓	DEBITS	DATE	ITEMS	POST. REF.	✓	CREDITS
					1967 May 31		S14		4 9 5 8 4 5

Report No. 12

Refer to the workbook and complete Report No. 12. After completing the report, continue with the following study assignment until the next report is required.

accounting procedure

The accounting procedure in recording the transactions of a merchandising business is, in general, the same as that involved in recording the transactions of any other enterprise. In a small merchandising business where the number of transactions is not large and all the bookkeeping may be done by one person, a standard two-column general journal or a combined cash journal may be used as the only book of original entry. However, if desired, a purchases journal and a sales journal may be used also. The purchases journal may be used for keeping a chronological record of purchases of merchandise on account, and the sales journal may be used for keeping a chronological record of sales of merchandise on account. All of the accounts may be kept in one general ledger, which may be either a bound book, a loose-leaf book, or a card file. The posting from a general journal or from the "General" columns of a combined cash journal may be completed daily or periodically; summary posting from the purchases and sales journals and from the special columns of a combined cash journal is done at the end of the month.

A trial balance should be taken at the end of each month as a means of proving the equality of the debit and credit account balances. The balance of the summary account for Accounts Receivable should be proved periodically, or at least at the end of each month. This may be done by determining the total of the unpaid sales tickets or charge slips that are kept in a customer's file. Likewise, the balance of the summary account for Accounts Payable should be proved periodically, or at least at the end of each month. This may be done by determining the total of the unpaid invoices that are kept in an unpaid invoice file.

This procedure will be illustrated by (1) recording a narrative of certain transactions for one month in a purchases journal, a sales journal, and a combined cash journal, (2) by posting to the ledger accounts, (3) by preparing a schedule of accounts receivable to reconcile the balance of the summary account for Accounts Receivable, and (4) by preparing a schedule of accounts payable to reconcile the balance of the summary account for Accounts Payable. (The end-of-month trial balance is not shown since the illustration does not involve all of the accounts in the general ledger.)

G. A. Rodgers is the owner of a small retail business operated under the name of "The Rodgers Store." A purchases journal, a sales journal, and a combined cash journal are used as books of original entry. All of the accounts are kept in a general ledger. Individual ledger accounts with customers and creditors are not kept; instead, the purchase invoices and the charge sales tickets are filed in the manner previously described. All sales are subject to a retail sales tax of 3 percent, whether for cash or on account. All sales on account are payable by the tenth of the following month unless otherwise agreed. A partial chart of accounts is reproduced at the top of page 157. It includes only the accounts needed to record certain transactions completed during March, 1967, the first month that Mr. Rodgers has owned and operated the business.

THE RODGERS STORE

PARTIAL CHART OF ACCOUNTS

*Assets**

   11 Cash
   12 Accounts Receivable
   18 Store Equipment

Liabilities

   23 Accounts Payable
   24 Sales Tax Payable

Revenue from Sales

   41 Sales
   041 Sales Returns and Allowances

Cost of Goods Sold

   51 Purchases
   051 Purchases Returns and Allowances

Words in italics represent headings and not account titles.

THE RODGERS STORE

PARTIAL NARRATIVE OF TRANSACTIONS

Thursday, March 2

Purchased store equipment on account from the Modern Store Equipment Co., 103 E. Jasper St., $1,121.60.

> Since this transaction involved a purchase of store equipment, it was recorded in the combined cash journal. (The purchases journal is used only for recording purchases of merchandise on account.)

Friday, March 3

Received invoice dated March 1 from Young's, 920 Iris Ave., for merchandise purchased, $172.05. Terms, 30 days net. (Assigned number "1" to this invoice.)

Saturday, March 4

Sold merchandise on account to John J. Lance, 206 "C" St., $20.20, tax 61 cents. Sale No. 1-1.

Sundry cash sales per cash register tape, $46, tax $1.38.

> Each Saturday the store's total cash sales for the week and related tax are recorded, using the cash register tape as the source of the amounts. This transaction was recorded in the combined cash journal by debiting Cash for the total amount received and by crediting Sales for the selling price of the merchandise and crediting Sales Tax Payable for the amount of the tax imposed on cash sales. This was recorded in the combined cash journal since only sales on account are entered in the sales journal.

Monday, March 6

Purchased merchandise from Levis Company, 1001 Garfield Ave., for cash, $86. Check No. 4.

> This transaction was recorded in the combined cash journal since only purchases of merchandise on account are recorded in the purchases journal.

Tuesday, March 7

Sold merchandise on account to William B. Sells, 908 High St., $22, tax 66 cents. Sale No. 1-2.

Wednesday, March 8

Gave William B. Sells credit for merchandise returned, $11, tax 33 cents.

This transaction increased sales returns and allowances and decreased sales tax payable and accounts receivable. It was recorded in the combined cash journal by debiting Sales Returns and Allowances for the amount of the merchandise returned, by debiting Sales Tax Payable for the amount of the sales tax, and by crediting Accounts Receivable for the total amount of the credit allowed Mr. Sells.

Thursday, March 9

Received invoice (No. 2) dated March 8 from Young's for merchandise purchased, $285. Terms, 30 days net.

Friday, March 10

Sold merchandise on account to Joseph F. Camm, 13 Wallace Ave., $16.60, tax 50 cents. Sale No. 2-1.

Saturday, March 11

Sundry cash sales for week, $142.90, tax $4.29.

Received a check for $20.81 from John J. Lance in payment of merchandise sold to him March 4.

Monday, March 13

Received credit for $18.10 from Young's for merchandise returned by agreement.

The credit applies to Invoice No. 2, dated March 8. This transaction had the effect of increasing purchases returns and allowances and decreasing accounts payable. It was recorded in the combined cash journal by debiting Accounts Payable and by crediting Purchases Returns and Allowances for the amount of the credit received from Young's.

Tuesday, March 14

Paid Rapid Transit, Inc., freight and drayage on merchandise purchased, $17.50. Check No. 5.

In the simple set of accounts maintained for The Rodgers Store, no separate account is used to record the cost of freight on merchandise purchases. Instead, the amount is debited to the purchases account. This treatment is acceptable since freight on purchases is really a part of the cost of goods purchased.

Wednesday, March 15

Received invoice (No. 3) dated March 13 from Carl B. Cooper & Son, Dayton, for merchandise purchased, $33. Terms, 60 days net.

Thursday, March 16

Paid Young's $172.05 in settlement of Invoice No. 1 dated March 1. Check No. 6.

Received $11.33 from William B. Sells in payment for merchandise sold March 7 less merchandise returned March 8.

Saturday, March 18

Sundry cash sales for week, $79.10, tax $2.37.

Monday, March 20

Paid Modern Store Equipment Co. $600 on account. Check No. 7.

Tuesday, March 21

Sold merchandise on account to Joseph F. Camm, $26, tax 78 cents. Sale No. 1-3.

Wednesday, March 22

Received invoice (No. 4) dated March 20 from Carl B. Cooper & Son for merchandise purchased, $52.10. Terms, 30 days net.

Thursday, March 23

Sold merchandise on account to John J. Lance, $37, tax $1.11. Sale No. 2-2.

Saturday, March 25

Sundry cash sales for week, $82.80, tax $2.48.

Monday, March 27

Sold merchandise on account to William B. Sells, $31.95, tax 96 cents. Sale No. 2-3.

Friday, March 31

Sundry cash sales, $46.20, tax $1.39.

Since this is the last day of the month, the amount of cash sales since March 25, including tax, was recorded.

Journalizing

The transactions completed by The Rodgers Store during the month of March were recorded in the combined cash journal reproduced on pages 160 and 161, the purchases journal reproduced on page 160, and the sales journal reproduced on page 161. (The footings of the combined cash journal reflect the amounts of more transactions than are actually recorded. The footings of the purchases journal and of the sales journal reflect only the amounts of the transactions recorded.)

COMBINED CASH JOURNAL

CASH		CK. NO.	DATE		DESCRIPTION	POST. REF.
REC. 11 DR.	DISB. 11 CR.		MO.	DAY		
			Mar.	2	Store Equipment	18
					Accts. Payable—Mod. Store Equip. Co.	23
4738				4	Cash Sales	✓
	8600	4		6	Purchases	51
				8	Sales Ret. and Allow. (Wm B. Sells)	041
					Sales Tax Payable	24
14719				11	Cash Sales	✓
2081				11	John J. Lance (on acct.)	✓
				13	Purchases Ret. and Allow. (Young's)	051
	1750	5		14	Purchases (freight)	51
	17205	6		16	Young's	✓
1133				17	William B. Sells (on acct.)	✓
8147				18	Cash Sales	✓
	60000	7		20	Modern Store Equipment Co.	✓
8528				25	Cash Sales	✓
4759				31	Cash Sales 919.84	✓
240083	148099					
240083	148099					
(11)	(11)					

The Rodgers Store — Combined Cash Journal (Left Page)

Posting

The accounts affected by the transactions narrated are reproduced on pages 162 and 163. The posting was completed from the books of original entry in the following order; first, the combined cash journal; second, the purchases journal; and third, the sales journal. After the columns of the combined cash journal were footed and the footings were proved, the totals were entered and the rulings were made as illustrated. Each entry in the General Debits and General Credits columns was posted individually

PURCHASES JOURNAL   PAGE 1

DATE	NO. OF INVOICE	FROM WHOM PURCHASED	POST. REF.	AMOUNT
1967 Mar 3	1	Young's		17205
9	2	Young's		28500
15	3	Carl B. Cooper & Son		3300
22	4	Carl B. Cooper & Son		5210
31		Purchases Dr.—Accounts Payable Cr.	51/23	54215

The Rodgers Store — Purchases Journal

GENERAL DEBITS	GENERAL CREDITS	ACCOUNTS PAY. 23 DR.	ACCOUNTS REC. 12 CR.	SALES 41 CR.	SALES TAX PAY. 24 CR.
112160					
	112160				
				4600	138
8600					
1100					
33			1133		
				14290	429
			2081		
	1810	1810			
1750		17205			
			1133		
				7910	237
		60000			
				8280	248
				4620	139
159258	285019	79015	4347	39700	1191
159258	285019	79015	4347	39700	1191
(✓)	(✓)	(23)	(12)	(41)	(24)

The Rodgers Store — Combined Cash Journal (Right Page)

to the proper account. The total of each of the six special columns was
posted to the account indicated by the column heading. The number of the
account to which the posting was made was written below the total. Since
the totals of the General Debits and General Credits columns were not
posted, a check mark (√) was made under each of these columns to so
indicate. The total of the single column in the purchases journal was posted

SALES JOURNAL   PAGE 1

DATE	NO. OF SALE	TO WHOM SOLD	POST. REF.	ACCOUNTS REC. DR.	SALES CR.	SALES TAX PAY. CR.
1967 Mar. 4	1-1	John J. Lance	✓	2081	2020	61
7	1-2	William B Sells	✓	2266	2200	66
10	2-1	Joseph F Camm	✓	1710	1660	50
21	1-3	Joseph F Camm	✓	2678	2600	78
23	2-2	John J Lance	✓	3811	3700	111
27	2-3	William B Sells	✓	3291	3195	96
				15837	15375	462
				15837	15375	462
				(12)	(41)	(24)

The Rodgers Store — Sales Journal

ACCOUNT Cash   ACCOUNT NO. 11

DATE	ITEMS	POST. REF.	✓	DEBITS	DATE	ITEMS	POST. REF.	✓	CREDITS
1967 Mar. 31	919.84	CJ1		2 4 0 0 8 3	1967 Mar. 31		CJ1		1 4 8 0 9 9

ACCOUNT Accounts Receivable   ACCOUNT NO. 12

DATE	ITEMS	POST. REF.	✓	DEBITS	DATE	ITEMS	POST. REF.	✓	CREDITS
1967 Mar. 31	114.90	S1		1 5 8 3 7	1967 Mar. 31		CJ1		4 3 4 7

ACCOUNT Store Equipment   ACCOUNT NO. 18

DATE	ITEMS	POST. REF.	✓	DEBITS	DATE	ITEMS	POST. REF.	✓	CREDITS
1967 Mar. 2		CJ1		1 1 2 1 6 0					

ACCOUNT Accounts Payable   ACCOUNT NO. 23

DATE	ITEMS	POST. REF.	✓	DEBITS	DATE	ITEMS	POST. REF.	✓	CREDITS
1967 Mar. 31		CJ1		7 9 0 1 5	1967 Mar. 2		CJ1		1 1 2 1 6 0
					31	873.60	P1		5 4 2 1 5
									1 6 6 3 7 5

ACCOUNT Sales Tax Payable   ACCOUNT NO. 24

DATE	ITEMS	POST. REF.	✓	DEBITS	DATE	ITEMS	POST. REF.	✓	CREDITS
1967 Mar. 8		CJ1		3 3	1967 Mar. 31		CJ1		1 1 9 1
					31	16.20	S1		4 6 2
									1 6 5 3

ACCOUNT Sales   ACCOUNT NO. 41

DATE	ITEMS	POST. REF.	✓	DEBITS	DATE	ITEMS	POST. REF.	✓	CREDITS
					1967 Mar. 31		CJ1		3 9 7 0 0
					31		S1		1 5 3 7 5
									5 5 0 7 5

ACCOUNT Sales Returns and Allowances   ACCOUNT NO. 041

DATE	ITEMS	POST. REF.	✓	DEBITS	DATE	ITEMS	POST. REF.	✓	CREDITS
1967 Mar. 8		CJ1		1 1 0 0					

The Rodgers Store — General Ledger Accounts

ACCOUNT *Purchases*								ACCOUNT NO. *51*	
DATE	ITEMS	POST. REF.	√	DEBITS	DATE	ITEMS	POST. REF.	√	CREDITS
1967 Mar. 6		CJ1		8 6 0 0					
14		CJ1		1 7 5 0					
31		P1		5 4 2 1 5					

ACCOUNT *Purchases Returns and Allowances*								ACCOUNT NO. *051*	
DATE	ITEMS	POST. REF.	√	DEBITS	DATE	ITEMS	POST. REF.	√	CREDITS
					1967 Mar. 13		CJ1		1 8 1 0

The Rodgers Store — General Ledger Accounts (Concluded)

as a debit to Purchases and also as a credit to Accounts Payable. The number of each of these accounts was noted in the Posting Reference column beside the total of the Amount column. After the three amount columns of the sales journal were footed and the footings were proved, the totals were entered and the rulings were made as illustrated. Each total was posted to the account indicated by the column heading, and the account number was shown below that total.

When more than one book of original entry is used, it is advisable to identify each book by means of an initial (or initials) preceding the page number. The following code was used in conjunction with the page number to indicate the source of each entry in the ledger accounts:

CJ = Combined cash journal
P = Purchases journal
S = Sales journal

Trial Balance

After the posting was completed, the accounts in the general ledger were footed where necessary, and the balances were entered in the Items column on the proper side. Usually a trial balance then would be prepared to prove the equality of the debit and credit account balances. However, since the illustration did not involve all of the general ledger accounts nor all of the transactions for the month, a trial balance of the general ledger of The Rodgers Store as of March 31, 1967, is not reproduced.

Schedule of Accounts Receivable

A list of customers showing the amount due from each one is known as a *schedule of accounts receivable*. It is usually advisable to prepare such a schedule at the end of each month. An example for The Rodgers Store as of March 31, 1967, is provided below. Such a schedule can be prepared easily by going through the cutomers' file and listing the names of the customers and the amount due from each. Should the total not be in agreement with the balance of the summary accounts receivable account, the error may be in either the file or the ledger account. The file may be incorrect in that either one or more sales tickets on which collection has been made have not been removed or that one or more uncollected ones are missing. Another possibility is that a memorandum of a partial collection was overlooked in preparing the list. The accounts receivable account could be incorrect, also, because of an error in posting or because of an error in a journal from which the totals were posted. In any event, the postings, journals, and sales tickets must be checked until the reason for the discrepancy is found so that the necessary correction can be made.

Schedule of Accounts Payable

A list of creditors showing the amount due to each one is known as a *schedule of accounts payable*. It is usually advisable to prepare such a schedule at the end of each month. An example for The Rodgers Store as of March 31, 1967, is provided below. Such a schedule can be prepared easily by going through the unpaid invoice file and listing the names of the creditors and the amount due to each. Should the total of the schedule not be in agreement with the balance of the summary accounts payable

The Rodgers Store
Schedule of Accounts Receivable
March 31, 1967

Joseph F. Camm	43 88
John J. Lance	38 11
William B. Sells	32 91
	1 14 90

The Rodgers Store
Schedule of Accounts Payable
March 31, 1967

Carl B. Cooper & Son	85 10
Modern Store Equipment Co.	5 21 60
Young's	2 66 90
	8 73 60

The Rodgers Store — Schedules of Accounts Receivable and Accounts Payable

account, the error may be in either the file or the ledger account. The file may be incorrect in that either one or more paid invoices have not been removed or in that one or more unpaid ones are missing. Another possibility is that a memorandum of a partial payment was overlooked in preparing the list. The accounts payable account could be incorrect, also, because of an error in posting or because of an error in a journal from which the total purchases was posted. In any event, the postings, journals, and invoices must be checked until the reason for the discrepancy is found so that the necessary correction can be made.

Merchandise Inventory

Apart from the fact that the foregoing illustration did not include any transactions or information about various operating expenses, Mr. Rodgers could not calculate his net profit or net loss for the month because the amount of the merchandise inventory at March 31 was not determined. Lacking this information, cost of goods sold could not be calculated. Since there was no inventory at the first of the month, the amount of the month's purchases of merchandise, $645.65, less the amount of purchases returns and allowances, $18.10, is the cost of the goods that were *available* for sale, $627.55. To calculate the cost of goods *sold*, however, the cost of the goods that remained on hand on March 31 would have to be deducted. The first step would have been to count the items of merchandise in the store at the end of that day. Next, these goods would have to have been assigned a reasonable share of the total purchases cost. Since Mr. Rodgers does not expect to calculate monthly net income (or net loss), he will not "take inventory" until the end of the year. This may be December 31, if he plans to keep his records on a calendar year basis, or it might be February 28 (or 29), if he wants to use a fiscal year that ends on the last day of February. Whatever the period chosen, a crucial step in the calculation of the periodic net income (or net loss) of a merchandising business under the accrual basis of accounting is the determination of the merchandise inventory at the end of the fiscal period — a point in time that is also the beginning of the next fiscal period.

When the end of the fiscal period does arrive and the cost to be assigned to the merchandise on hand at that time is calculated, the amount of this calculation will have to be recorded in an asset account. The title of the account usually used is "Merchandise Inventory." This account will be debited; the related credit is made to an account with the title "Expense and Revenue Summary" — a temporary owner's equity account used in summarizing the accounts whose balances enter into the determination of the net income (or loss) for a period. The manner of using the expense and revenue summary account in the end-of-period process of adjusting and closing the books of a retail merchandising business will be explained and illustrated in Chapters 9 and 10.

Report No. 13

Refer to the workbook and complete Report No. 13. After completing the report, you may proceed with the textbook discussion in Chapter 7 until the next report is required.

---

chapter seven

accounting for notes and interest

A major characteristic of modern business is the extensive use of credit. Each day hundreds of millions of transactions occur that involve the sale of goods or services in return for promises to pay at a later date for what was received. Sales of this type are said to be "on credit" or "on account"; they are often described as "charge sales." To facilitate such transactions, the use of *credit cards* has become commonplace. The majority of credit transactions do not involve a written promise to pay a specified amount of money. Often the buyer signs a sales slip or sales ticket, but this is done as an acknowledgment of the receipt of the merchandise or service. When "opening an account" the prospective customer may sign a form or document that obligates him to pay for all purchases that he (and, often, members of his family) may make, but this is a general promise to pay if and when something is purchased.

While not nearly as commonplace as transactions that involve "open account" credit, the use of *promissory notes* (usually just called *notes*) is an important business practice. A promise to repay a loan of money nearly always takes the form of a note. The extension of credit for periods of more than 60 days, or when large amounts of money are involved, usually entails the use of notes. Such notes nearly always have certain legal characteristics that cause them to be *negotiable instruments*. In order to be considered a negotiable instrument, a promissory note must:

(a) Be in writing and signed by the person or persons agreeing to make payment.

(b) Be an unconditional promise to pay a certain amount of money.

(c) Be payable to the order of a specified person or firm, or to bearer.

(d) Be payable either on demand or at a definite time.

A promissory note is illustrated below. It will be observed that this note has all of the characteristics listed above. It should also be understood that to John Copes it is a *note payable*, while to Wayne Tyson it is a *note receivable*. John Copes is known as the *maker* of the note because he is the one who promises to pay. Wayne Tyson is called the *payee* of the note because he is the one who is to receive the specified amount of money.

The note illustrated is interest bearing. This is often, though not always, the case. Sometimes no rate of interest is specified, but it is likely that a transaction in which a nominally non-interest-bearing note is involved will entail some interest. For example, a borrower might give a $1,000 note payable in 60 days to a bank in return for a loan of $990. The $10 difference between the amount received and the amount that must be repaid when the note matures is, in reality, interest. Such a difference is described as *prepaid interest*. When a bank is involved in such a transaction, the difference between the amount received and the amount to be repaid may be referred to as *bank discount*.

$385 75   INDIANAPOLIS, INDIANA   *April 6*   19 *67*

Ninety days   AFTER DATE *I* PROMISE TO PAY TO

THE ORDER OF *Wayne Tyson*

Three hundred eighty-five 75/100 DOLLARS

PAYABLE AT *Citizens Savings Bank*

VALUE RECEIVED WITH INTEREST AT *6* %

No. *5* DUE *July 5, 1967*   *John Copes*

Model Filled-In Promissory Note

Calculating Interest

In calculating interest on notes, it is necessary to take the following factors into consideration:

(a) The principal of the note.

(b) The rate of interest.

(c) The time.

The principal is the face amount of the note — the amount that the maker promises to pay at maturity, apart from any specified interest. The principal is the base on which the interest is calculated.

The rate of interest is usually expressed in the form of a percentage, such as 4 percent or 6 percent. Ordinarily the rate is an annual percentage rate, but in some cases the rate is quoted on a monthly basis, such as 1 percent a month. A rate of 1 percent a month is equivalent to a rate of 12 percent a year payable monthly. When a note is interest bearing but the rate is not specified on the face of the note, it is subject to the legal rate, which varies under the laws of different states.

The days or months from the date of issue of a note to the date of its maturity (or the interest payment date) is the time for which the interest is to be computed. Thus, if a note is payable in 60 days with interest, each and every day is considered in determining the date due, and the exact number of days is used in calculating interest.

When the time in a note is specified in months, the interest should be calculated on the basis of months rather than days. For example, if a note is payable 3 months from date, the interest should be calculated on the basis of 3 months or ¼ of a year. However, when the due date is specified in a note, the time should be computed by figuring the exact number of days that will elapse from the date of the note to the date of its maturity. The interest should then be computed on the basis of this number of days. For example, if a note is dated April 1 and the due date is specified as July 1, the time should be computed in the manner shown at the right.

Days in April...........	30
Date of note, April......	1
Days remaining in April..	29
Days in May...........	31
Days in June...........	30
Note matures on July....	1
Total time in days.......	91

In this computation notice that the date of maturity was counted but the date of the note was not counted. If the note had specified "3 months after date" instead of July 1, the interest should be computed on the basis of 90 days instead of 91 days.

In the case of long-term notes, the interest may be payable periodically, such as semiannually or annually.

In computing interest it is customary to consider 360 days as a year. Most banks and business firms follow this practice, though some banks and government agencies use 365 days as the base in computing daily interest. In any case, the formula for computing interest is:

PRINCIPAL × RATE × TIME (usually a fraction of a 360-day year) = AMOUNT OF INTEREST

The 60-Day, 6 Percent Method. There are many short cuts that may be used in computing interest on the basis of a 360-day year. The interest on any amount for 60 days at 6 percent can be determined simply by moving the decimal point in the amount two places to the left. The reason for this is that 60 days is ⅙ of a year and the interest on any amount at 6 percent for $\frac{1}{6}$ of a year is the same as the interest at 1 percent for a full year. Thus, the interest on $241.30 for 60 days at 6 percent is $2.41.

The 60-day, 6 percent method may be used to advantage in many cases even though the actual time may be more or less than 60 days. The following examples will serve to illustrate this fact:

FACTORS

(a) Principal of note, $1,000
(b) Time, 30 days
(c) Rate of interest, 6%

CALCULATION

When the decimal point is moved two places to the left the result is $10
30 days = $\frac{1}{2}$ of 60 days; so the interest amounts to $\frac{1}{2}$ of $10 or $5

FACTORS

(a) Principal of note, $1,000
(b) Time, 120 days
(c) Rate of interest, 6%

CALCULATION

When the decimal point is moved two places to the left the result is $10
120 days = 2 times 60 days; so the interest amounts to 2 times $10 or $20

The 60-day, 6 percent method may also be used to advantage when the actual rate is more or less than 6 percent. The following examples will serve to illustrate this fact:

FACTORS

(a) Principal of note, $1,000
(b) Time, 30 days
(c) Rate of interest, 3%

CALCULATION

Interest at 6% for 60 days = $10
Interest at 6% for 30 days = $5
Interest at 3% = $\frac{1}{2}$ of $5 or $2.50

FACTORS

(a) Principal of note, $1,000
(b) Time, 120 days
(c) Rate of interest, 8%

CALCULATION

Interest at 6% for 60 days = $10
Interest at 6% for 120 days = $20
Interest at 8% = $1\frac{1}{3}$ times $20 or $26.67

Sometimes it is helpful to determine the interest for 6 days at 6 percent and to use the result as the basis for calculating the actual interest. The interest on any sum for 6 days at 6 percent may be determined simply by moving the decimal point three places to the left. For example, the interest on $1,000 at 6 percent for 6 days is $1. If the actual time were 18 days instead of 6 days, the interest would be three times $1 or $3. This method differs from the 60-day, 6 percent method only in that 6 days is used in the basic computation instead of 60 days.

Published tables are available for reference use in determining the amount of interest on stated sums at different rates for any length of time. Such tables are widely used by financial institutions and may also be used by other firms.

Present Value. The *present value* or *present worth* of a note is its value on any day between the date of the note and its maturity. If a note is interest bearing, the present value may be determined by adding the accrued interest to the face of the note. If a note is non-interest bearing, the present value may be determined by subtracting interest at the discount rate from the face value of the note. This interest is computed for the time that will elapse from the present date to the date of maturity.

It may be necessary to determine the present value of a note **(1)** when the note is being transferred for credit or **(2)** when it is being sold for cash. Consider the following alternative transactions involving the note illustrated on page 168:

> **(a)** May 16, Wayne Tyson transferred the note to the Stanton Hardware Co. Mr. Stanton agreed to allow him credit for its present value; or
>
> **(b)** May 16, Wayne Tyson sold the note to the First National Bank at a discount of 7 percent.

In transaction (a) the note is transferred for credit at its present value. The factors involved in computing its present value are as follows:

FACTORS

(a) Principal of note, $385.75
(b) Time interest has accrued, 40 days (April 6 to May 16)
(c) Rate of interest, 6%

CALCULATION

Interest accrued on $385.75 at 6% for 40 days = $2.57
$385.75 + $2.57 = $388.32, present value

In transaction (b) the note was sold to the First National Bank at a discount of 7 percent. Such a transaction is often referred to as *discounting a note*. It is the custom of banks to calculate the discount on the maturity value of a note. The amount of the discount is then subtracted from the maturity value to find the present value of the note.

FACTORS

(a) Principal of note, $385.75
(b) Time from date of note to date of maturity, 90 days (April 6 to July 5)
(c) Rate of interest, 6%
(d) Time from date of discount to date of maturity, 50 days (May 16 to July 5)
(e) Rate of discount, 7%

CALCULATION

Interest on $385.75 at 6% for 90 days = $5.79
$385.75 + $5.79 = $391.54, maturity value
Discount on $391.54 at 7% for 50 days = $3.81
$391.54 − $3.81 = $387.73, present value

The interest is computed on the face of the note, while the discount is computed on the maturity value of the note. Interest collected in advance by a bank is called bank discount. Bank discount should not be confused with either *trade discount* or *cash discount*. Trade discount is a discount from the list price of merchandise, while cash discount is a discount allowed for the payment of an invoice within a specified time. Discounting a note receivable at the bank is a method of borrowing money and using the note as security. Since the party discounting the note must endorse it, he is liable for its maturity value in case the maker does not pay it at maturity. This possible future obligation is known as a *contingent liability*.

Accounting for Notes Receivable

The following types of transactions involve notes receivable:

(a) Note received in exchange for merchandise or other property.
(b) Note received from customer in return for an extension of time for payment of obligation.
(c) Note received as security for cash loan.
(d) Note discounted prior to maturity.
(e) Note collected at maturity.
(f) Note renewed at maturity.
(g) Note dishonored.

Note Received in Exchange for Merchandise or Other Property. A note may be accepted in exchange for merchandise or other property. For example, W. J. Stanton accepted a 60-day, 5 percent note for $101.48 in exchange for hardware sold to Bill Crawford. This transaction was recorded in the books of the Stanton Hardware Co. by debiting Notes Receivable and by crediting Sales for $101.48.

Note Received from Customer to Obtain an Extension of Time for Payment. When a customer wishes to obtain an extension of time for the payment of his account, he may be willing to issue a note for all or part of the amount due. A merchant may be willing to accept a note in such a case because the note will be a written acknowledgment of the debt and, if cash is needed before the note matures, it may be possible to discount the note at the bank.

C. D. Jacob owes the Stanton Hardware Co. $422.36 on open account. The account is past due and Mr. Stanton insists upon a settlement. Mr. Jacob offers to give his 60-day, 6 percent note. Mr. Stanton accepts Mr. Jacob's offer; the note is dated April 10. It was recorded in the books of the Stanton Hardware Co. as indicated by the following general journal entry:

```
April 10.  Notes Receivable.................................  422.36
              Accounts Receivable............................          422.36
              Received note from C. D. Jacob.
```

If, instead of giving a note for the full amount, Mr. Jacob gave a check for $22.36 and a note for the balance, the transaction should be recorded in Mr. Stanton's books as indicated by the following general journal entry:

```
April 10.  Cash...........................................   22.36
           Notes Receivable...............................  400.00
              Accounts Receivable............................          422.36
              Received check and note from C. D. Jacob.
```

(While the foregoing entry is shown in general journal form, it actually would be recorded in the combined cash journal or other appropriate book of original entry being used. This observation applies to all illustrations of entries involving the receipt and disbursement of cash.)

Note Received as Security for Cash Loan. Loans may be secured by notes receivable. For example, Mr. Stanton might lend Clark Tibbs, an employee, $100 on his 90-day, 4 percent note. Such a transaction may be recorded in the books of the Stanton Hardware Co. as indicated by the following general journal entry:

```
April  1. Notes Receivable..............................    100.00
             Cash........................................              100.00
                  Loaned Clark Tibbs $100.
```

If it is the practice of a firm to make frequent loans to employees, it is generally advisable to keep a separate account for such notes. An appropriate title for such an account is Notes Receivable from Employees.

Note Discounted Prior to Maturity. As previously explained, a note may be discounted at a bank prior to its maturity. It sometimes happens that a merchant is in need of money and, in order to obtain it, he may discount at a bank one or more notes that he owns. Suppose, for example, that on May 1 Mr. Stanton discounted at the First National Bank the note received from Bill Crawford on April 29 and received credit for the proceeds. The rate of discount was 6 percent. The proceeds were computed as follows:

```
Face value of note...............................................   $101.48
Interest at 5% for 60 days.......................................       .85
Maturity value of note...........................................   $102.33
```
Discount period May 1 to June 28 = 58 days
$102.33 at 6% for 58 days = 99¢
$102.33 − 99¢ = $101.34, proceeds

Since the note had been accepted originally by Mr. Stanton at its face value of $101.48 and the proceeds from discounting the note amounted to only $101.34, the difference of 14 cents represents interest expense, which should be debited to an account so titled. This transaction should be recorded in the books of the Stanton Hardware Co. as indicated by the following general journal entry:

```
May 1. Cash.......................................   101.34
           Interest Expense......................      .14
           Notes Receivable......................              101.48
                Discounted Bill Crawford's note at the bank.
```

If the proceeds from discounting the note had amounted to more than the face of the note, the difference would represent a gain which should be credited to a revenue account titled *Interest Earned* (or *Interest Income*).

Contingent Liability on Notes Discounted. In discounting the Crawford note at the bank it was necessary for Mr. Stanton to endorse the note. This endorsement had the effect of guaranteeing payment of the note at maturity, because Mr. Stanton would have to pay it if Mr. Crawford should fail to do so. The Stanton Hardware Co. acquired a *contingent liability* — contingent upon Mr. Crawford's failure to pay the note at maturity.

In preparing a balance sheet, it is customary to determine the total amount of any notes that have been discounted but have not yet been paid by their makers (because their maturity dates have not yet arrived) and to indicate the resulting contingent liability. This is usually accomplished by means of a footnote on the balance sheet. The usual plan is to place an asterisk (*) after the amount of the asset notes receivable and to state the amount of the contingent liability at the bottom of the report. For example, if the notes receivable amounted to $12,000 and notes discounted but not yet paid amounted to $2,000, the following statement should be added to the balance sheet in a footnote:

*Contingent liability on notes discounted, $2,000.

If a note that was discounted at a bank is not paid at maturity, the bank will immediately inform the person or firm that endorsed the note and request payment.

Note Collected at Maturity. When a note receivable matures, it may be collected by the holder or he may leave it at his bank for collection. If the maker of the note resides in another locality, the note may be forwarded to a bank in his locality for collection. It is customary for banks to charge a fee for making such collections. Usually the maker is notified a few days before the maturity of a note so that he may know the due date and the amount that must be paid.

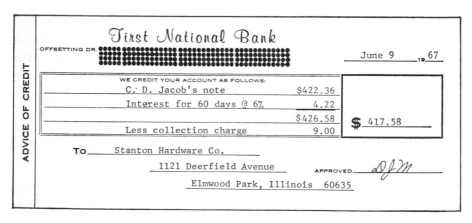

Credit Advice

If Clark Tibbs pays his note in full plus the interest when both are due, the transaction should be recorded in the books of the Stanton Hardware Co. as indicated by the following general journal entry:

```
June 30.  Cash..............................................  101.00
              Notes Receivable...............................            100.00
              Interest Earned................................              1.00
              Received $101 from Clark Tibbs in settlement of his
              note for $100 and interest $1.
```

Suppose Mr. Stanton left C. D. Jacob's note for $422.36 at the First National Bank for collection and on June 9 received the notice of collection reproduced at the bottom of page 174.

The transaction should be recorded as indicated by the following general journal entry:

```
June 9.  Cash...............................................  417.58
             Collection Expense..............................    9.00
             Notes Receivable................................            422.36
             Interest Earned.................................              4.22
             Received credit for the proceeds of C. D. Jacob's
             note collected by the bank.
```

Note Renewed at Maturity. If the maker of a note is unable to pay the amount due at maturity, he may be permitted to renew all or part of the note. If, instead of paying his note for $100 at maturity, Clark Tibbs was permitted to pay the interest and renew the note for another 90 days at the same rate of interest, the transaction should be recorded in the books of the Stanton Hardware Co. as indicated by the following general journal entry:

```
June 30.  Notes Receivable (new note)........................  100.00
          Cash...............................................    1.00
              Notes Receivable (old note)....................            100.00
              Interest Earned................................              1.00
              Received a new note for $100 from Clark Tibbs in
              renewal of his note due today and $1 in cash in pay-
              ment of the interest on the old note.
```

Note Dishonored. If the maker of a note refuses or is unable to pay or renew it at maturity, the note is said to be *dishonored.* It thereby loses the quality of negotiability which, in effect, means that it loses its legal status as a note receivable. Usually, the amount is transferred from the notes receivable account to the accounts receivable account pending final disposition of the obligation involved. Suppose, for example, that W. J. Stanton was unable to collect a non-interest-bearing note for $300 received a few weeks before from Ronald Jackson, a customer. The following entry should be made in the books of the Stanton Hardware Co.:

```
July 17.  Accounts Receivable................................  300.00
              Notes Receivable................................            300.00
              Ronald Jackson's note dishonored.
```

If the claim against Mr. Jackson should turn out to be completely worthless, the $300 will have to be removed from the accounts receivable account and recognized as a bad debt loss. The manner of accounting for this type of transaction will be discussed in the next chapter.

Notes Receivable Register

When many notes are received in the usual course of business, it may be advisable to keep an auxiliary record of such notes that will provide more detailed information than a ledger account. Such an auxiliary record is usually known as a *notes receivable register*. One form of a notes receivable register is reproduced below and at the bottom of page 177. The notes recorded in the illustration were those received by the W. D. Wilcox Co. during the period indicated by the record.

The information recorded in the register is obtained directly from the notes received. The notes are numbered consecutively as they are entered in the register. (This number should not be confused with the maker's number.) The due date of each note is calculated and entered in the proper When Due column. The interest to maturity is calculated and entered in the Interest Amount column. When a note is discounted, the name of the bank at which it is discounted and the date are entered in the Discounted columns. When a remittance is received in settlement of a note, the date is entered in the Date Paid column.

Notes Receivable Account

The information recorded in the notes receivable account should agree with that entered in the notes receivable register. The account shown on page 177 contains a record of the notes that were entered in the notes receivable

PAGE *12*   NOTES RECEIVABLE REGISTER

DATE RECEIVED	NO.	BY WHOM PAYABLE	WHERE PAYABLE BANK OR FIRM	ADDRESS	DATE MADE MO.	DAY	YEAR
1967 Mar. 28	1	Riegert & Briem	Central Trust	City	Mar. 28		1967
30	2	William Ross	Valley Savings Bank	Hamilton	Mar. 30		1967
30	3	O. P. Meyer	State Bank, Inc.	Dayton	Mar. 30		1967
Apr. 1	4	M. Van Horn	West Side Savings	City	Apr. 1		1967
May 1	5	A. Canter & Co.	Central Trust	City	May 1		1967
3	6	E. M. Kelly	Third National Bank	Middlefield	Apr. 29		1967
18	7	A. V. Brown	Citizens Bank	City	May 18		1967
25	8	Hardy Brothers	State Bank, Inc.	Dayton	May 23		1967
29	9	O. P. Meyer	State Bank, Inc.	Dayton	May 29		1967

Notes Receivable Register (Left Page)

register of the W. D. Wilcox Co. Notice that each note is identified by the number assigned to the note. If the notes are not numbered, each note should be identified by writing the name of the maker in the Items column of the account.

NOTES RECEIVABLE

1967				1967			
Mar. 28	No. 1		180.00	May 27	No. 1		180.00
30	No. 2		200.00	29	No. 4		492.50
30	No. 3		250.00	29	No. 2		200.00
Apr. 1	No. 4		492.50	29	No. 3		250.00
May 1	No. 5		350.00	29	No. 7		300.00
3	No. 6		286.50				1,422.50
18	No. 7		300.00				
25	No. 8		218.60				
29	No. 9		200.00				
		1,055.10	2,477.60				

Proving the Notes Receivable Account

Periodically (usually at the end of each month) the notes receivable account should be proved by comparing the balance of the account with the total of the notes owned as shown by the notes receivable register. A schedule of the notes owned on May 31 is given below.

Notice that the total of this schedule is the same as the balance of the notes receivable account illustrated above.

SCHEDULE OF NOTES OWNED

No. 5......................	$ 350.00
No. 6......................	286.50
No. 8......................	218.60
No. 9......................	200.00
Total.................	$1,055.10

NOTES RECEIVABLE REGISTER   PAGE 12

TIME	WHEN DUE				AMOUNT	INTEREST		DISCOUNTED		DATE PAID	REMARKS
	J	M J	J	D		RATE	AMT.	BANK	DATE		
60 da.		27			18000	6%	180			May 27	
60 da.		29			20000	—				May 29	Sent for coll. 5/22
60 da.		29			25000	6%	250			May 29	Renewal for $200
90 da.			30		49250	6%	739	Second National	May 29		
60 da.			30		35000	6%	350				
90 da.			28		28650	6%	430				
60 da.			17		30000	—		Second National	May 29		
60 da.			22		21860	—					
60 da.			28		20000	6%	200				Renewal of Note No. 3

Notes Receivable Register (Right Page)

Chapter 7 / Accounting for Notes and Interest   177

Endorsement of Notes

A promissory note is usually payable to a specified person or firm, though some notes are made payable to "Bearer." If the note is payable to the order of a specified party, he must *endorse* the note to transfer the promise to pay to another party. The two major types of endorsements are **(1)** the *blank endorsement* and **(2)** the *full endorsement*. When the payee signs only his name on the left end of the back of the note, he is endorsing it in blank. If, instead, he writes the words "Pay to the order of" followed by the name of a specified party and his signature, he is giving a full endorsement. The legal effect of both types of endorsement is much the same. However, a blank endorsement makes a note payable to the bearer, while a full endorsement identifies the party to whose order payment is to be made.

Under certain circumstances the maker of a note may arrange for an additional party to join in the promise to pay, either as a *cosigner* or as an endorser of the note. In the first instance, this other party signs his name below that of the maker of the note on its face. In the second case, the other party makes a blank endorsement on the back of the note, called an *accommodation endorsement*. In either event the payee of the note has two persons to look to for payment. This presumably adds security to the note.

If a partial payment is made on a note, it is common practice to record the date of the payment and the amount paid on the back of the note. This is called *endorsing the payment*.

Shown at the right is a reproduction of the back of a promissory note originally made payable to the order of James Crown. The maker of the note (whoever he was) was able to get Clifford Getz to become an accommodation endorser. Later, the payee, Crown, transferred the note to E. B. Craft by a full endorsement. On April 15, $100 was paid on the note.

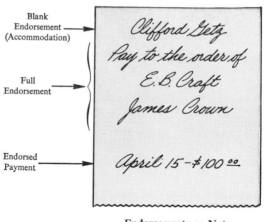

Endorsements on Note

Accounting for Notes Payable

The following types of transactions involve notes payable:

    (a) Note issued in exchange for merchandise or other property.

    (b) Note issued to a creditor in return for an extension of time for payment of obligation.

(c) Note issued as security for cash loan.
(d) Note paid at maturity.
(e) Note renewed at maturity.

Note Issued in Exchange for Merchandise or Other Property. A note may be issued in exchange for merchandise, long-lived assets, or other property. For example, W. J. Stanton issues a 30-day, 6 percent interest-bearing note for $265 to the Murdock Store Equipment Co. in exchange for store equipment purchased April 1. This transaction was recorded in the books of the Stanton Hardware Co. by debiting Store Equipment and by crediting Notes Payable for $265.

Note Issued to a Creditor in Return for Extension of Time for Payment. When a firm wishes to obtain an extension of time for the payment of an account, a note for all or part of the amount due may be acceptable to the creditor. Assume, for example, that the Stanton Hardware Co. owes Slater & Co. $291.50 and by agreement on May 14 a check on the First National Bank for $41.50 and a 90-day, 5 percent interest-bearing note for $250 are issued. This transaction should be recorded in the books of the Stanton Hardware Co. as indicated by the following general journal entry:

```
May 14. Accounts Payable.............................    291.50
           Cash.........................................           41.50
           Notes Payable...............................          250.00
           Issued check for $41.50 and note for $250 to Slater
           & Co.
```

Note Issued as Security for Cash Loan. Many firms experience periods in which receipts from customers in the usual course of business are not adequate to finance their operations. During such periods, it may be necessary to borrow money from banks. Business firms commonly borrow money from banks on short-term notes to help finance their business operations. Assume, for example, that on May 15, W. J. Stanton borrows $2,000 from the First National Bank on a 60-day, 6 percent interest-bearing note. The transaction should be recorded in general journal form as follows:

```
May 15. Cash........................................    2,000.00
           Notes Payable..............................          2,000.00
           Borrowed $2,000 at the bank on a 60-day, 6%
           note.
```

Commercial banks often deduct interest in advance. If, instead of the transaction described above, Mr. Stanton had issued a $2,000, 60-day, non-interest-bearing note which the bank had discounted at 6 percent, the bank account of the Stanton Hardware Co. would have increased $1,980, and interest expense of $20 would have been recorded as follows:

```
May 15. Cash........................................    1,980.00
           Interest Expense...........................       20.00
           Notes Payable..............................          2,000.00
           Discounted at 6% a $2,000, 60-day, non-interest-
           bearing note.
```

| DATE ISSUED | | NO. | TO WHOM PAYABLE | WHERE PAYABLE | | DATE MADE | | |
				BANK OR FIRM	ADDRESS	MO.	DAY	YEAR
1967 Mar.	15	1	L. J. Schaefer Co.	Valley Savings Bank	Hamilton	Mar.	15	1967
May	16	2	Carbonell Supply	Third National Bank	Middlefield	May	16	1967
	20	3	Third National Bank	" "	" City	May	20	1967
	22	4	Dickson and Brooks	" "	" "	May	22	1967
	22	5	Thompson Trucking	" "	" "	May	22	1967
	29	6	Third National Bank	" "	" "	May	29	1967

Notes Payable Register (Left Page)

Note Paid at Maturity. When a note payable matures, payment may be made directly to the holder or to a bank where the note was left for collection. The maker will know who the payee is but he may not know who the holder is at maturity because the payee may have transferred the note to another party or he may have left it with a bank for collection. When a note is left with a bank for collection, it is customary for the bank to mail the maker a notice of maturity. For example, the Murdock Store Equipment Co. might forward the one-month, 6 percent note of W. J. Stanton for $265 (dated April 1) to the First National Bank for collection, and the bank might notify Mr. Stanton by sending a notice similar to the one reproduced below.

FIRST NATIONAL BANK

YOUR NOTE DESCRIBED BELOW WILL BE DUE→

MAKER - CO-SIGNER - COLLATERAL	NUMBER	DATE DUE		AMOUNT
W. J. Stanton Stanton Hardware Co.	24-007	5-1-67	Prin. Int. Total	$265.00 1.33 $266.33

ENDORSER

TO ⌐ W. J. Stanton
Stanton Hardware Co.
1121 Deerfield Avenue
Elmwood Park, Illinois 60635 ⌐

NOTE: PLEASE BRING THIS NOTICE WITH YOU.

Notice of Maturity of Note

If, upon receiving this notice, Mr. Stanton issued a check to the bank for $266.33 in payment of the note and interest, the transaction should be recorded in the books of the Stanton Hardware Co. as indicated by the following general journal entry:

TIME	WHEN DUE												AMOUNT	INTEREST		DATE PAID	REMARKS
	J	F	M	A	M	J	J	A	S	O	N	D		RATE	AMOUNT		
90 days						13							150 00	—		June 13	In settlement of Jan. 15 inv.
60 days							15						378 65	6%	3 79		
90 days								18					1000 00	6%	15 00		
3 mos.								22					200 00	6%	3 00		
6 mos.											22		200 00	6%	6 00		Purchased used truck
60 days								28					2500 00	6%	25 00		

Notes Payable Register (Right Page)

May 1. Notes Payable	265.00	
Interest Expense	1.33	
Cash		266.33

Paid note issued April 1 to the Murdock Store
Equipment Co., plus interest.

Note Renewed at Maturity. If the maker is unable to pay a note in full at maturity, he may arrange to renew all or a part of the note. For example, on August 12 Mr. Stanton might pay the $3.13 interest and $50 on the principal of the note for $250 issued to Slater & Co. on May 14 and give them a new 60-day, 5 percent note for $200. This transaction should be recorded as indicated in the following general journal entry:

Aug. 12. Notes Payable (old note)	250.00	
Interest Expense	3.13	
Cash		53.13
Notes Payable (new note)		200.00

Issued a check for $53.13 and a note for $200 to Slater & Co. in settlement of a note for $250 plus interest.

Notes Payable Register

When many notes are issued in the usual course of business, it may be advisable to keep an auxiliary record of such notes that will provide more detailed information than a ledger account. Such an auxiliary record is usually known as a *notes payable register*. One form of such a register is reproduced on the previous page and above. The notes recorded in the illustration were those issued by the W. D. Wilcox Co. during the period indicated by the record.

The information recorded in the register may be obtained directly from the note before it is mailed or given to the payee, or from a note stub. Blank notes are usually made up in pads with stubs attached on which spaces are provided for recording such essential information as amount, payee, where payable, date, time, rate of interest, and number. The due date of each note is calculated and entered in the proper When Due column of the register. The interest at maturity is also calculated and entered in the Interest Amount column. When a note is paid, the date is entered in the Date Paid column.

Notes Payable Account

The information recorded in the notes payable account should agree with that recorded in the notes payable register. The following account contains a record of the notes that were entered in the notes payable register of the W. D. Wilcox Co.

NOTES PAYABLE

1967				1967				
June 13	No. 1		150.00	Mar. 15	No. 1			150.00
				May 16	No. 2			378.65
				20	No. 3			1,000.00
				22	No. 4			200.00
				22	No. 5			200.00
				29	No. 6			2,500.00
							4,278.65	*4,428.65*

Proving the Notes Payable Account

Periodically (usually at the end of each month) the notes payable account should be proved by comparing the balance of the account with the total notes outstanding as shown by the notes payable register. A schedule of the notes outstanding on June 30 is given below. Notice that the total of this schedule is the same as the balance of the notes payable account.

SCHEDULE OF NOTES OUTSTANDING

No. 2..........................	$ 378.65
No. 3..........................	1,000.00
No. 4..........................	200.00
No. 5..........................	200.00
No. 6..........................	2,500.00
Total........................	$4,278.65

Accrued Interest Receivable

While interest on a note literally accrues day by day, it is impractical to keep a daily record of such accruals. If the life of a note receivable is entirely within the accounting period, no record need be made of interest until the amount is received.

If, however, the business owns some interest-bearing notes receivable at the end of the accounting period, neither the net income for the period nor the assets at the end of the period will be correctly stated unless the interest accrued on notes receivable is taken into consideration. It is, therefore, customary to adjust the accounts by debiting Accrued Interest Receivable and by crediting Interest Earned for the amount of interest that has accrued to the end of the period. The amount of the accrual may be computed by reference to the notes themselves or to the record provided by a notes receivable register. Suppose, for example, that at the end of a fiscal year ending June 30, a business owns four interest-bearing notes. The amount of each note, the date of issue, the rate of interest, the number of days from issue date to June 30, and the interest accrued on June 30 are shown in the following schedule:

SCHEDULE OF ACCRUED INTEREST ON NOTES RECEIVABLE

PRINCIPAL	DATE OF ISSUE	RATE OF INTEREST	DAYS FROM ISSUE DATE TO JUNE 30	ACCRUED INTEREST JUNE 30
$350.00	April 15	6%	76	$4.43
200.00	May 4	5%	57	1.58
248.50	May 31	6%	30	1.24
500.00	June 15	6%	15	1.25
Total accrued interest on notes receivable.................				$8.50

The entry, in general journal form, to record the interest accrued on June 30 is as follows:

June 30. Accrued Interest Receivable.......................	8.50	
Interest Earned.................................		8.50
Interest accrued on notes receivable as of June 30.		

In preparing the financial statements at the end of the year, the balance of the interest earned account (which will include the $8.50 interest earned but not yet received) will be reported in the income statement, while the balance of the account with Accrued Interest Receivable will be reported in the balance sheet as a current asset.

Accrued Interest Payable

Neither the expenses of a period nor the liabilities at the end of the period will be correctly stated unless the interest accrued on notes payable is taken into consideration. The mechanics of calculating the amount of interest accrued on notes payable are the same as in the case of notes receivable. If a notes payable register is kept, it should provide the information needed in computing the amount of interest accrued on notes payable. If the total amount of such accrued interest was calculated to be $23.18, and the fiscal period ended June 30, the proper adjusting entry may be made in general journal form as follows:

June 30. Interest Expense.....................................	23.18	
Accrued Interest Payable.......................		23.18
Interest accrued on notes payable as of June 30.		

In preparing the financial statements at the end of the year, the balance of the interest expense account (which will include the $23.18 interest incurred but not yet paid) will be reported in the income statement, while the balance of the account with Accrued Interest Payable will be reported in the balance sheet as a current liability.

Drafts and Trade Acceptances

In addition to promissory notes, there are some other documents or instruments which are sometimes used in connection with the extension of business credit or the settlement of business obligations that have certain qualities in common with notes. Examples include drafts (some versions of which are called "bills of exchange") and trade acceptances. Essentially, a *draft* is an order by one party (the *drawer*) to another party (the *drawee*) to pay a specified amount of money to a third party (the *payee*). There are several varieties of drafts. An ordinary bank check is a draft. Commercial banks often have money on deposit in other banks. Withdrawals are made by using *bank drafts*. When a seller of goods is not well acquainted with a buyer in a different locality, he may draw a *sight draft* (one that is to be paid as soon as the drawee sees it) on the buyer and attach to the draft the *bill of lading* that relates to the property involved. (A bill of lading is prepared by the transporting company, such as a railroad, trucking company, or airline.) Usually the buyer is ordered to pay a bank. The draft and attached bill of lading are sent to this bank. An employee of the bank "presents" these documents to the buyer (the drawee of the draft). It is only by paying ("honoring") such a draft that the buyer can get the bill of lading and thereby obtain the property. The bank remits the amount collected (less a fee for the service) to the seller. The accounting for all this is usually quite simple. The seller either waits until he is paid and then records the collection as a cash sale, or he treats the sale as having been on account when the shipment was made, followed by a cash collection. On the other hand, the buyer accounts for the transaction as a cash purchase — usually a purchase of merchandise, but other property such as equipment might be involved.

Drafts of the type referred to are not essentially credit instruments; rather, they are devices used to facilitate the transfer of money from one person or firm to another under certain circumstances. The characteristic that these drafts have in common with notes is that normally they are negotiable instruments. This is because they are in writing, use the proper legal phraseology, specify the amount involved, are signed, dated, etc.

When one party orders another to make payment at some later date (for example, "60 days after sight" or "60 days after date") and the party addressed agrees to do so in writing on the face of the instrument, it becomes, in effect, a promissory note. Instruments of this type are known as *time drafts* or *trade acceptances*. They may be accounted for in the same manner as notes — notes receivable from the standpoint of the drawer of the instrument and notes payable from the standpoint of the one who accepts it. Normally, time drafts and trade acceptances do not specifically call for any interest. However, like non-interest-bearing notes, interest will arise if discounting of drafts and trade acceptances is involved — which is often the case.

Report No. 14

Complete Report No. 14 in the workbook and submit your working papers to the instructor for approval. Then continue with the next study assignment in Chapter 8 until Report No. 15 is required.

---

chapter eight

the accrual basis of accounting applied to a retail business

A business enterprise that purchases and sells goods on account, maintains a stock of merchandise, and has long-lived assets must account for periodic income or loss on the accrual basis. This is a necessity both for the sake of measuring the success of the business from the standpoint of the owner and in order to comply with federal and state income tax laws. Several of the features of this type of accounting have been introduced in the preceding pages. A more detailed consideration of these procedures and the introduction of the other major practices that constitute accrual accounting will be presented in this and the two following chapters. To make the discussion realistic, it will center around the accounting records of a retail appliance business called The Adams Appliance Store, owned and operated by R. L. Adams. It should be recognized, however, that most of the principles and procedures discussed and illustrated are equally applicable to many other types of businesses.

principles and procedures

The discussion will continue to be a blend of accounting principles and bookkeeping practices. It is important to keep in mind that the principles relate to goals and objectives while bookkeeping practices are designed to attain these goals and objectives. Such procedures as double entry and the use of business papers, journals, and ledger accounts are employed to make the record-keeping process complete, orderly, and as error-free as possible. While most accounting principles are broad enough to allow considerable flexibility, it is in the area of bookkeeping procedures that wide latitude is found. Within limits, the records for each business can be styled to meet the particular requirements of the management.

Accrual Accounting

The *accrual basis of accounting* consists of recording revenue in the period in which it is earned and expenses in the period in which they are incurred. The receipt or disbursement of cash in the same period may or may not be involved. Revenue is considered to be earned when, in exchange for something of value, money is received or a legal claim to money comes into existence. To a merchant, this normally means the time at which the customer buys the goods and either pays for them or agrees to pay for them. In terms of changes in the accounting elements, revenue arises or accrues when an increase in cash or in a receivable causes an increase in owner's equity (except in cases where the increase is due to an investment of assets in the business by the owner). In comparable terms, expense accrues or is incurred when either a reduction in some asset or an increase in a liability causes the owner's equity to be reduced (except in cases where the owner's withdrawal of assets reduces the owner's equity).

In keeping business records the accountant must think in terms of time intervals. He must be sure that revenue and expense are accounted for in the proper accounting period. Within a period, the recognition of many types of revenue and expense at precisely the moment this revenue or expense arises is not so important nor is it usually practicable. For example, the expense of having a salaried employee literally accrues minute by minute during each working day; but if the salary will be paid by the end of the period, no record is made of the expense until it is paid. If, on the other hand, the worker was not paid by the end of the period, the accountant should record the liability and expense at that time. A lag in recording revenue and expense is not serious within the accounting period, but steps must be taken at the end of the period to be sure that all revenue earned and expenses incurred are recorded. These steps consist of making what are called *end-of-period adjustments* in the accounts.

The accrual basis of accounting is widely used because it is suited to the needs of enterprises employing it. It involves the period-by-period matching of revenue with the expenses that caused or aided in producing revenue. The revenue from sales, for example, must be matched against the cost of the goods sold and the various expenses that were incurred in conducting the business. A simple matching of cash received from customers during a period with the cash paid for goods purchased in that period would be almost meaningless in most cases. The collections might relate to sales of a prior period and the payments to purchases of the current period, or vice versa. The expense related to most long-lived assets does not arise when the property is acquired; the expense occurs as the usefulness of the property is gradually exhausted. The accrual basis recognizes changes in many types of assets and liabilities in computing net income for a specified period — not just changes in the cash account.

The Chart of Accounts

The importance of classifying accounts in an orderly and systematic manner, identifying each account by assigning it a number to assist in locating it in the ledger, and maintaining a list of the accounts — called a *chart of accounts* — has been discussed and illustrated in preceding chapters. The chart of accounts for the retail business that is used as a basis of the discussion and illustration in this chapter and in the two chapters that follow is shown at the top of page 189.

The pattern of numbers or code shown in the illustration is fairly typical of the arrangement used by many businesses. However, numerous variations are possible. Sometimes letters as well as numbers are made a part of the code. When numbers are used, it is not uncommon for special columns in journals to be headed by just the number, rather than the name, of the account involved. In a system of records that requires numerous accounts, the use of account numbers virtually displaces account names for all but statement purposes.

The nature of many of the accounts included in the chart of accounts for The Adams Appliance Store should be apparent as they have been described and their use has been illustrated. However, the chart includes certain accounts that are needed in recording several types of transactions and events that have either not yet been considered, or only briefly mentioned. These accounts will be discussed prior to illustrating the accounting records of The Adams Appliance Store.

CHART OF ACCOUNTS

*Assets**

Cash

111 Columbia National Bank
112 Petty Cash Fund

Receivables

121 Notes Receivable
122 Accrued Interest Receivable
123 Accounts Receivable
    0120 Allowance for Bad Debts

Merchandise Inventory

130 Merchandise Inventory

Prepaid Expenses

140 Prepaid Insurance
150 Stationery and Supplies

Long-Lived Assets

180 Store Equipment
    0180 Accumulated Depreciation
        —Store Equipment
190 Delivery Equipment
    0190 Accumulated Depreciation
        —Delivery Equipment

Liabilities

210 Notes Payable
220 Accrued Interest Payable
230 Accounts Payable
240 Sales Tax Payable
250 FICA Taxes Payable
260 Employees' Income Taxes Payable
270 FUTA Taxes Payable
280 State Unemployment Taxes Payable

Owner's Equity

310 R. L. Adams, Capital
031 R. L. Adams, Drawing
320 Expense and Revenue Summary

Revenue from Sales

410 Sales
    0410 Sales Returns and Allowances

Cost of Goods Sold

510 Purchases
    0511 Purchases Returns and Allowances
    0512 Purchases Discount

Operating Expenses

610 Rent Expense
611 Depreciation Expense
612 Salaries and Commissions Expense
613 Payroll Tax Expense
614 Heating and Lighting Expense
615 Stationery and Supplies Expense
616 Telephone and Telegraph Expense
617 Advertising Expense
618 Bad Debts Expense
619 Insurance Expense
620 Truck Expense
621 Charitable Contributions Expense
622 Miscellaneous Expense

Other Revenue

710 Interest Earned

Other Expenses

810 Interest Expense

*Words in italics represent headings and not account titles.

Accounting for Bad Debts

Businesses that sell goods or services on account realize that all of the customers may not pay all that they owe. The amounts that cannot be collected are called *bad debts*, *bad debts expense*, or *loss from bad debts*. The last designation is slightly misleading because, while the amounts that cannot be collected are certainly losses, they are losses that may reasonably be expected since they ensue as a result of selling on account to encourage a larger volume of sales. The amount of such losses depends to a large degree upon the credit policy of a business. The seller should avoid the two extremes of either having such a "liberal" credit policy that bad debts become excessive, or having such a "tight" credit policy that bad debt losses are minimized at the sacrifice of a larger volume of sales and greater net income.

It would be possible to wait until it was certain that the amount due from a customer would never be collected before writing off the amount by a debit to Bad Debts Expense and by a credit to Accounts Receivable. This procedure is sometimes followed. However, it is considered to be better accounting to estimate the amount of bad debt losses that will eventually result from the sales of a period and to treat the estimated amount of expected losses as an expense of that same period. This is accomplished by using a *contra* account entitled Allowance for Bad Debts (sometimes called Allowance for Doubtful Accounts or Reserve for Bad Debts). This account is contra to the receivable accounts which means its balance will be deducted from the total of the receivable accounts. At the end of the accounting period, an estimate of the expected bad debt losses is made, and an adjusting entry is made by debiting Bad Debts Expense and by crediting Allowance for Bad Debts. To illustrate, suppose that in view of past experience, it is expected that there will be a loss of an amount equal to one half of one percent of the sales on account during the year. If such sales amounted to $100,000, the estimated bad debt losses would be $500 which should be recorded as follows:

Dec. 31. Bad Debts Expense.............................	500.00	
Allowance for Bad Debts......................		500.00
Bad debts expense provision for the year.		

The amount of the debit balance in the bad debts expense account is reported in the income statement as an operating expense. The amount of the credit balance in the allowance for bad debts account is reported in the balance sheet as a deduction from the sum of the receivables. This arrangement serves to show the net amount of receivables that is expected to be collected.

It should be apparent that the credit part of the adjusting entry cannot be made directly to one of the receivable accounts because, at the time this entry is made, there is no way of knowing exactly which of the debtors will not pay. Experience gives virtual assurance that some of the amounts due will be uncollectible but only time will reveal which ones.

When it is determined that a certain account will not be collected, an entry should be made to write off the account and to charge the loss against the allowance. Suppose, for example, that on April 22 of the next year, it is determined that $85 owed by Lee Klise cannot be collected. Perhaps he died sometime before and it is found that he left no property, or perhaps he became bankrupt, or he left town and cannot be traced. Whatever the circumstance, if it is fairly certain that the amount will not be collected, the following journal entry should be made:

April 22. Allowance for Bad Debts........................	85.00	
Accounts Receivable..........................		85.00
To write off account of Lee Klise found to be uncollectible.		

The chart of accounts for The Adams Appliance Store includes Allowance for Bad Debts, Account No. 0120, and Bad Debts Expense, Account

No. 618, to provide for recording bad debts expense and subsequent write-offs of the uncollectible accounts.

Accounting for Prepaid Expenses

The term *prepaid expense* is largely self-explanatory. It refers to something that has been bought that is properly considered an asset when acquired, but which will eventually be consumed or used up and thus become an expense. Prepaid (unexpired) insurance and supplies of various sorts are leading examples. At the end of the period, the portion of such assets that has expired or has been consumed must be determined and an entry made debiting the proper expense accounts and crediting the proper prepaid expense accounts.

The chart of accounts for The Adams Appliance Store includes two prepaid expense accounts, Prepaid Insurance, Account No. 140, and Stationery and Supplies, Account No. 150. These accounts are classified as assets in the chart of accounts. The account with Prepaid Insurance should be debited for the cost of the insurance purchased. At the end of the year the account should be credited for the portion of the cost that relates to the year then ending with an offsetting debit to Insurance Expense, Account No. 619. The account with Stationery and Supplies should be debited for the cost of stationery and supplies purchased. At the end of the year the account should be credited for the cost of stationery and supplies consumed or used during the year with an offsetting debit to Stationery and Supplies Expense, Account No. 615.

Accounting for Depreciation

Depreciation accounting is the process of attempting to allocate the cost of most long-lived assets to the periods benefited by the use of these assets. Most long-lived assets eventually become useless to the business either because they wear out or because they become inadequate or obsolete. Sometimes all three of these causes combine to make the assets valueless except, perhaps, for some small value as scrap or junk.

Generally, in computing depreciation, no consideration is given to what the assets might bring if they were to be sold. Assets of this type are acquired to be used and not to be sold. During their useful life their resale value is of no consequence unless the business is about to cease. For a going business, the idea is to allocate the net cost of the assets over the years they are expected to serve. By "net cost" is meant original cost less estimated scrap or salvage value. Inasmuch as the possibility of scrap or salvage value is commonly ignored, it is usually the original cost of the assets that is allocated.

It should be apparent that depreciation expense can be no more than an estimate. Usually there is no way of knowing just how long an asset will serve. However, with past experience as a guide, the estimates can be reasonably reliable.

There are several ways of calculating the periodic depreciation write-off. Traditionally, the so-called *straight line method* has been widely used. With this method, the original cost (or cost less any expected scrap value) of an asset is divided by the number of years the asset is expected to serve to find the amount that is to be considered as depreciation expense each year. It is common practice to express depreciation as a percentage of the original cost of the asset. For example, in the case of an asset with a 10-year life, 10 percent of the original cost should be written off each year; for a 20-year asset, 5 percent should be written off.

There are some depreciation methods that permit larger write-offs in the earlier years of the life of the asset. In 1954 the Internal Revenue Code was revised to permit taxpayers to use certain of these methods in calculating net income subject to tax, though the methods can be used in the case of new assets only. This change in the law has stimulated the use of these "reducing-charge" methods. ("Reducing-charge" means a successively smaller write-off each year.) However, the straight line method has been very popular in the past, and it has a number of virtues including simplicity. Straight line depreciation is widely used. The straight line method of accounting for depreciation is used by The Adams Appliance Store.

Depreciation expense is recorded by an end-of-period adjusting entry that involves debiting one or more depreciation expense accounts and crediting one or more accumulated depreciation (sometimes called allowance for depreciation) accounts. The latter accounts are contra accounts — contra to the accounts for the assets that are being depreciated. In theory there would be no objection to making the credits directly to the asset accounts themselves (in the same way that the asset accounts for prepaid expenses are credited to record their decreases). However, in order that the original cost of the assets will be clearly revealed, any portions of this cost written off are credited to the contra accounts. The amounts of the credit balances of the contra accounts are reported in the balance sheet as deductions from the costs of the assets to which they relate.

The credit balances in the accumulated depreciation accounts get larger year by year. When the amounts become equal to the cost of the assets, no more depreciation may be taken.

The difference between the allowance for bad debts account and the accumulated depreciation account should be recognized. Both are credited by adjusting entries at the end of the period. In both cases, the offsetting debits go to expense accounts. In both cases, the balances in the contra accounts are shown in the balance sheet as subtractions from the amounts of the assets to which they relate. However, the allowance for bad debts account is debited whenever anticipated bad debts materialize. The balance of this allowance account does not get continually larger. (If it does, this indicates that the estimate of bad debt losses has been excessive.) In contrast, the credit balances of the accumulated depreciation accounts will get larger year by year, often for many years. The credit balances remain in these accounts for as long as the assets to which they relate are kept in service.

Since The Adams Appliance Store has two classes of long-lived assets that are subject to depreciation, store equipment and delivery equipment, there are two contra accounts, Accumulated Depreciation — Store Equipment, Account No. 0180, and Accumulated Depreciation — Delivery Equipment, Account No. 0190. Although depreciation expense could be classified by the type of asset to which the depreciation relates, just one account, Depreciation Expense, Account No. 611, is used by The Adams Appliance Store.

Purchases Discount

Purchase invoices representing purchases on account may be subject to discount if paid within a specified time. Retailers may be allowed a discount by wholesalers on invoices that are paid within a specified time, such as five days, ten days, or fifteen days, from the date of the invoice. This is known as a *cash discount* and it should not be confused with trade discounts allowed by wholesalers.

Trade discounts are the discounts allowed retailers from the list or catalog prices of wholesalers. Such trade discounts are usually shown as deductions on the invoice and only the net amount is recorded as the purchase price. If the invoice is subject to an additional discount for cash, it will be indicated on the invoice under the heading of "Terms." For example, the terms may be specified as "2/10, n/30," which means that if paid within ten days from the date of the invoice a discount of 2 percent may be deducted, otherwise the net amount of the invoice (after any trade discounts) is payable within thirty days.

To facilitate the payment of invoices in time to be entitled to any discount offered, Mr. Adams follows the policy of filing each invoice in an unpaid invoice file according to the date it should be paid. It is, therefore, only necessary to refer to the file each day to determine which invoices are due on that date and which may be subject to discount. Any amount of cash discount deducted when paying an invoice should be recorded as a credit to Purchases Discount, Account No. 0512. Thus, if an invoice for $140, subject to a discount of 2 percent if paid within ten days, is paid within the specified time, the payment should be recorded by debiting Accounts Payable for $140, by crediting the bank account for $137.20, and by crediting Purchases Discount for $2.80. The purchases discount account has a credit balance and (along with Purchases Returns and Allowances) is reported as a deduction from the gross amount of purchases in the cost of goods sold section of the income statement. Some businesses report the credit balance in the purchases discount account as "other revenue." Although this latter practice is not uncommon, the trend definitely favors the practice of regarding discount earned for prompt payment of purchase invoices as a deduction from the gross amount of purchases rather than as other revenue.

Accounts with Creditors and Customers

As previously explained, a record of the amounts due to creditors for purchases on account and the amounts due from customers for sales on account may be kept without maintaining a separate ledger account for each creditor and for each customer. A file of unpaid vendors' invoices and another of sales slips for sales on account may suffice. Many merchants, however, prefer to keep a separate ledger account for each creditor and for each customer.

Subsidiary Ledgers. When the character of the enterprise and the volume of business are such that it is necessary to keep relatively few accounts, it may be satisfactory to keep all of the accounts together in a single general ledger, which may be bound, loose-leaf, or cards. However, when the volume of business and the number of transactions warrant employment of more than one bookkeeper to keep the records, it may be advisable to subdivide the ledger. In some businesses it is necessary to keep separate accounts with thousands of customers and creditors. In such cases it usually is considered advisable to segregate the accounts with customers and the accounts with creditors from the other accounts and to keep them in separate ledgers known as *subsidiary ledgers*.

Balance-Column Account Form. A special account form known as the balance-column account form is widely used in keeping the individual accounts with customers and creditors. While the standard account form, shown in the illustration on page 12, may be used satisfactorily for customers' and creditors' accounts, most accountants favor the use of the *balance-column account form* shown on page 195 for such accounts. It will be noted that three parallel amount columns are provided for recording debits, credits, and balances. Following each entry the new balance may be determined and recorded in the Balance column, or if preferred, the balance may be determined and recorded at the end of each month. A check (√) column is provided preceding the amount columns. This column may be used in checking postings to the account.

DATE	ITEMS	POST. REF.	√	DEBITS	CREDITS	BALANCE

NAME

ADDRESS

Balance-Column Account Form

Control Accounts

When subsidiary ledgers are kept for creditors and for customers, it is customary to keep *control accounts* for the subsidiary ledgers in the general ledger. Thus, if accounts with creditors are kept in a subsidiary accounts payable ledger, a control account for accounts payable should be kept in the general ledger; if accounts with customers are kept in a subsidiary accounts receivable ledger, a control account for accounts receivable should be kept in the general ledger. The use of control accounts in the general ledger makes it possible to take a trial balance of the general ledger accounts without reference to the subsidiary ledgers.

Accounts Payable Control. The accounts payable control account provides a summary of the information recorded in the individual accounts with creditors kept in a subsidiary accounts payable ledger. Transactions affecting creditors' accounts are posted separately to the individual accounts in the subsidiary ledger. These transactions may also be posted separately, or may be summarized periodically and the totals posted, to the control account in the general ledger. The balance of the accounts payable control account may be proved by preparing a schedule of the individual account balances in the accounts payable ledger.

Accounts with creditors normally have credit balances. If a creditor's account has a debit balance, the balance may be circled or be written in red ink. In preparing the schedule of accounts payable, the total of the accounts with debit balances should be deducted from the total of the accounts with credit balances, and the difference should agree with the balance of the accounts payable control account.

Accounts Receivable Control. The accounts receivable control account provides a summary of the information recorded in the individual accounts with customers kept in a subsidiary accounts receivable ledger. Transactions affecting customers' accounts are posted separately to the individual accounts in the subsidiary ledger. These transactions may also be posted separately, or may be summarized periodically and the totals posted, to the control account in the general ledger. The balance of the accounts receivable control account may be proved by preparing a schedule of the individual account balances in the accounts receivable ledger.

Accounts with customers normally have debit balances. If a customer's account has a credit balance, the balance may be circled or be written in red ink. In preparing the schedule of accounts receivable, the total of the accounts with credit balances should be deducted from the total of the accounts with debit balances and the difference should agree with the balance of the accounts receivable control account.

Posting from the Books of Original Entry

Posting to the individual accounts with creditors and customers in the subsidiary ledgers may be done either from the books of original entry or directly from vouchers or other documents that represent the transactions. When the posting is done from the books of original entry, each item should, of course, be posted separately to the proper account and as the posting is completed the proper cross-reference should be made in the Posting Reference column of the book of original entry and in the Posting Reference column of the ledger account. Under this plan the voucher or other document that represents the transaction may be filed after the transaction is recorded in the appropriate book of original entry. As each transaction is recorded in a book of original entry, care must be taken to enter all of the information that will be needed when posting.

Posting from Vouchers or Other Documents

When the posting is done directly from the vouchers or other documents that represent the transactions, the transactions usually will be recorded first in the proper books of original entry, after which the vouchers or other documents will be referred to the bookkeeper in charge of the creditors' and customers' accounts for direct posting.

Posting to the Individual Accounts with Creditors

It is necessary to post all items that represent increases or decreases in the amount owed to each creditor. A list of vouchers or other documents that usually represent transactions completed with creditors is shown at the top of page 197. The usual posting reference is also indicated.

The purchase invoices and charge-back invoices are usually numbered consecutively as they are received and issued. These numbers should not be confused with the numbers used by the vendor (creditor). The check

Voucher or Document	Transaction Represented	Posting Reference
(a) Purchase invoice No. 1	Purchase	P 1
(b) Charge-back invoice No. 1	Return or allowance	CB 1
(c) Check stub No. 1	Payment on account	Ck 1
(d) Note issued No. 1	Temporary settlement of account	N 1

stubs should be numbered consecutively to agree with the numbers of the checks issued. As the posting is completed, the proper cross-reference should be made in the Posting Reference column of the account and on the voucher or other document. If a loose-leaf ledger is used and accounts with creditors are kept in alphabetic order, the posting may be indicated by means of a distinctive check mark on the voucher or other document.

Posting to the Individual Accounts with Customers

It is necessary to post all items that represent increases or decreases in the amount owed by each customer. Following is a list of vouchers or other documents that usually represent transactions completed with customers. The usual posting reference is also indicated.

Voucher or Document	Transaction Represented	Posting Reference
(a) Sale ticket No. 1	Sale	S 1
(b) Credit memo No. 1	Return or allowance	CM 1
(c) Remittance received	Collection on account	C
(d) Note received	Temporary settlement of account	N

The sales tickets usually are prepared in duplicate or triplicate and are numbered consecutively. Each salesperson may use a different series of numbers. One copy is retained for the use of the bookkeeper and another copy is given to the customer.

Credit memorandums issued to customers in connection with sales returns or allowances are usually prepared in duplicate and are numbered consecutively. One copy goes to the customer and the other copy is retained for the use of the bookkeeper.

Remittances received from customers may consist of cash or cash items, such as checks, bank drafts, and money orders. When the remittance is in the form of cash, it is customary to issue a receipt. The receipt may be issued in duplicate, in which case the duplicate copy will provide the information needed for the purpose of posting to the customer's account. Sometimes receipt stubs are used to record the information for posting purposes. When the remittance is in the form of a check, it is not necessary to issue a receipt as the canceled check will serve as a receipt for the customer.

Posting a credit to the customer's account may be made directly from the check or from a list of checks received. Sometimes all remittances received daily are listed in such a manner as to provide the information needed for posting purposes. When this plan is followed, the bookkeeper need not handle the remittances at all. It is a quite common practice to use a form of monthly statement of account in which the upper portion (containing the customer's name and address) is to be detached and sent in along with the remittance. The amount of the remittance is noted on this slip of paper which then contains all the information needed to post the correct credit to the proper customer's account. If the customer does not send in (or bring in) the top part of the statement, a receipt or memo is prepared to serve the same purpose. This procedure is especially suitable when it is possible to separate the functions of **(1)** handling the cash and cash items, and **(2)** recording the credits to the customers' accounts.

As the posting is completed, the proper cross-reference should be made in the Posting Reference column of the account and on the voucher or other document. If a loose-leaf ledger is used and accounts with customers are kept in alphabetic order, the posting may be indicated by means of a distinctive check mark or by initialing the voucher or other document.

Accountants generally prefer to post from the basic documents rather than from the books of original entry to the individual accounts with creditors and customers because such procedure provides better control and promotes accuracy. When a purchase invoice is recorded in a purchases journal by one person and is posted directly from the invoice to the proper creditor's account by another person, it is unlikely that both persons will make the same mistake. Even if the posting is done by the person who also keeps the purchases journal, there is less likelihood of making a mistake than when the posting is done from the purchases journal. If a mistake were made in recording the amount of the invoice in the purchases journal, the same mistake would almost certainly be made in posting from the purchases journal to the creditor's account. The same reasoning may be applied to the recording of sales transactions and all other transactions that affect accounts with creditors and customers.

Statement of Account

When merchandise is sold on account, it is customary to render a monthly statement of account to each charge customer. Usually the statements are mailed as soon as they can be completed following the close of each month. In order that statements may be mailed on the first of each month, some firms follow the policy of including transactions completed up to the 25th of the preceding month. Such statements are an aid to collection. When a remittance is not received from the customer within the usual credit period, a copy of the statement of account may be referred to the credit department for such action as the credit manager may wish to take. A model filled-in copy of a statement of account is reproduced below. This is a statement of the account of R. T. Rusk for the month ended December 31. It shows **(1)** the balance at the beginning of the month

STATEMENT

THE
Adams Appliance Store

14 NORTH FOURTH STREET

R. T. Rusk
1659 Forest View Dr.
City

PLEASE DETACH THIS PORTION AND RETURN WITH YOUR REMITTANCE ▼

DATE	REFERENCE	CHARGES	CREDITS	BALANCE
Dec. 1			BALANCE FORWARD	689.08
24	Mdse.	473.49		1,162.57
26	Cash		300.00	862.57

Statement of Account

amounting to $689.08; **(2)** a charge of $473.49 for a sale of $459.70 plus tax of $13.79 made on December 24; **(3)** a credit of $300 for cash received on December 26; and **(4)** the balance at the close of the month amounting to $862.57. Note that the customer is asked to tear off the upper portion of the statement and to send it along with his remittance.

Report No. 15

Complete Report No. 15 in the workbook and submit your working papers to the instructor for approval. After completing the report, continue with the following study assignment until the next report is required.

---

application of accounting principles

The accrual basis of accounting as applied to a merchandising enterprise is illustrated on the following pages by a reproduction of the records of The Adams Appliance Store, owned and operated by R. L. Adams. The records include the following:

BOOKS OF ORIGINAL ENTRY	BOOKS OF FINAL ENTRY
Combined cash journal	General ledger
Purchases journal	Accounts receivable ledger
Sales journal	Accounts payable ledger

AUXILIARY RECORDS

Petty cash disbursements record
Checkbook
Employees' earnings records

Combined Cash Journal

The form of combined cash journal used is the same as the one illustrated on pages 160 and 161, except that the first two amount columns are used in recording banking transactions including deposits and checks. These columns serve the same purpose as though they were headed Cash Receipts and Disbursements. Mr. Adams follows the practice of depositing all cash receipts in a checking account at the Columbia National Bank and of making all disbursements by check (except for the payment of small items, which may be paid from a petty cash fund). For these reasons, a bank account rather than a cash account is kept in the general ledger. The posting to the bank account is from the combined cash journal, the account being debited for the total receipts (deposits) and being credited for the total disbursements (checks).

All items entered in the General Debits and Credits columns of the combined cash journal are posted individually to the proper accounts in the general ledger. No individual posting to the general ledger is required from any of the other amount columns. Instead, the totals of these columns are posted at the end of the month.

Purchases Journal

The form of purchases journal used is the same as the one illustrated on page 146. It was described in detail in Chapter 6. All transactions involving the purchase of merchandise *on account* are recorded in this journal. Because the posting of the individual credits to the accounts with creditors is done directly from the purchase invoices, the only posting required from the purchases journal is the total purchases for each month. This involves a debit to Purchases, Account No. 510, and a credit to Accounts Payable, Account No. 230.

Sales Journal

The form of sales journal used is the same as the one illustrated on page 153. It was described in detail in Chapter 6. All transactions involving the sale of merchandise *on account* are recorded in this journal. Because the posting of individual charges to the accounts with customers is done directly from the sales tickets, the only posting required from the sales journal is the total sales for each month. This involves a debit to Accounts Receivable, Account No. 123, and credits to Sales, Account No. 410, and to Sales Tax Payable, Account No. 240.

General Ledger

A general ledger with the accounts arranged in numerical order is used. A chart of the accounts appears on page 189. The standard account form is used in the general ledger.

Accounts Receivable Ledger

An accounts receivable ledger with the accounts for customers arranged in alphabetic order is used. The balance-column account form is used in this ledger. Posting to the individual accounts with customers is done directly from the sales tickets or other documents. As each item is posted, the balance is extended immediately so that reference to the account of any customer at any time will reveal without any delay the amount due from him. This is important since it is often necessary to determine the status of a particular customer's account before extending additional credit.

Accounts Payable Ledger

An accounts payable ledger with the accounts for creditors arranged in alphabetic order is used. The balance-column account form is used in this ledger. Posting to the individual accounts with creditors is done directly from the invoices or other documents. As each item is posted, the balance is extended immediately so that reference to the account of any creditor at any time will reveal the amount owed to that creditor.

Auxiliary Records

As previously stated, certain auxiliary records are used, including a petty cash disbursements record and a checkbook. The form of petty cash disbursements record is similar to that illustrated on pages 56 and 57. A record of deposits made and checks issued is kept on the check stubs as well as in the combined cash journal. At the end of each month, when the summary posting from the combined cash journal has been completed, the balance of the bank checking account in the ledger should be the same as the balance recorded on the check stubs. The earnings records maintained for each of Mr. Adams' four employees are similar to the one illustrated on page 84. (To conserve space, these records are not reproduced in this chapter.)

Accounting Procedure

The books of account containing a record of the transactions completed during the month of December are reproduced on pages 212 to 226. These books include the combined cash journal, the purchases journal, the sales journal, the petty cash disbursements record, the general ledger, the accounts receivable ledger, and the accounts payable ledger. Before recording any transactions for December, the balance of the bank checking account was entered in the combined cash journal and the balance in the petty cash fund was entered in the petty cash disbursements record. The balance at the beginning of the month of December is shown in each of the accounts in the general, accounts receivable, and accounts payable ledgers. These balances along with those at the end of the month are summarized in the trial balances and schedules reproduced on pages 226 and 227.

Following is a narrative of the transactions completed during December. Transactions of a type that have not been previously introduced are analyzed to show their effect upon the accounts.

THE ADAMS APPLIANCE STORE

NARRATIVE OF TRANSACTIONS

Monday, December 2

Issued checks as follows:

No. 978, Glick Realty Co., $500, in payment of December rent.

No. 979, The Pennsylvania Railroad Co., $42.19, in payment of freight on merchandise purchased.

Both checks were recorded in the combined cash journal. Check No. 978 was recorded by debiting Rent Expense, Account No. 610, and by crediting the bank account. Check No. 979 was recorded by debiting Purchases, Account No. 510, and by crediting the bank account. Since the freight charge increases the cost of the merchandise, the purchases account should be debited.

Note that the account titles were written in the Description column. The account numbers were inserted in the Posting Reference column when the individual posting was completed at the end of the week.

Tuesday, December 3

Bought merchandise from the Ferguson Electric Co., Ferguson, $369.50, per Invoice No. 121 of November 30. Terms, net 30 days.

After receiving the merchandise and checking the invoice, the transaction was recorded in the purchases journal. A check mark was placed in the Posting Reference column to indicate that individual posting is not done from the purchases journal. The invoice was then posted directly to the credit of the Ferguson Electric Co. account in the accounts payable ledger, after which the invoice was filed in an unpaid invoice file according to its due date.

Wednesday, December 4

Received check from R. F. Webber, $205.90.

The credit was immediately posted to the customer's account. The remittance was then recorded in the combined cash journal by debiting the bank account and by crediting Accounts Receivable. The name of the customer was written in the Description column. Since the credit had already been posted to the customer's account, a check mark was placed in the Posting Reference column.

Thursday, December 5

Sold merchandise on account as follows:

No. 271A, R. F. Webber, 51 Webster Woods, City, $209.75, tax $6.29.

No. 257B, C. F. Abbott, 5245 Kingwood, City, $239.95, tax $7.20.
No. 235C, E. T. Busch, 9440 Arban, City, $1,284.40, tax $38.53.

Unless otherwise specified, all charge sales are payable on the 10th of the following month. No cash discount is allowed. These transactions were recorded in the sales journal. A check mark was placed in the Posting Reference column to indicate that individual posting is not done from the sales journal. The sales tickets were then posted directly to the proper customers' accounts in the accounts receivable ledger, after which each ticket was filed under the name of the customer for future reference. The numbers of the sales tickets indicate that there are three salespersons identified by the letters A, B, and C. Each of these persons uses a separate pad of sales tickets numbered consecutively.

Friday, December 6

Issued checks as follows:

No. 980, Globe Publishing Co., $53.37, in payment for circulars to be used for advertising purposes.
No. 981, State Treasurer, $376.45, in payment of sales taxes for November.

Both checks were recorded in the combined cash journal by debiting the proper accounts and by crediting the bank account. Check No. 980 was charged to Advertising Expense and Check No. 981 was charged to Sales Tax Payable. The numbers of the checks were written in the Check No. column and the titles of the accounts to be charged were written in the Description column.

Bought merchandise from the Clayshire Electric Co., Richmond Heights, $1,390, per Invoice No. 122 of December 6. Terms, net 30 days.

Sold merchandise on account as follows:

No. 259B, R. J. Winston, Des Peres, $374.75, tax $11.24.

Saturday, December 7

Cash sales for the week:

SALESPERSON	MERCHANDISE	TAX	TOTAL
A	$299.75	$ 8.99	$308.74
B	379.70	11.39	391.09
C	199.95	6.00	205.95
	$879.40	$26.38	$905.78

As each cash sale was completed a sales ticket was prepared. This ticket provided the information needed in recording the sale on the cash register when ringing up the amount of cash received. As each amount was thus recorded it was added to the previous total of cash sales made by each salesperson on a mechanical accumulator in the register. Usually the total cash sales are recorded daily, but to save time and to avoid unnecessary duplication of entries the total cash sales are here recorded at the end of each week and on the last day of the month. This transaction was recorded in the combined cash journal by debiting the bank account for $905.78 and by crediting Sales for $879.40 and Sales Tax Payable for $26.38.

Made petty cash disbursements as follows:

Postage stamps, $10. Petty Cash Voucher No. 62.

Collect telegram, $1.40. Petty Cash Voucher No. 63.

Messenger fee, $2. Petty Cash Voucher No. 64.

All disbursements from the petty cash fund are recorded in the petty cash disbursements record. This record is ruled so as to facilitate the classification of such expenditures. It will be noted that the cost of the postage stamps was recorded as a charge to Stationery and Supplies, Account No. 150, the cost of the telegram to Telephone and Telegraph Expense, Account No. 616, and the messenger fees to Miscellaneous Expense, Account No. 622.

END-OF-THE-WEEK WORK

(1) Proved the footings of the combined cash journal. **(2)** Deposited $1,111.68 in the Columbia National Bank and proved the bank balance ($8,793.26). **(3)** Posted each entry individually from the General Debits and Credits columns of the combined cash journal to the proper general ledger accounts. When Check No. 981, issued December 6, was posted to the account with Sales Tax Payable, the account was in balance; hence, it was ruled with a double line as illustrated on page 219. **(4)** Proved the footings of the petty cash disbursements record and proved the balance of the petty cash fund ($111.60). **(5)** Proved the footings of the sales journal.

Monday, December 9

Issued checks as follows:

No. 982, Clayshire Electric Co., $1,350, on account.

No. 983, Ferguson Electric Co., $500, on account.

Checks Nos. 982 and 983 were recorded in the combined cash journal by debiting Accounts Payable and by crediting the bank account, the names of the creditors being written in the Description column. Check marks were placed in the Posting Reference column to indicate that checks issued to creditors are not posted individually from the combined cash journal. The checks were posted directly to the proper creditors' accounts in the accounts payable ledger from the check stubs.

Tuesday, December 10

Issued Check No. 984 for $234.80 to the Columbia National Bank, a U.S. depositary, in payment of the following taxes:

Employees' income taxes withheld during November..........		$176.80
FICA taxes imposed —		
On employees (withheld during November)................	$ 29.00	
On the employer.......................................	29.00	58.00
Total...		$234.80

This transaction resulted in decreases in FICA taxes payable and in employees' income taxes payable with a corresponding decrease in the bank account; hence, it was recorded in the combined cash journal by debiting FICA Taxes Payable for $58 and Employees' Income Taxes Payable for $176.80, and by crediting the bank account for $234.80.

Sold merchandise on account as follows:

No. 275A, C. A. Weis, 5520 Wren, City, $329.95, tax $9.90.

Wednesday, December 11

Received the following remittances from customers:

R. G. Barry, $400, on account.
J. L. Fox, $250, on account.
W. L. Vedder, $61.54, in full payment of account.

Thursday, December 12

Made the following disbursements from the petty cash fund:

Boy Scouts of America, $5. Petty Cash Voucher No. 65.
R. L. Adams, $10, for personal use. Petty Cash Voucher No. 66.

Friday, December 13

Received the following invoices for merchandise purchased on account:

Mack Electric Co., 4581 Gravois, City, $992, per Invoice No. 123 of December 13. Terms, 2/10, n/30.
Tipton Electric Co., Lemay, $495.50, per Invoice No. 124 of December 12. Terms, net 30 days.

Saturday, December 14

Cash sales for the week:

SALESPERSON	MERCHANDISE	TAX	TOTAL
A	$ 404.90	$12.15	$ 417.05
B	524.75	15.74	540.49
C	374.75	11.24	385.99
	$1,304.40	$39.13	$1,343.53

Issued Check No. 985 payable to Payroll for $825.45.

Mr. Adams follows the policy of paying his employees on the 15th and last day of each month. Since December 15 fell on Sunday, the employees were paid on the 14th. The following statement was prepared from the payroll record:

PAYROLL STATEMENT FOR PERIOD ENDED DECEMBER 15

Total wages and commissions earned during period.............		$925.96
Employees' taxes to be withheld:		
Employees' income taxes................................	$ 84.20	
FICA taxes, 4.5% of $362.50............................	16.31	100.51
Net amount payable to employees.........................		$825.45
Employer's payroll taxes:		
FICA taxes, 4.5% of $362.50............................		$16.31
Unemployment compensation taxes —		
State unemployment taxes, 2.7% of $175.................		4.73
FUTA tax, 0.4% of $175...............................		.70
Total......................................		$21.74

The earnings of two employees had reached the $6,600 point in an earlier month. Accordingly, only $362.50 of the wages and commissions earned during the period is subject to the FICA tax. All but one employee had reached the State Unemployment and FUTA tax limits in an earlier month. As a result, only $175 of wages and commissions earned during the period is subject to these unemployment taxes.

Two entries were required to record the payroll in the combined cash journal — one to record the total earnings of the employees, the amounts withheld for FICA taxes and income taxes, and the net amount paid; the other to record the social security taxes imposed on the employer.

END-OF-THE-WEEK WORK

(1) Proved the footings of the combined cash journal. **(2)** Deposited $2,055.07 in the Columbia National Bank and proved the bank balance ($7,938.08). **(3)** Posted each entry individually from the General Debits and Credits columns of the combined cash journal to the proper general ledger accounts. When Check No. 984, issued December 10, was posted to the accounts with FICA Taxes Payable and Employees' Income Taxes Payable, the accounts were found to be in balance; hence, each account was ruled with a double line as illustrated on page 219. **(4)** Proved the footings of the petty cash disbursements record and proved the balance of the petty cash fund ($96.60). **(5)** Proved the footings of the sales journal.

Monday, December 16

Issued checks as follows:

No. 986, General Appliance Co., $600, on account.
No. 987, Mack Electric Co., $593.75, on account.

Tuesday, December 17

Received the following remittances from customers:

R. J. Winston, $946.98, on account.
J. S. Nicholson, $453.10, in full payment of account.
John F. White, $461.18 and a 30-day, 5 percent note dated December 16 payable to R. L. Adams for $2,000.

Mr. Adams agreed to accept the $2,000 note in order to extend the time of settlement of Mr. White's obligation. The transaction was recorded in the combined cash journal by a debit to the bank account for $461.18, a debit to Notes Receivable, Account No. 121, for $2,000, and a credit to Accounts Receivable for the total, $2,461.18. In posting to Mr. White's account in the Accounts Receivable ledger, two lines were used; one to show the amount of the cash receipt, and another to record the receipt of the note.

Wednesday, December 18

Sold merchandise on credit as follows:

No. 239C, W. L. Vedder, 1017 Veronica, Baden, $469.70, tax $14.09.
No. 277A, W. V. Peters, Webster Groves, $959.80, tax $28.79.
No. 262B, R. J. Powell, 1685 Avignon Ct., City, $859.60, tax $25.79.

Issued Check No. 988 to Milner Garage, $58.50, in payment of storage, gasoline, oil, and service.

> This check was recorded in the combined cash journal by crediting the bank account and by debiting Truck Expense, Account No. 620.

Thursday, December 19

Made petty cash disbursements as follows:

Advertising, $6. Petty Cash Voucher No. 67.
Supplies, $8.35. Petty Cash Voucher No. 68.
Miscellaneous expense, $1.75. Petty Cash Voucher No. 69.

Bought merchandise from Morganford Appliance Co., 4214 Arsenal, City, $981.75, per Invoice No. 125 of December 19. Terms, 2/30, n/60.

Friday, December 20

Issued charge-back Invoice No. 791 for $40 to Tipton Electric Co., for merchandise returned; to be applied on Invoice No. 124 received December 13.

> This transaction was recorded in the combined cash journal by debiting Accounts Payable and by crediting Purchases Returns and Allowances. It was also posted directly to the account of the Tipton Electric Co. in the accounts payable ledger from the charge-back invoice.

Saturday, December 21

Issued Check No. 989 for $1,000 to Mr. Adams for personal use.

Cash sales for the week:

SALESPERSON	MERCHANDISE	TAX	TOTAL
A	$ 549.75	$16.49	$ 566.24
B	549.90	16.50	566.40
C	529.90	15.90	545.80
	$1,629.55	$48.89	$1,678.44

END-OF-THE-WEEK WORK

(1) Proved the footings of the combined cash journal. (2) Deposited $3,539.70 in the Columbia National Bank and proved the bank balance ($9,225.53). (3) Posted each entry individually from the General Debits and Credits columns of the combined cash journal to the proper general ledger accounts. (4) Proved the footings of the petty cash disbursements record and proved the balance of the petty cash fund ($80.50). (5) Proved the footings of the sales journal.

Monday, December 23

Issued Check No. 990 for $972.16 to Mack Electric Co. in payment of its invoice of December 13, less 2 percent discount.

The amount of the check is computed as follows:

Amount of invoice............................	$992.00
Discount, 2%...............................	19.84
Balance due................................	$972.16

This transaction was recorded in the combined cash journal by debiting Accounts Payable for $992 and by crediting Purchases Discount for $19.84 and crediting the bank account for $972.16. In posting the check directly to the account of the Mack Electric Co. in the accounts payable ledger, the amount of the check was entered on one line and the amount of the discount on another line.

Tuesday, December 24

Sold merchandise on credit as follows:

No. 269B, R. F. Webber, 51 Webster Woods, City, $1,059.50, tax $31.79.

No. 281A, R. T. Rusk, 1659 Forest View Dr., City, $459.70, tax $13.79.

No. 256C, J. L. Fox, 5374 Delmar, City, $609.65, tax $18.29.

Thursday, December 26

Received the following remittances from customers:

R. J. Powell, $1,000, on account.
R. T. Rusk, $300, on account.

Made petty cash disbursements as follows:

Advertising, $4.80. Petty Cash Voucher No. 70.
Supplies, $9.13. Petty Cash Voucher No. 71.
Miscellaneous expense, $2.90. Petty Cash Voucher No. 72.

Friday, December 27

Issued Credit Memorandum No. 12 for $61.54 to R. J. Powell for merchandise returned. (Sales price of merchandise, $59.75, tax $1.79.)

Issued Check No. 991 for $382.40 to the Globe Publishing Co. in payment of advertising bill.

Issued Check No. 992 for $453.10 to the Columbia National Bank for J. S. Nicholson's check which was returned unpaid (NSF).

J. S. Nicholson's check was received on December 17, and was deposited in the bank December 21. The bank returned the check with a notice advising that the maker did not have sufficient funds on deposit to cover the check. Check No. 992 was recorded in the combined cash journal by debiting Accounts Receivable and by crediting the bank account. The amount of the check was debited immediately to Mr. Nicholson's account in the accounts receivable ledger. The notation "NSF" was made in the Items column, and the number of the check (992) was shown in the Posting Reference column beside the $453.10 debit to Mr. Nicholson's account.

Saturday, December 28

Cash sales for the week:

SALESPERSON	MERCHANDISE	TAX	TOTAL
A	$ 594.50	$17.84	$ 612.34
B	674.50	20.24	694.74
C	429.90	12.90	442.80
	$1,698.90	$50.98	$1,749.88

Issued checks as follows:

No. 993, The Bell Telephone Co., $21.65, for telephone service.

No. 994, The Union Gas & Electric Co., $64.90, for gas and electricity.

END-OF-THE-WEEK WORK

(1) Proved the footings of the combined cash journal. (Since a page of the combined cash journal was filled at this point, the totals of the amount columns were recorded on the double ruled line at the bottom of the page, after which they were carried forward and entered at the top of the next page.) (2) Deposited $3,049.88 in the Columbia National Bank and proved the bank balance ($10,381.20). (3) Posted each entry individually from the General Debits and Credits columns of the combined cash journal to the proper general ledger accounts. (4) Proved the footings of the petty cash disbursements record and proved the balance of the petty cash fund ($63.67). (5) Proved the footings of the sales journal.

Monday, December 30

Received invoice from Mack Electric Co., 4581 Gravois, City, $396.50, for merchandise purchased per Invoice No. 126 of December 27. Terms, 2/10, n/30.

Tuesday, December 31

Received the following invoices:

Cabany Electric Co., Maplewood, $670.50, merchandise purchased per Invoice No. 127 of December 30. Terms, 2/30, n/60.

Watson Safe & Lock Co., Chicago, $435, safe purchased per invoice of December 30. Terms, 2/30, n/60.

The invoice received from the Cabany Electric Co. was recorded in the purchases journal in the usual manner. The invoice received from the Watson Safe & Lock Co. was recorded in the combined cash journal by debiting Store Equipment and by crediting Accounts Payable. In this enterprise the purchases journal is used only for recording invoices covering merchandise purchased on credit.

Cash sales:

SALESPERSON	MERCHANDISE	TAX	TOTAL
A	$414.90	$12.45	$ 427.35
B	289.95	8.70	298.65
C	274.75	8.24	282.99
	$979.60	$29.39	$1,008.99

Issued Check No. 995 payable to Payroll for $909.26.

PAYROLL STATEMENT FOR PERIOD ENDED DECEMBER 31

Total wages and commissions earned during period..........		$1,021.67
Employees' taxes to be withheld:		
Employees' income taxes................................	$96.10	
FICA taxes, 4.5% of $362.50..........................	16.31	112.41
Net amount payable to employees........................		$ 909.26
Employer's payroll taxes:		
FICA taxes, 4.5% of $362.50..........................		$ 16.31
Unemployment compensation taxes —		
State unemployment taxes, 2.7% of $175.................		4.73
FUTA tax, 0.4% of $175.............................		.70
Total...		$ 21.74

Issued Check No. 996 for $61.33 to replenish the petty cash fund.

The following statement of the petty cash disbursements for December served as a voucher authorizing the issuance of the check to replenish the petty cash fund:

STATEMENT OF PETTY CASH DISBURSEMENTS FOR DECEMBER

R. L. Adams, drawing	$10.00
Stationery and supplies...	27.48
Telephone and telegraph expense...................................	1.40
Advertising expense..	10.80
Charitable contributions expense...................................	5.00
Miscellaneous expense..	6.65
Total disbursements..	$61.33

Before the above statement was prepared the petty cash disbursements record was proved by footing the amount columns, the totals were entered in ink, and the record was ruled with single and double lines. The balance was then brought down below the double rules. The amount received to replenish the fund was added to the balance and the total, $125, was entered in the Description column.

The amount of the check issued was entered in the combined cash journal by debiting the proper accounts and by crediting the bank account. It should be remembered that no posting is done from the petty cash disbursements record; the proper accounts will be charged for the petty cash disbursements when the posting is completed from the combined cash journal.

ROUTINE END-OF-THE-MONTH WORK

(1) Proved the footings and entered the totals in the combined cash journal and the sales journal; entered the total in the purchases journal. **(2)** Deposited $1,008.99 in the Columbia National Bank and proved the
(continued on page 216)

DEPOSITS 111 DR.	CHECKS 111 CR.	CK. NO.	MO.	DAY	DESCRIPTION	POST. REF.
					Balance 8,653.59	
					AMOUNTS FORWARDED	
	500 00	978	Dec	2	Rent Expense	610
	42 19	979		2	Purchases	510
205 90				4	R. F. Webber	✓
	53 37	980		6	Advertising Expense	617
	376 45	981		6	Sales Tax Payable	240
905 78				7	Cash sales for week 8,793.26	✓
1 111 68	972 01					
	1 350 00	982		9	Clayshire Electric Co.	✓
	500 00	983		9	Ferguson Electric Co.	✓
	234 80	984		10	FICA Taxes Payable	250
					Employees' Income Taxes Payable	260
400 00				11	R. G. Barry	✓
250 00				11	J. L. Fox	✓
61 54				11	W. L. Vedder	✓
1 343 53				14	Cash sales for week	✓
	825 45	985		14	Salaries and Commissions Expense	612
					FICA Taxes Payable	250
					Employees' Income Taxes Payable	260
				14	Payroll Tax Expense	613
					FICA Taxes Payable	250
					FUTA Taxes Payable	270
					State Unemployment Taxes Payable 7,938.08	280
3 166 75	3 851 26					
	600 00	986		16	General Appliance Co	✓
	593 75	987		16	Mack Electric Co	✓
946 98				17	R. J. Winston	✓
453 10				17	J. S. Nicholson	✓
461 18				17	Notes Receivable—John F. White	121
	58 50	988		18	Truck Expense	620
				20	Purchases R. and A. – Tipton El. Co	0511
	1 000 00	989		21	R. L. Adams, Drawing	031
1 678 44				21	Cash sales for week 9,225.53	✓
6 706 45	6 134 51					
	972 16	990		23	Purchases Disc – Mack Electric Co	0512
1 000 00				26	R. J. Powell	✓
300 00				26	R. T. Rusk	✓
				27	Sales R. and A. – R. J. Powell	0410
					Sales Tax Payable	240
	382 40	991		27	Advertising Expense	617
	453 10	992		27	Accounts Rec. – J. S. Nicholson	123
1 749 88				28	Cash sales for week	✓
	21 65	993		28	Telephone and Telegraph Exp.	616
	64 90	994		28	Heating and Lighting Expense 10,391.20	614
9 756 33	8 028 72			28	Carried forward	
9 756 33	8 028 72					

The Adams Appliance Store — Combined Cash Journal (Left Page)

GENERAL DEBITS	GENERAL CREDITS	ACCOUNTS PAY. 230 DR.	ACCOUNTS REC. 123 CR.	SALES 410 CR.	SALES TAX PAY. 240 CR.
50000					
4219					
			20590		
5337					
37645					
97201			20590	87940 / 87940	2638 / 2638
		135000			
		50000			
5800					
17680					
			40000		
			25000		
			6154		
				130440	3913
92596					
	1631				
	8420				
2174					
	1631				
	70				
	473				
215451	12225	175000	91744	213370	6551
		60000			
		59375			
			94698		
			45310		
200000			246118		
5850					
	4000	4000			
100000					
521301	16225	308375	477770	162955 / 381335	4889 / 11440
	1984	99200			
			100000		
			3000		
5975			6154		
179					
38240					
45310					
				169890	5098
	2165				
	6490				
619660	18209	407575	614024	551225	16538
619660	18209	407575	614024	551225	16538

The Adams Appliance Store — Combined Cash Journal (Right Page)

Chapter 8 / Accrual Basis Applied to a Retail Business   213

COLUMBIA NATIONAL BANK		CK. NO.	DATE MO. DAY	DESCRIPTION	POST. REF.
DEPOSITS 111 DR.	CHECKS 111 CR.				
				Balance 10,381.20	
975633	802872			AMOUNTS FORWARDED	
			Dec. 31	Store Equipment	180
				Accounts Pay.-Walton, Safe, and Lock Co.	230
100899			31	Cash sales, 12/29-31	✓
	90926	995	31	Salaries and Commissions Expense	612
				FICA Taxes Payable	250
				Employees' Income Taxes Payable	260
			31	Payroll Tax Expense	613
				FICA Taxes Payable	250
				FUTA Taxes Payable	270
				State Unemployment Taxes Payable	280
	6133	996	31	R. L. Adams, Drawing	031
				Stationery and Supplies	150
				Telephone and Telegraph Exp.	616
				Advertising Expense	617
				Charitable Contributions Expense	621
1076532	899931			Miscellaneous Expense 10,419.60	622
1076532	899931				
(111)	(111)				

DAY	DESCRIPTION	VOU. NO.	TOTAL AMOUNT	031	150
	AMOUNTS FORWARDED Balance 125.00				
7	Postage stamps	62	1000		1000
7	Collect telegram	63	140		
7	Messenger fee	64	200		
	111.60		1340		1000
12	Boy Scouts of America	65	500		
12	R. L. Adams, Drawing	66	1000	1000	
	96.60		2840	1000	1000
19	Advertising	67	600		
19	Supplies	68	835		835
19	Miscellaneous expense	69	175		
	80.50		4450	1000	1835
26	Advertising	70	480		
26	Supplies	71	913		913
26	Miscellaneous expense	72	290		
	63.67		6133	1000	2748
			6133	1000	2748
31	Balance		63.67		
31	Received in fund		61.33		
	Total		125.00		

GENERAL		ACCOUNTS PAY. 230 DR.	ACCOUNTS REC. 123 CR.	SALES 410 CR.	SALES TAX PAY. 240 CR.
DEBITS	CREDITS				
619660	18209	407575	614024	551225	16538
43500					
	43500				
				97960	2939
102167					
	1631				
	9610				
2174					
	1631				
	70				
	473				
1000					
2748					
140					
1080					
500					
665					
773634	75124	407575	614024	649185	19477
773634	75124	407575	614024	649185	19477
(✓)	(✓)	(230)	(123)	(410)	(240)

DISTRIBUTION OF CHARGES					
616	617	621	622	ACCOUNT	AMOUNT
140					
140			200		
		500			
140		500	200		
	600				
140	600	500	175		
	480				
			290		
140	1080	500	665		
140	1080	500	665		

DATE	NO. OF INVOICE	FROM WHOM PURCHASED	POST. REF.	AMOUNT
19— Dec 3	121	Ferguson Electric Co.	✓	369 50
6	122	Clayshire Electric Co.	✓	1390 00
13	123	Mack Electric Co.	✓	992 00
13	124	Tipton Electric Co.	✓	495 50
19	125	Morganford Appliance Co.	✓	981 75
30	126	Mack Electric Co.	✓	396 50
31	127	Cabany Electric Co.	✓	670 50
		Purchases Dr.—Accounts Payable Cr.	510/230	5295 75

The Adams Appliance Store — Purchases Journal

DATE	NO. OF SALE	TO WHOM SOLD	POST. REF.	ACCOUNTS REC. 123 DR.	SALES 410 CR.	SALES TAX PAY. 240 CR.
19— Dec 5	271a	R.F. Webber	✓	216 04	209 75	6 29
5	2578	C.F. Abbott	✓	247 15	239 95	7 20
5	2350	E.J. Busch	✓	1322 93	1284 40	38 53
6	2598	R.J. Winston	✓	385 99	374 75	11 24
10	2750	C.A. Weis	✓	339 85	329 95	9 90
18	2390	W.L. Vedder	✓	483 79	469 70	14 09
18	277a	W.V. Peters	✓	988 59	959 80	28 79
18	2628	R.J. Powell	✓	885 39	859 60	25 79
24	2698	R.F. Webber	✓	1091 29	1059 50	31 79
24	281a	R.J. Rusk	✓	473 49	459 70	13 79
24	2560	J.L. Fox	✓	627 94	609 65	18 29
				7062 45	6856 75	205 70
				(123)	(410)	(240)

The Adams Appliance Store — Sales Journal

bank balance ($10,419.60). **(3)** Completed the individual posting from the General Debits and Credits columns of the combined cash journal. **(4)** Completed the summary posting of the columnar totals of the combined cash journal, the purchases journal, and the sales journal to the proper accounts in the general ledger. **(5)** Ruled the combined cash journal, the purchases journal, and the sales journal. **(6)** Prepared a trial balance and schedules of accounts receivable and accounts payable.

(continued on page 227)

ACCOUNT *Columbia National Bank*   ACCOUNT NO. 111

DATE	ITEMS	POST. REF.	✓	DEBITS	DATE	ITEMS	POST. REF.	✓	CREDITS
19– Dec. 1	Balance	✓		865359	Dec. 31		CJ48		899931
31	10,419.60	CJ48		1076532					
				1941791					

ACCOUNT *Petty Cash Fund*   ACCOUNT NO. 112

DATE	ITEMS	POST. REF.	✓	DEBITS	DATE	ITEMS	POST. REF.	✓	CREDITS
19– Dec. 1	Balance	✓		12500					

ACCOUNT *Notes Receivable*   ACCOUNT NO. 121

DATE	ITEMS	POST. REF.	✓	DEBITS	DATE	ITEMS	POST. REF.	✓	CREDITS
19– Dec. 17		CJ47		200000					

ACCOUNT *Accounts Receivable*   ACCOUNT NO. 123

DATE	ITEMS	POST. REF.	✓	DEBITS	DATE	ITEMS	POST. REF.	✓	CREDITS
19– Dec. 1	Balance	✓		736064	19– Dec. 31		CJ48		614024
27		CJ47		45310					
31	8,735.95	J44		706245					
				1487619					

ACCOUNT *Allowance for Bad Debts*   ACCOUNT NO. 0120

DATE	ITEMS	POST. REF.	✓	DEBITS	DATE	ITEMS	POST. REF.	✓	CREDITS
					19– Dec. 1	Balance	✓		20045

ACCOUNT *Merchandise Inventory*   ACCOUNT NO. 130

DATE	ITEMS	POST. REF.	✓	DEBITS	DATE	ITEMS	POST. REF.	✓	CREDITS
19– Dec. 1	Balance	✓		2884245					

ACCOUNT *Prepaid Insurance*   ACCOUNT NO. 140

DATE	ITEMS	POST. REF.	✓	DEBITS	DATE	ITEMS	POST. REF.	✓	CREDITS
19– Dec. 1	Balance	✓		43110					

The Adams Appliance Store — General Ledger

ACCOUNT *Stationery and Supplies*   ACCOUNT NO. *150*

DATE	ITEMS	POST. REF.	✓	DEBITS	DATE	ITEMS	POST. REF.	✓	CREDITS
19– Dec. 1	Balance	✓		2 2 3 2 2					
31		CJ48		2 7 4 8 2 5 0 7 0					

ACCOUNT *Store Equipment*   ACCOUNT NO. *180*

DATE	ITEMS	POST. REF.	✓	DEBITS	DATE	ITEMS	POST. REF.	✓	CREDITS
19– Dec. 1	Balance	✓		2 0 8 5 0 0					
31		CJ48		4 3 5 0 0 2 5 2 0 0 0					

ACCOUNT *Accumulated Depreciation—Store Equipment*   ACCOUNT NO. *0180*

DATE	ITEMS	POST. REF.	✓	DEBITS	DATE	ITEMS	POST. REF.	✓	CREDITS
					19– Dec. 1	Balance			6 4 6 5 0

ACCOUNT *Delivery Equipment*   ACCOUNT NO. *190*

DATE	ITEMS	POST. REF.	✓	DEBITS	DATE	ITEMS	POST. REF.	✓	CREDITS
19– Dec. 1	Balance	✓		2 9 8 4 0 0					

ACCOUNT *Accumulated Depreciation—Delivery Equipment*   ACCOUNT NO. *0190*

DATE	ITEMS	POST. REF.	✓	DEBITS	DATE	ITEMS	POST. REF.	✓	CREDITS
					19– Dec. 1	Balance	✓		1 9 3 9 6 0

ACCOUNT *Notes Payable*   ACCOUNT NO. *210*

DATE	ITEMS	POST. REF.	✓	DEBITS	DATE	ITEMS	POST. REF.	✓	CREDITS
					19– Dec. 1	Balance	✓		8 6 3 9 0

ACCOUNT *Accounts Payable*   ACCOUNT NO. *230*

DATE	ITEMS	POST. REF.	✓	DEBITS	DATE	ITEMS	POST. REF.	✓	CREDITS
19– Dec. 31		CJ48		4 0 7 5 7 5	19– Dec. 1	Balance	✓		2 8 2 6 8 0
					31		CJ48		4 3 5 0 0
					31		P32		5 2 9 5 7 5
						4,481.80			8 5 5 7 5 5

The Adams Appliance Store — General Ledger (Continued)

ACCOUNT Sales Tax Payable   ACCOUNT NO. 240

DATE	ITEMS	POST. REF.	✓	DEBITS	DATE	ITEMS	POST. REF.	✓	CREDITS
19— Dec. 6		CJ47		37645	19— Dec. 1	Balance	✓		37645
27		CJ47		179	31		CJ48		19477
					31		S44		20570
						398.68			40047

ACCOUNT FICA Taxes Payable   ACCOUNT NO. 250

DATE	ITEMS	POST. REF.	✓	DEBITS	DATE	ITEMS	POST. REF.	✓	CREDITS
19— Dec. 10		CJ47		5800	19— Dec. 1	Balance	✓		5800
					14		CJ47		1631
					14		CJ47		1631
					31		CJ48		1631
					31		CJ48		1631
									6524

ACCOUNT Employees' Income Taxes Payable   ACCOUNT NO. 260

DATE	ITEMS	POST. REF.	✓	DEBITS	DATE	ITEMS	POST. REF.	✓	CREDITS
19— Dec. 10		CJ47		17680	19— Dec. 1	Balance	✓		17680
					14		CJ47		8420
					31		CJ48		9610
									18030

ACCOUNT FUTA Taxes Payable   ACCOUNT NO. 270

DATE	ITEMS	POST. REF.	✓	DEBITS	DATE	ITEMS	POST. REF.	✓	CREDITS
					19— Dec. 1	Balance	✓		5140
					14		CJ47		70
					31		CJ48		70
									5280

ACCOUNT State Unemployment Taxes Payable   ACCOUNT NO. 280

DATE	ITEMS	POST. REF.	✓	DEBITS	DATE	ITEMS	POST. REF.	✓	CREDITS
					19— Dec. 1	Balance	✓		1890
					14		CJ47		473
					31		CJ48		473
									2836

ACCOUNT R. L. Adams, Capital   ACCOUNT NO. 310

DATE	ITEMS	POST. REF.	✓	DEBITS	DATE	ITEMS	POST. REF.	✓	CREDITS
					19— Dec. 1	Balance	✓		4778942

The Adams Appliance Store — General Ledger (Continued)

ACCOUNT *R. L. Adams, Drawing*   ACCOUNT NO. 031

DATE	ITEMS	POST. REF.	✓	DEBITS	DATE	ITEMS	POST. REF.	✓	CREDITS
19– Dec. 1	Balance	✓		8 1 5 4 80					
21		CJ47		1 0 0 0 00					
31		CJ48		1 0 00					
				9 1 6 4 80					

ACCOUNT *Sales*   ACCOUNT NO. 410

DATE	ITEMS	POST. REF.	✓	DEBITS	DATE	ITEMS	POST. REF.	✓	CREDITS
					19– Dec. 1	Balance	✓		10 5 8 3 5 52
					31		CJ48		6 4 9 1 85
					31	S44			6 8 5 6 75
									11 9 1 8 4 12

ACCOUNT *Sales Returns and Allowances*   ACCOUNT NO. 0410

DATE	ITEMS	POST. REF.	✓	DEBITS	DATE	ITEMS	POST. REF.	✓	CREDITS
19– Dec. 1	Balance	✓		3 0 7 65					
27		CJ47		5 9 75					
				3 6 7 40					

ACCOUNT *Purchases*   ACCOUNT NO. 510

DATE	ITEMS	POST. REF.	✓	DEBITS	DATE	ITEMS	POST. REF.	✓	CREDITS
19– Dec. 1	Balance	✓		6 8 9 1 1 14					
2		CJ47		4 2 19					
31		P32		5 2 9 5 75					
				7 4 2 4 9 08					

ACCOUNT *Purchases Returns and Allowances*   ACCOUNT NO. 0511

DATE	ITEMS	POST. REF.	✓	DEBITS	DATE	ITEMS	POST. REF.	✓	CREDITS
					19– Dec. 1	Balance	✓		5 6 5 13
					20		CJ47		4 0 00
									6 0 5 13

ACCOUNT *Purchases Discount*   ACCOUNT NO. 0512

DATE	ITEMS	POST. REF.	✓	DEBITS	DATE	ITEMS	POST. REF.	✓	CREDITS
					19– Dec. 1	Balance	✓		4 0 3 76
					23		CJ47		1 9 84
									4 2 3 60

The Adams Appliance Store — General Ledger (Continued)

ACCOUNT Rent Expense   ACCOUNT NO. 610

DATE	ITEMS	POST. REF.	✓	DEBITS	DATE	ITEMS	POST. REF.	✓	CREDITS
19— Dec. 1	Balance	✓		5 5 0 0 0 0					
2		CJ47		5 0 0 0 0					
				6 0 0 0 0 0					

ACCOUNT Salaries and Commissions Expense   ACCOUNT NO. 612

DATE	ITEMS	POST. REF.	✓	DEBITS	DATE	ITEMS	POST. REF.	✓	CREDITS
19— Dec. 1	Balance	✓		2 0 8 2 8 9 4					
14		CJ47		9 2 5 9 6					
31		CJ48		1 0 2 1 6 7					
				2 2 7 7 6 5 7					

ACCOUNT Payroll Tax Expense   ACCOUNT NO. 613

DATE	ITEMS	POST. REF.	✓	DEBITS	DATE	ITEMS	POST. REF.	✓	CREDITS
19— Dec. 1	Balance	✓		1 1 4 9 3 5					
14		CJ47		2 1 7 4					
31		CJ48		2 1 7 4					
				1 1 9 2 8 3					

ACCOUNT Heating and Lighting Expense   ACCOUNT NO. 614

DATE	ITEMS	POST. REF.	✓	DEBITS	DATE	ITEMS	POST. REF.	✓	CREDITS
19— Dec. 1	Balance	✓		5 7 8 2 0					
28		CJ47		6 4 9 0					
				6 4 3 1 0					

ACCOUNT Telephone and Telegraph Expense   ACCOUNT NO. 616

DATE	ITEMS	POST. REF.	✓	DEBITS	DATE	ITEMS	POST. REF.	✓	CREDITS
19— Dec. 1	Balance	✓		2 1 7 1 5					
28		CJ47		2 1 6 5					
31		CJ48		1 4 0					
				2 4 0 2 0					

ACCOUNT Advertising Expense   ACCOUNT NO. 617

DATE	ITEMS	POST. REF.	✓	DEBITS	DATE	ITEMS	POST. REF.	✓	CREDITS
19— Dec. 1	Balance	✓		4 2 6 1 8 0					
6		CJ47		5 3 3 7					
27		CJ47		3 8 2 4 0					
31		CJ48		1 0 8 0					
				4 7 0 8 3 7					

The Adams Appliance Store — General Ledger (Continued)

ACCOUNT *Truck Expense* — ACCOUNT NO. 620

DATE	ITEMS	POST. REF.	√	DEBITS	DATE	ITEMS	POST. REF.	√	CREDITS
19— Dec. 1	Balance	√		473 60					
18		CJ47		58 50					
				532 10					

ACCOUNT *Charitable Contributions Expense* — ACCOUNT NO. 621

DATE	ITEMS	POST. REF.	√	DEBITS	DATE	ITEMS	POST. REF.	√	CREDITS
19— Dec. 1	Balance	√		280 00					
31		CJ48		5 00					
				285 00					

ACCOUNT *Miscellaneous Expense* — ACCOUNT NO. 622

DATE	ITEMS	POST. REF.	√	DEBITS	DATE	ITEMS	POST. REF.	√	CREDITS
19— Dec. 1	Balance	√		371 10					
31		CJ48		6 65					
				377 75					

ACCOUNT *Interest Earned* — ACCOUNT NO. 710

DATE	ITEMS	POST. REF.	√	DEBITS	DATE	ITEMS	POST. REF.	√	CREDITS
					19— Dec. 1	Balance	√		32 15

ACCOUNT *Interest Expense* — ACCOUNT NO. 810

DATE	ITEMS	POST. REF.	√	DEBITS	DATE	ITEMS	POST. REF.	√	CREDITS
19— Dec. 1	Balance	√		46 05					

The Adams Appliance Store — General Ledger (Concluded)

NAME *C. F. Abbott*
ADDRESS *5245 Kingwood, City*

DATE	ITEMS	POST. REF.	√	DEBITS	CREDITS	BALANCE
19— Dec. 5		S2S78		247 15		247 15

NAME *R. G. Barry*
ADDRESS *14811 Point Dr., City*

DATE	ITEMS	POST. REF.	√	DEBITS	CREDITS	BALANCE
19— Dec. 1	Dr. Balance	√				1183 98
11		C			400 00	783 98

The Adams Appliance Store — Accounts Receivable Ledger

NAME *E. J. Busch*
ADDRESS *9440 Arban, City*

DATE	ITEMS	POST. REF.	√	DEBITS	CREDITS	BALANCE
19– Dec 5		S235C		132293		132293

NAME *J. L. Fox*
ADDRESS *5374 Delmar, City*

DATE	ITEMS	POST. REF.	√	DEBITS	CREDITS	BALANCE
19– Dec 1	Dr. Balance	√				53550
11		C			25000	28550
24		S256C		62794		91344

NAME *J. S. Nicholson*
ADDRESS *875 Glenway Dr., City*

DATE	ITEMS	POST. REF.	√	DEBITS	CREDITS	BALANCE
19– Dec 1	Dr. Balance	√				45310
17		C			45310	–0–
27	N S F	Cb 992		45310		45310

NAME *W. V. Peters*
ADDRESS *Webster Groves*

DATE	ITEMS	POST. REF.	√	DEBITS	CREDITS	BALANCE
19– Dec 1	Dr. Balance	√				20590
18		S277a		98859		119449

NAME *R. J. Powell*
ADDRESS *1685 Avignon Ct., City*

DATE	ITEMS	POST. REF.	√	DEBITS	CREDITS	BALANCE
19– Dec 1	Dr. Balance	√				61748
18		S262B		88539		150287
26		C			100000	50287
27		CM12			6154	44133

NAME *R. J. Rusk*
ADDRESS *1659 Forest View Dr., City*

DATE	ITEMS	POST. REF.	√	DEBITS	CREDITS	BALANCE
19– Dec 1	Dr. Balance	√				68908
24		S281a		47349		116257
26		C			30000	86257

The Adams Appliance Store — Accounts Receivable Ledger (Continued)

NAME *W. L. Vedder*
ADDRESS *1017 Veronica, Baden*

DATE	ITEMS	POST. REF.	✓	DEBITS	CREDITS	BALANCE
19— Dec. 1	Dr. Balance	✓				6154
11		C			6154	—0—
18		S239C		48379		48379

NAME *R. F. Webber*
ADDRESS *51 Webster Woods, City*

DATE	ITEMS	POST. REF.	✓	DEBITS	CREDITS	BALANCE
19— Dec. 1	Dr. Balance	✓				20590
4		C			20590	—0—
5		S271a		21604		21604
24		S2698		109129		130733

NAME *C. A. Weis*
ADDRESS *5520 Wren, City*

DATE	ITEMS	POST. REF.	✓	DEBITS	CREDITS	BALANCE
19— Dec. 10		S275a		33985		33985

NAME *John F. White*
ADDRESS *23 Stratford Ln., City*

DATE	ITEMS	POST. REF.	✓	DEBITS	CREDITS	BALANCE
19— Dec. 1	Dr. Balance	✓				246118
17		C			46118	
17		N			200000	—0—

NAME *R. J. Winston*
ADDRESS *Des Peres*

DATE	ITEMS	POST. REF.	✓	DEBITS	CREDITS	BALANCE
19— Dec. 1	Dr. Balance	✓				94698
6		S2598		38599		133297
17		C			94698	38599

The Adams Appliance Store — Accounts Receivable Ledger (Concluded)

NAME *Cabany Electric Co.*
ADDRESS *Maplewood*

DATE	ITEMS	POST. REF.	✓	DEBITS	CREDITS	BALANCE
19— Dec. 31	12/30 – 2/30, n/60	P127			670 50	670 50

NAME *Clayshire Electric Co.*
ADDRESS *Richmond Hts.*

DATE	ITEMS	POST. REF.	✓	DEBITS	CREDITS	BALANCE
19— Dec. 1	Cr. Balance	✓				356 80
6	12/6 – n/30	P122			1390 00	1746 80
9		Ck 912		1350 00		396 80

NAME *Ferguson Electric Co.*
ADDRESS *Ferguson*

DATE	ITEM!	POST. REF.	✓	DEBITS	CREDITS	BALANCE
19— Dec. 1	Cr. Balance	✓				601 25
3	11/30 – n/30	P121			369 50	970 75
9		Ck 913		500 00		470 75

NAME *General Appliance Co.*
ADDRESS *Rock Hill*

DATE	ITEMS	POST. REF.	✓	DEBITS	CREDITS	BALANCE
19— Dec. 1	Cr. Balance	✓				800 00
16		Ck 986		600 00		200 00

NAME *Mack Electric Co.*
ADDRESS *4581 Gravois, City*

DATE	ITEMS	POST. REF.	✓	DEBITS	CREDITS	BALANCE
19— Dec. 1	Cr. Balance	✓				593 75
13	12/13 – 2/10, n/30	P123			992 00	1585 75
16		Ck 917		593 75		992 00
23		Ck 990		972 16		
23	Discount			19 84		—0—
30	12/27 – 2/10, n/30	P126			396 50	396 50

NAME *Morganford Appliance Co.*
ADDRESS *4214 Arsenal, City*

DATE	ITEMS	POST. REF.	✓	DEBITS	CREDITS	BALANCE
19— Dec. 19	12/19 – 2/30, n/60	P125			981 75	981 75

The Adams Appliance Store — Accounts Payable Ledger

NAME *Tipton Electric Co*
ADDRESS *Lemay*

DATE	ITEMS	POST. REF.	√	DEBITS	CREDITS	BALANCE
19— Dec. 1	Cr. Balance	√				47500
13	12/12 – n/30	P124			49550	97050
20		CB791		4000		93050

NAME *Watson Safe and Lock Co.*
ADDRESS *Chicago*

DATE	ITEMS	POST. REF.	√	DEBITS	CREDITS	BALANCE
19— Dec. 31	12/30 – 2/30, n/60	CJ48			43500	43500

The Adams Appliance Store — Accounts Payable Ledger (Concluded)

The Adams Appliance Store
Schedule of Accounts Receivable

	Nov. 30, 19—	Dec. 31, 19—
C. F. Abbott		24715
R. G. Barry	118398	78398
E. J. Busch		132293
J. L. Fox	53550	91344
J. S. Nicholson	45310	45310
W. V. Peters	20590	119449
R. J. Powell	61748	44133
R. T. Rusk	68908	86257
W. L. Vedder	6154	48379
R. F. Webber	20590	130733
C. A. Weis		33985
John F. White	246118	
R. G. Winston	94698	38599
	736064	773595
	736064	873595

The Adams Appliance Store — Schedule of Accounts Receivable

The Adams Appliance Store
Schedule of Accounts Payable

	Nov. 30, 19—	Dec. 31, 19—
Cabany Electric Co.		67050
Clayshire Electric Co.	35680	39680
Ferguson Electric Co.	60125	47075
General Appliance Co.	80000	20000
Mack Electric Co.	59375	39650
Morganford Appliance Co.		98175
Tipton Electric Co.	47500	93050
Watson Safe and Lock Co.		43500
	282680	448170
	282680	448180

The Adams Appliance Store — Schedule of Accounts Payable

The Adams Appliance Store
Trial Balance

Account	Acct. No.	November 30, 19— Dr. Balance	November 30, 19— Cr. Balance	December 31, 19— Dr. Balance	December 31, 19— Cr. Balance
Columbia National Bank	111	865359		1041960	
Petty Cash Fund	112	12500		12500	
Notes Receivable	121			200000	
Accounts Receivable	123	736064		873595	
Allowance for Bad Debts	0120		20045		20045
Merchandise Inventory	130	2884245		2884245	
Prepaid Insurance	140	43110		43110	
Stationery and Supplies	150	22322		25070	
Store Equipment	180	208500		252000	
Accum. Deprec.—Store Equipment	0180		64650		64650
Delivery Equipment	190	298400		298400	
Accum. Deprec.—Delivery Equipment	0190		193960		193960
Notes Payable	210		86390		86390
Accounts Payable	230		282680		448180
Sales Tax Payable	240		37645		39868
FICA Taxes Payable	250		5800		6524
Employees' Income Taxes Payable	260		17680		18030
FUTA Taxes Payable	270		5140		5280
State Unemployment Taxes Payable	280		1890		2836
R. L. Adams, Capital	310		4778942		4778942
R. L. Adams, Drawing	031	815480		916480	
Sales	410		10583552		11918412
Sales Returns and Allowances	0410	30765		36740	
Purchases	510	6891114		7424908	
Purchases Returns and Allow.	0511		56513		60513
Purchases Discount	0512		40376		42360
Rent Expense	610	550000		600000	
Salaries and Commissions Exp.	612	2082894		2277631	
Payroll Tax Expense	613	114935		119283	
Heating and Lighting Expense	614	57820		64310	
Telephone and Telegraph Expense	616	21715		24020	
Advertising Expense	617	426180		470837	
Truck Expense	620	47360		53210	
Charitable Contributions Expense	621	28000		28500	
Miscellaneous Expense	622	37110		37775	
Interest Earned	710		3215		3215
Interest Expense	810	4605		4605	
		16178478	16178478	17689205	17689205

The Adams Appliance Store — Trial Balance

Report No. 16

Complete Report No. 16 in the workbook and submit your working papers to the instructor for approval. After completing this report, continue with the textbook discussion in Chapter 9 until the next report is required.

chapter nine

the periodic summary

One of the major reasons for keeping accounting records is to accumulate information that will make it possible to prepare periodic summaries of both **(1)** the revenue and expenses of the business during a specified period and **(2)** the assets, liabilities, and owner's equity of the business at a specified date. A trial balance of the general ledger accounts will provide most of the information that is required for these summaries (the income statement and the balance sheet). However, the trial balance does not supply the data in a form that is easily interpreted, nor does it reflect changes in the accounting elements that have not been represented by ordinary business transactions. Therefore, at the end of a fiscal period it is necessary, first, to determine the kind and amounts of changes that the accounts do not reflect and to adjust the accounts accordingly and, second, to recast the information into the form of an income statement and a balance sheet. These two steps are often referred to as "the periodic summary."

end-of-period work sheet

It has already been mentioned that an end-of-period work sheet is a device that assists the accountant in three ways. It facilitates **(1)** the preparing of the financial statements, **(2)** the making of needed adjustments in the accounts, and **(3)** the closing of the temporary owner's equity accounts. In most cases the accountant is under some pressure to produce the income statement and the balance sheet as soon as possible after the period has ended. The end-of-period work sheet is of greatest assistance in helping the accountant meet this need for promptness. The help that the work sheet gives in making adjustments and in closing the accounts is secondary in importance.

Work sheets are not financial statements; they are devices used to assist the accountant in performing certain of his tasks. Ordinarily it is only the accountant who uses (or even sees) a work sheet. For this reason a work sheet (sometimes called a *working trial balance*) is usually prepared in lead pencil.

A Work Sheet for a Retail Store

While an end-of-period work sheet can be in any of several forms, a common and widely used arrangement involves ten amount columns. The amount columns are used in pairs. The first pair of amount columns is for the trial balance. The data to be recorded consist of the name, number, and debit or credit balance of each account. Debit balances should be entered in the left-hand column and credit balances in the right-hand column. The second pair of amount columns is used to record needed end-of-period adjustments. The third pair of amount columns is used to show the account balances as adjusted. This pair of amount columns is headed "Adjusted Trial Balance" because its purpose is to show that the debit and credit account balances as adjusted are equal in amount. The fourth pair of amount columns is for the adjusted balances of the expense and revenue accounts. This pair of columns is headed "Income Statement" since the amounts shown will be reported in that statement. The fifth, and last, pair of amount columns is headed "Balance Sheet" and shows the adjusted account balances that will be reported in that statement.

To illustrate the preparation and use of the end-of-period work sheet, the example of the accounts of The Adams Appliance Store will be continued. The journals and ledgers for this business for the month of December were reproduced in the preceding chapter. In this chapter the income statement for the year and the balance sheet at the end of the year will be reproduced, showing the use of a work sheet as a device for summarizing the data to be presented in those statements.

The Work Sheet for The Adams Appliance Store

The end-of-year work sheet for this business is reproduced on pages 232 and 233. Following is a description and discussion of the steps that were followed in the preparation of this work sheet. Each step should be studied carefully with frequent reference to the work sheet itself.

Trial Balance Columns. The trial balance of the general ledger accounts as of December 31 was entered in the first pair of amount columns. This trial balance is the same as the one shown on page 227 except that all of the account titles were included in the work sheet list even though certain of the accounts had no balance at this point.

The Trial Balance Debits and Credits columns were totaled. The totals should be equal. If not, the cause of any discrepancy must be found and corrected before the preparation of the work sheet can proceed.

Adjustments Columns. The second pair of amount columns on the work sheet was used to record certain entries that were necessary to reflect various changes that had occurred during the year in some of the accounting elements. In this case, adjustments were needed: **(1)** to remove the amount of the beginning-of-year merchandise inventory and to record the amount of the end-of-year inventory; **(2)** to record the amounts of interest earned but not collected, and of interest expense incurred but not paid; **(3)** to record the portions of prepaid insurance expired, and of stationery and supplies used during the year; **(4)** to record the estimated depreciation expense for the year; and **(5)** to record the estimated amount of expected bad debt losses.

Eight complete entries involving eight debits and nine credits were made in the Adjustments columns to reflect these changes. When an account was debited, the amount was entered on the same horizontal line as the name of the account and in the Adjustments Debits column. Amounts credited were entered, of course, in the Credits column. Each such entry made on the work sheet was identified by a small letter in parentheses to facilitate cross-reference. Following is an explanation of each of the entries:

Entry (a): In order to remove the amount of the beginning inventory of merchandise from the asset account and at the same time to include it in the determination of net income for the current year, Expense and Revenue Summary, Account No. 320, was debited, and Merchandise Inventory, Account No. 130, was credited for $28,842.45. This amount was the calculated cost of the inventory at the end of the preceding year (the beginning of the year under consideration). The amount had been in the merchandise inventory account as a debit since the accounts were adjusted as of December 31 a year ago.

Entry (b): This entry recorded the calculated cost of the merchandise on hand December 31 — often referred to as the year-end inventory. The calculation was based on a physical count of the merchandise in stock at the close of the year. The cost of the merchandise in stock was recorded by debiting Merchandise Inventory, Account No. 130, and by crediting Expense and Revenue Summary, Account No. 320, for $31,604.50.

Entry (c): This entry recorded the accrued interest that had been earned but not received by debiting Accrued Interest Receivable, Account No. 122, and by crediting Interest Earned, Account No. 710, for $4.17. The December 31 trial balance shows that Notes Receivable had a debit balance of $2,000. This was the amount of a 5 percent, 30-day note dated December 16, signed by John F. White. From December 16 to December 31 was 15 days. Interest at 5 percent per year on $2,000 for 15 days is $4.17.

Entry (d): This entry recorded the accrued interest expense that had been incurred but not paid by debiting Interest Expense, Account No. 810, and by crediting Accrued Interest Payable, Account No. 220, for $8.06. The December 31 trial balance shows that Notes Payable had a credit balance of $863.90. This related to a 6 percent, six-month note dated November 5. From November 5 to December 31 was 56 days. Interest at the rate of 6 percent per year on $863.90 for 56 days is $8.06.

Entry (e): This entry recorded the insurance expense for the year by debiting Insurance Expense, Account No. 619, and by crediting Prepaid Insurance, Account No. 140, for $215.55. The December 31 trial balance shows that Prepaid Insurance had a debit balance of $431.10. This amount was the cost of a two-year policy dated January 2 of the year under consideration. By December 31 one year had elapsed and, thus, one half of the premium paid had become an expense.

Entry (f): This entry recorded the calculated cost of the stationery and supplies used during the year by debiting Stationery and Supplies Expense, Account No. 615, and by crediting Stationery and Supplies, Account No. 150, for $210.70. The December 31 trial balance shows that Stationery and Supplies had a debit balance of $250.70. This amount was the sum of the cost of any stationery and supplies on hand at the start of the year, plus

The Adams Appliance Store

Work Sheet

For the Year Ended December 31, 19—

Account	Acct. No.	Trial Balance Debits	Trial Balance Credits	Adjustments Debits	Adjustments Credits	Adj. Trial Balance Debits	Adj. Trial Balance Credits	Income Statement Debits	Income Statement Credits	Balance Sheet Debits	Balance Sheet Credits
Columbia National Bank	111	1041960				1041960				1041960	
Petty Cash Fund	112	12500				12500				12500	
Notes Receivable	121	200000				200000				200000	
Accrued Interest Receivable	122			(c) 417		417				417	
Accounts Receivable	123	873595				873595				873595	
Allowance for Bad Debts	0120		20045		(b) 46125		66170				66170
Merchandise Inventory	130	2884245		(a) 3160450	(a) 2884245	3160450				3160450	
Prepaid Insurance	140	43110			(e) 21555	21555				21555	
Stationery and Supplies	150	250070			(f) 21070	229000				229000	
Store Equipment	160	252000				252000				252000	
Accumulated Deprec.—Store Equip.	0180		64650		(g) 20850		85500				85500
Delivery Equipment	190	298400				298400				298400	
Accumulated Deprec.—Delivery Equip.	0190		193960		(g) 74600		268560				268560
Accumulated Deprec.—Office Equip.	0290		86390				86390				86390
Notes Payable	210										
Accrued Interest Payable	220				(d) 806		806				806
Accounts Payable	230		448180				448180				448180
Sales Tax Payable	240		39868				39868				39868
FICA Taxes Payable	250		6524				6524				6524
Employees' Inc. Taxes Payable	260		18030				18030				18030
FUTA Taxes Payable	270		5280				5280				5280
State Unemployment Taxes Pay.	220		2836				2836				2836
R.L. Adams Capital	310		4778942				4778942				4778942
R.L. Adams Drawing	031	916480				916480				916480	
Expense and Revenue Summary	320			(a) 2884245	(a) 3160450	2884245	3160450	2884245	3160450		
Sales	410		11918412				11918412		11918412		
Sales Returns and Allow.	0410	36740				36740		36740			
Purchases	510	7424908				7424908		7424908			

The Adams Appliance Store — Ten-Column Work Sheet

Account	No.	Trial Balance Dr	Trial Balance Cr	Adjustments Dr	Adjustments Cr	Adjusted Trial Balance Dr	Adjusted Trial Balance Cr	Income Statement Dr	Income Statement Cr	Balance Sheet Dr	Balance Sheet Cr
Purchases Returns and Allow.	0511		60513				60513		60513		
Purchases Discount	0512		42360				42360		42360		
Rent Expense	610	600000				600000		600000			
Depreciation Expense	611			(g) 95450		95450		95450			
Salaries and Commissions Exp.	612	2277657				2277657		2277657			
Payroll Tax Expense	613	119283				119283		119283			
Heating and Lighting Expense	614	64310				64310		64310			
Stationery and Supplies Expense	615			(f) 21070		21070		21070			
Telephone and Telegraph Expense	616	24020				24020		24020			
Advertising Expense	617	470837				470837		470837			
Bad Debts Expense	618			(e) 46125		46125		46125			
Insurance Expense	619			(e) 21555		21555		21555			
Truck Expense	620	53210				53210		53210			
Charitable Contributions Expense	621	28500				28500		28500			
Miscellaneous Expense	622	37775				37775		37775			
Interest Earned	710		3215		(c) 417		3632		3632		
Interest Expense	810	4605		(a) 806		5411		5411			
		17689205	17689205	6230118	6230118	20992453	20992453	1421096	1518367	5807016	6781357
Net Income								974271			974271
								1518367	1518367	6781357	6781357

the cost of stationery and supplies purchased during the year. A physical count of the stationery and supplies on hand December 31 was made and the cost determined to be $40. Thus, stationery and supplies that cost $210.70 ($250.70 — $40) had been used during the year.

Entry (g): This entry recorded the calculated depreciation expense for the year by debiting Depreciation Expense, Account No. 611, for $954.50 and by crediting Accumulated Depreciation — Store Equipment, Account No. 0180, for $208.50 and crediting Accumulated Depreciation — Delivery Equipment, Account No. 0190, for $746. The December 31 trial balance shows that Store Equipment had a debit balance of $2,520. This balance represented the $2,085 cost of various items of property that had been owned the entire year plus the $435 cost of the safe that was purchased on December 31. Mr. Adams follows the policy of not calculating any depreciation on assets that have been owned for less than a month. Thus, depreciation expense for the year on store equipment related to property that had been owned for the entire year. Its cost was $2,085. This equipment is being depreciated at the rate of 10 percent a year. Ten percent of $2,085 is $208.50.

The December 31 trial balance shows that the delivery equipment account had a debit balance of $2,984. This was the cost of a delivery truck that had been owned the entire year. The truck is being depreciated at the rate of 25 percent per year. Twenty-five percent of $2,984 is $746.

Entry (h): This entry recorded the estimated bad debts expense for the year by debiting Bad Debts Expense, Account No. 618, and by crediting Allowance for Bad Debts, Account No. 0120, for $461.25. Guided by past experience, Mr. Adams estimated that bad debt losses will be approximately one percent of the total sales on account for the year. Investigation of the records revealed that such sales amounted to $46,125.10. One percent of $46,125.10 is $461.25.

After making the required entries in the Adjustments columns of the work sheet, the columns were totaled to prove the equality of the debit and credit entries.

Adjusted Trial Balance Columns. The third pair of amount columns of the work sheet was used for the *adjusted trial balance*. To determine the balance of each account after making the required adjustments, it was necessary to take into consideration the amounts recorded in the first two pairs of amount columns. When an account balance was not affected by entries in the Adjustments columns, the amount in the Trial Balance columns was extended directly to the Adjusted Trial Balance columns.

When an account balance was affected by an entry in the Adjustments columns, the balance recorded in the Trial Balance columns was increased or decreased, as the case might be, by the amount of the adjusting entry. For example, Accumulated Depreciation — Store Equipment was listed in the Trial Balance Credits column as $646.50. Since there was an entry of $208.50 in the Adjustments Credits column, the amount extended to the Adjusted Trial Balance Credits column was found by addition to be $855 ($646.50 + $208.50). Prepaid Insurance was listed in the Trial Balance Debits column as $431.10. Since there was an entry of $215.55 in the Adjustments Credits column, the amount to be extended to the Adjusted Trial Balance Debits column was found by subtraction to be $215.55 ($431.10 − $215.55).

There is one exception to the procedure described above that relates to the debit and the credit on the line for Expense and Revenue Summary, Account No. 320, in the Adjustments columns. While the $2,762.05 excess of the $31,604.50 credit (the amount of the end-of-year merchandise inventory) over the $28,842.45 debit (the amount of the beginning-of-year merchandise inventory) could be extended to the Adjusted Trial Balance Credits column, it is better to extend both the debit and the credit amounts into the Adjusted Trial Balance columns. The reason is that both amounts are used in the preparation of the income statement and, accordingly, it is helpful to have both amounts appear in the Income Statement columns. Therefore, both amounts are shown in the Adjusted Trial Balance columns.

The Adjusted Trial Balance columns were totaled to prove the equality of the debits and credits.

Income Statement Columns. The fourth pair of amount columns of the work sheet was used to show the amounts that will be reported in the income statement. The manner of extending the debit and credit amounts on the line for Expense and Revenue Summary was mentioned previously. The amounts for sales, purchases returns and allowances, purchases discount, and interest earned were extended to the Income Statement Credits column. The amounts for sales returns and allowances, purchases, and all of the expenses were extended to the Income Statement Debits column.

The Income Statement columns were totaled. The difference between the totals of these columns is the amount of the increase or the decrease in owner's equity due to net income or net loss during the accounting period. If the total of the credits exceeds the total of the debits, the difference represents the increase in owner's equity due to net income; if the total of the debits exceeds the total of the credits, the difference represents the decrease in owner's equity due to net loss.

Reference to the Income Statement columns of The Adams Appliance Store work sheet will show that the total of the credits amounted to

$151,853.67 and the total of the debits amounted to $142,110.96. The difference, amounting to $9,742.71, was the amount of the net income for the year.

Balance Sheet Columns. The fifth pair of amount columns of the work sheet was used to show the amounts that will be reported in the balance sheet. The Balance Sheet columns were totaled. The difference between the totals of these columns also is the amount of the net income or the net loss for the accounting period. If the total of the debits exceeds the total of the credits, the difference represents a net income for the accounting period; if the total of the credits exceeds the total of the debits, the difference represents a net loss for the period. This difference should be the same as the difference between the totals of the Income Statement columns.

Reference to the Balance Sheet columns of the work sheet will show that the total of the debits amounted to $67,813.57 and the total of the credits amounted to $58,070.86. The difference of $9,742.71 represented the amount of the net income for the year.

Completing the Work Sheet. The difference between the totals of the Income Statement columns and the totals of the Balance Sheet columns should be recorded on the next horizontal line below the totals. If the difference represents net income, it should be so designated and recorded in the Income Statement Debits and in the Balance Sheet Credits columns. If, instead, a net loss has been the result, the amount should be so designated and entered in the Income Statement Credits and in the Balance Sheet Debits columns. Finally, the totals of the Income Statement and Balance Sheet columns, after the net income (or net loss) has been recorded, are entered, and a double line is ruled immediately below the totals.

Proving the Work Sheet. The work sheet provides proof of the arithmetical accuracy of the data it summarizes. The totals of the Trial Balance columns, the Adjustments columns, and the Adjusted Trial Balance columns must be equal in each case. The difference between the totals of the Income Statement columns must be exactly the same as the amount of the difference between the totals of the Balance Sheet columns.

The reason why the same amount must be inserted to cause both the Income Statement columns and the Balance Sheet columns to be in balance was mentioned in Chapter 5. Stated slightly differently, the explanation is found in the basic difference between the balance sheet accounts and the income statement accounts, and in an understanding of the real nature of net income (or net loss). The reality of net income is that the assets have increased, or that the liabilities have decreased, or that some combination of both events has taken place during a period of time. Day by day most of these changes have been recorded in the asset and liability accounts in order that they may be kept up-to-date. However, the effect of the changes on the owner's equity element is not recorded in the permanent owner's equity account. Instead, the changes are recorded in the temporary owner's equity accounts — the revenue and expense accounts.

Thus, at the end of the period after the accounts have been adjusted, each of the asset and liability accounts reflects the amount of that element *at the end of the period.* If, however, there have been no capital investments during the period and any withdrawals have been charged to a drawing account, the balance of the owner's capital account is the amount of his equity *at the beginning of the period.* (All of the changes in owner's equity are shown in the revenue and expense accounts and in the drawing account.)

As applied to the work sheet, this must mean that the Balance Sheet column totals are out of balance by the amount of the change in owner's equity that is due to net income or net loss for the period involved. If there was net income, the assets, in total, are either that much larger, or the liabilities are that much smaller, or some combination of such changes has resulted. In other words, the asset and liability accounts reflect the net income of the period, but the owner's capital account, at this point, does not. It is only after the temporary accounts are closed at the end of the period and the net amount of the income for the period has been transferred to the owner's capital account that the latter account reflects the net income of the period.

The owner's capital account lacks two things to bring its balance up-to-date (like the balances of the asset and liability accounts): **(1)** the decrease due to any withdrawals during the period which is reflected in the debit balance of the drawing account and **(2)** the increase due to any net income for the period. On the work sheet the debit balance of the drawing account is extended to the Balance Sheet Debits column. Thus, all that is needed to cause the Balance Sheet columns to be equal is the amount of the net income for the year — the same amount that is the difference between the totals of the Income Statement columns.

Report No. 17

Complete Report No. 17 in the workbook and submit your working papers to the instructor for approval. After completing the report, continue with the following study assignment until the next report is required.

the financial statements

The financial statements usually consist of **(1)** an income statement and **(2)** a balance sheet. The purpose of an income statement is to summarize the results of operations during an accounting period. The income statement provides information as to the sources of revenue, types of expenses, and the amount of the net income or the net loss for the period. The purpose of a balance sheet is to provide information as to the status of a business at a specified date. The balance sheet shows the kinds and amounts of assets and liabilities and the owner's equity in the business at a specified point of time — usually at the close of business on the last day of the accounting period.

The Income Statement

A formal statement of the results of the operation of a business during an accounting period is called an *income statement*. Other titles commonly used for this statement include *profit and loss statement, income and expense statement, revenue and expense statement, operating statement,* and *report of earnings*. Whatever the title, the purpose of the statement or report is to show the types and amounts of revenue and expenses that the business had during the period involved, and the resulting net income or net loss for this accounting period.

Importance of the Income Statement. The income statement is now generally considered to be the most important financial statement of a business. A business cannot exist indefinitely unless it has profit or net income. The income statement is essentially a "report card" of the enterprise. The statement provides a basis for judging the overall effectiveness of the management. Decisions as to whether to continue a business, to expand it, or to contract it are often based upon the results as reported in the income statement. Actual and potential creditors are interested in income statements because one of the best reasons for extending credit or for making a loan is that the business is profitable.

Various government agencies are interested in income statements of businesses for a variety of reasons. Regulatory bodies are concerned with the earnings of the enterprises they regulate, because a part of the regulation usually relates to the prices, rates, or fares that may be charged. If the enterprise is either exceptionally profitable or unprofitable, some change in the allowed prices or rates may be needed. Income tax authorities, both federal and local, have an interest in business income statements. Net income determination for tax purposes differs somewhat from the calculation of net income for other purposes, but, for a variety of reasons, the tax authorities are interested in both sets of calculations.

Form of the Income Statement. The form of the income statement depends, in part, upon the type of business. For merchandising businesses, the so-called "ladder type" is commonly used. This name is applied because the final net income is calculated on a step-by-step basis. The amount of gross sales is shown first with sales returns and allowances deducted. The difference is *net sales*. Cost of goods sold is next subtracted to arrive at *gross margin* (sometimes called *gross profit*). The portion of the statement down to this point is sometimes called the "trading section." Operating expenses are next listed, and the total of their amounts is subtracted to arrive at the amount of the *net operating income*. Finally, the amounts of any "other" revenue are added and any "other" expenses are subtracted to arrive at the final amount of net income (or net loss).

It is essential that the statement be properly headed. The name of the business (or of the individual if a professional practice or if the owner operates a business in his own name) should be shown first. The name of the statement is then shown followed by the period of time that the statement covers. It is common practice to state this as, for example, "For the Year Ended December 31, 1967" (or whatever the period and ending date happen to be).

The income statement presented to the owner (or owners) of a business, and to potential creditors or other interested parties is usually in typewritten form. Very often, however, the accountant prepares the original statement in pencil or ink on ruled paper. This is used by the typist in preparing typewritten copies. The income statement for The Adams Appliance Store for the year ended December 31, 19--, is shown on page 240. The information needed in preparing the statement was obtained from the work sheet shown on pages 232 and 233.

Income Statement Analysis. There are various procedures employed to assist in the interpretation of income statements. One device is to present income statements for two or more comparable periods in comparative form. If the figures for two periods are shown in adjacent columns, a third column showing the amount of increase or decrease in each element may be shown. This will call attention to changes which may be of major significance.

Another analytical device is to express all, or at least the major, items on the statement as a percent of net sales and then compare these percent-

THE ADAMS APPLIANCE STORE
Income Statement
For the Year Ended December 31, 19__

Operating revenue:			
Sales............................			$119,184.12
Less sales returns and allowances..			367.40
Net sales.........................			$118,816.72
Cost of goods sold:			
Merchandise inventory, January 1....		$ 28,842.45	
Purchases......................	$74,249.08		
Less: Pur. returns and all.. $605.13			
Purchases discount.. 423.60	1,028.73		
Net purchases...................		73,220.35	
Merchandise available for sale......		$102,062.80	
Less merch. inv., December 31....		31,604.50	
Cost of goods sold.............			70,458.30
Gross margin on sales................			$ 48,358.42
Operating expenses:			
Rent expense....................		$ 6,000.00	
Depreciation expense..............		954.50	
Salaries and commissions expense....		22,776.57	
Payroll tax expense...............		1,192.83	
Heating and lighting expense.......		643.10	
Stationery and supplies expense.....		210.70	
Telephone and telegraph expense...		240.20	
Advertising expense...............		4,708.37	
Bad debts expense...............		461.25	
Insurance expense...............		215.55	
Truck expense....................		532.10	
Charitable contributions expense.....		285.00	
Miscellaneous expense.............		377.75	
Total operating expenses.........			38,597.92
Net operating income................			$ 9,760.50
Other expenses:			
Interest expense..................		$ 54.11	
Other revenue:			
Interest earned...................		36.32	17.79
Net income........................			$ 9,742.71

The Adams Appliance Store — Income Statement

ages for two or more periods. For example, if the net sales of $118,816.72 for The Adams Appliance Store for the year just ended are treated as 100 percent, the cost of goods sold which amounted to $70,458.30 was equal to 59 percent of net sales; the gross margin on sales which amounted to $48,358.42 was equal to 41 percent of net sales; operating expenses which amounted to $38,597.92 were equal to 32.5 percent of net sales; net operating income which amounted to $9,760.50 was equal to 8.21 percent of net sales; and net income which amounted to $9,742.71 was equal to 8.20 percent of net sales. A comparison of these percentages with the same data for one or more prior years would reveal trends that would surely be of interest, and perhaps of real concern, to the management of the business.

The Balance Sheet

A formal statement of the assets, liabilities, and owner's equity in a business at a specified date is known as a *balance sheet*. The title of the statement had its origin in the equality of the elements, that is, in the balance between the sum of the assets and the sum of the liabilities and owner's equity. Sometimes the balance sheet is called a *statement of assets and liabilities*, a *statement of condition*, or a *statement of financial position*. Various other titles are used occasionally.

Importance of the Balance Sheet. The balance sheet of a business is of considerable interest to various parties for several reasons. The owner or owners of a business are interested in the kinds and amounts of assets and liabilities, and the amount of the owner's equity or capital element.

Creditors of the business are interested in the financial condition of the enterprise, particularly as it pertains to the claims they have and the prospects for prompt payment. Potential creditors or possible lenders are concerned about the financial position of the business. Their decision as to whether to extend credit or to make loans to the business may depend, in large part, upon the condition of the enterprise as revealed by a balance sheet.

Persons considering buying an ownership interest in a business are greatly interested in the character and amount of the assets and liabilities, though this interest is probably secondary to their concern about the future earnings possibilities.

Finally, various regulatory bodies are interested in the financial condition of the businesses that are under their jurisdiction. Examples of regulated businesses include banks, insurance companies, public utilities, railroads, and airlines.

Assets

Current assets:

Cash..............................		$10,544.60
Notes receivable....................	$ 2,000.00	
Accrued interest receivable...........	4.17	
Accounts receivable.................	8,735.95	
Total receivables.................	$10,740.12	
Less allowance for bad debts........	661.70	10,078.42
Merchandise inventory...............		31,604.50
Prepaid insurance....................		215.55
Stationery and supplies..............		40.00
Total current assets................		$52,483.07

Long-lived assets:

Store equipment.....................	$ 2,520.00		
Less accumulated depreciation.......	855.00	$ 1,665.00	
Delivery equipment...................	$ 2,984.00		
Less accumulated depreciation.......	2,685.60	298.40	
Total long-lived assets.............			1,963.40
Total assets.........................			$54,446.47

The Adams Appliance Store — Balance Sheet (Left Side)

Form of the Balance Sheet. Traditionally, balance sheets have been presented either in *account form* or in *report form*. When the account form is followed, the assets are listed on the left side of the page (or on the left of two facing pages) and the liabilities and owner's equity on the right. This form is similar to the debit-side and credit-side arrangement of the standard ledger account. The balance sheet of The Adams Appliance Store as of December 31, 19--, in account form is reproduced above and on the opposite page. The data for the preparation of the statement were secured from the work sheet.

When the report form of the balance sheet is followed, the assets, liabilities, and owner's equity elements are exhibited in that order on the page. The balance sheet of Howard C. Miller, Architect, was shown in report form on page 120. This arrangement is generally superior when the statement is typed on regular letter-size paper (8½" x 11").

Whichever form is used, it is essential that the statement have the proper heading. This means that three things must be shown: **(1)** The name of the business must be given (or name of the individual if the business or

APPLIANCE STORE
Sheet
31, 19__

Liabilities

Current liabilities:

Notes payable.....................	$ 863.90	
Accrued interest payable.............	8.06	
Accounts payable....................	4,481.80	
Sales tax payable...................	398.68	
FICA taxes payable..................	65.24	
Employees' income taxes payable.....	180.30	
FUTA taxes payable................	52.80	
State unemployment taxes payable....	28.36	
Total current liabilities.............		$ 6,079.14

Owner's Equity

R. L. Adams, capital:

Capital, January 1..................		$47,789.42	
Net income........................	$ 9,742.71		
Less withdrawals...................	9,164.80	577.91	
Capital, December 31			48,367.33

Total liabilities and owner's equity....... $54,446.47

The Adams Appliance Store — Balance Sheet (Right Side)

professional practice is carried on in the name of an individual), followed by **(2)** the name of the statement — usually just "Balance Sheet," and finally **(3)** the date — month, day, and year. Sometimes the expression "As of Close of Business December 31, 1967" (or whatever date is involved) is included. It must be remembered that a balance sheet relates to a particular moment of time.

Classification of Data in the Balance Sheet. The purpose of the balance sheet and of all other financial statements and reports is to convey as much information as possible. This aim is furthered by some classification of the data being reported. As applied to balance sheets, it has become almost universal practice to classify both assets and liabilities as between those that are considered "current" and those that are considered "noncurrent" or "long-lived."

Current Assets. *Current assets* include cash and all other assets that may be reasonably expected to be realized in cash or sold or consumed during the normal operating cycle of the business. In a merchandising business the current assets usually will include cash, receivables, such as notes and accounts receivable, merchandise inventory, and temporary investments. Prepaid expenses, such as unexpired insurance and unused stationery and supplies, are also generally treated as current assets. This is not because such items will be realized in cash, but because they will probably be consumed in a relatively short time.

The asset cash may be represented by one or more accounts, such as bank checking accounts, bank savings accounts, or a petty cash fund. Reference to The Adams Appliance Store balance sheet will show that cash is listed at $10,544.60. Reference to the work sheet will show that this is made up of two items: the balance in the checking account at the Columbia National Bank, $10,419.60, and the amount of the petty cash fund, $125.

Temporary investments refer to those assets that have been acquired with money that would otherwise have been temporarily idle and unproductive. Such investments usually take the form of corporate stocks, bonds, or notes, or any of several types of government bonds. Quite often the policy is to invest in securities that can be liquidated in a short time with little chance of loss. So-called *marketable securities* are often favored. Assets of the same type may be owned by a business for many years, and, under such circumstances, they would not be classified as temporary investments. It is the matter of intention that indicates whether the investments are to be classified as temporary and included in the current assets or considered as long-term investments and either be included in the long-lived asset classification or in a separate classification entitled *Permanent Investments*.

Reference to the balance sheet of The Adams Appliance Store on pages 242 and 243 reveals that the current assets of this business consisted of cash, notes receivable, accrued interest receivable, accounts receivable, merchandise inventory, prepaid insurance, and stationery and supplies.

Long-Lived Assets. Property that is used in the operation of a merchandising business may include such assets as land, buildings, office equipment, store equipment, and delivery equipment. Such assets are called *long-lived assets*. Of these assets only land is really permanent; however, all of these assets have a useful life that is comparatively long.

Reference to the balance sheet of The Adams Appliance Store will show that the long-lived assets of the business consist of store equipment and delivery equipment. In each case, the amount of the accumulated depreciation is shown as a deduction from the cost of the equipment. The difference represents the *book value* of the equipment. This is the amount that will be written off as depreciation expense in future periods.

Current Liabilities.   *Current liabilities* include those obligations that will be due in a short time and paid with monies provided by the current assets. As of December 31, the current liabilities of The Adams Appliance Store consisted of notes payable, accrued interest payable, accounts payable, sales tax payable, FICA taxes payable, employees' income taxes payable, FUTA taxes payable, and state unemployment taxes payable.

Long-Term Liabilities.   *Long-term liabilities* (sometimes called *fixed liabilities*) include those obligations that will not be due for a relatively long time.   The most common of the long-term liabilities is mortgages payable.

A mortgage payable is a debt or an obligation that is secured by a *mortgage*, which provides for the conveyance of certain property upon failure to pay the debt at maturity.   When the debt is paid, the mortgage becomes void.   It will be seen, therefore, that a mortgage payable differs little from an account payable or a note payable except that the creditor holds the mortgage as security for the payment of the debt.   Usually debts secured by mortgages run for a longer period of time than ordinary notes payable or accounts payable.   A mortgage payable should be classified as a long-term liability if the maturity date extends beyond the normal operating cycle of the business (usually a year).   The Adams Appliance Store has no long-term liabilities.

Owner's Equity.   As previously explained, accounts relating to the owner's equity element may be either permanent or temporary owner's equity accounts.   The permanent owner's equity accounts used in recording the operations of a particular enterprise depend upon the type of legal organization, that is, whether the enterprise is organized as a sole proprietorship, as a partnership, or as a corporation.

In the case of a sole proprietorship, one or more accounts representing the owner's interest or equity in the assets may be kept.   Reference to the chart of accounts, shown on page 189, will reveal that the following accounts are classified as owner's equity accounts:

Account No. 310, R. L. Adams, Capital
Account No. 031, R. L. Adams, Drawing
Account No. 320, Expense and Revenue Summary

Account No. 310 reflects the amount of Mr. Adams' equity.   It may be increased by additional investments or by the practice of not withdrawing cash or other assets in an amount as large as the net income of the enterprise; it may be decreased by withdrawals in excess of the amount of the net income or by sustaining a net loss during one or more accounting periods.   Usually there will be no changes in the balance of this account during the accounting period, in which case the balance represents the owner's investment in the business as of the beginning of the accounting period and until such time as the books are closed at the end of the accounting period.

Account No. 031 is Mr. Adams' drawing account. This account is charged for any withdrawals of cash or other property for personal use. It is a temporary account in which is kept a record of the owner's personal drawings during the accounting period. Ordinarily such drawings are made in anticipation of earnings rather than as withdrawals of capital. The balance of the account, as shown by the trial balance at the close of an accounting period, represents the total amount of the owner's drawings during the period.

Reference to the work sheet shown on pages 232 and 233 will reveal that the balance of Mr. Adams' drawing account is listed in the Balance Sheet Debits column. This is because there is no provision on a work sheet for making deductions from owner's equity except by listing them in the Debits column. Since the balance of the owner's capital account is listed in the Balance Sheet Credits column, the listing of the balance of the owner's drawing account in the Debits column is equivalent to deducting the amount from the balance of the owner's capital account.

Account No. 320 is used only at the close of the accounting period for the purpose of summarizing the temporary owner's equity accounts. Sometimes this account is referred to as a *clearing account*. No entries should appear in the account before the books are closed at the end of the accounting period.

The owner's equity section of the balance sheet of The Adams Appliance Store is arranged to show the major changes that took place during the year in the owner's equity element of the business. Mr. Adams' interest in the business amounted to $47,789.42 at the beginning of the period. His interest was increased $9,742.71 as the result of profitable operations, and decreased $9,164.80 as the result of withdrawals during the year. Thus, the owner's equity element of the business on December 31 amounted to $48,367.33.

Balance Sheet Analysis. The information provided by a balance sheet can be analyzed in several ways to assist in judging the financial condition and soundness of the business. A few of the major analytical procedures will be briefly considered.

A balance sheet as of one date may be compared with a balance sheet as of another date to determine the amount of the increase or the decrease in any of the accounts or groups of accounts. Sometimes balance sheets as of two or more dates are prepared in comparative form by listing the amounts as of different dates in parallel columns. Thus, if balance sheets as of the close of two succeeding calendar years are compared, it is possible to determine the amount of the increase or the decrease during the intervening period in any of the accounts or groups of accounts involved. If such a comparison reveals an increase in accounts receivable, it may indicate that collections during the later period were not as favorable as they were during the preceding period. If the comparison reveals an increase in accounts payable, it may indicate an inability to pay current bills because of insufficient cash. If the comparison reveals an increase in the current assets without a corresponding increase in the liabilities, it may indicate an improved financial position or status.

Too much emphasis should not be placed upon an increase or a decrease in cash. Some individuals are inclined to judge the results of operations largely by the cash balance. This practice may be misleading. The net results of operations can be properly determined only by comparison of all the assets and the liabilities. The ability of a business to meet its current obligations may be determined largely by an analysis of its current assets, particularly those assets that are sometimes referred to as the quick assets. *Quick assets* include cash and all other current assets that are readily realizable in cash, such as temporary investments in the form of marketable securities.

The relation of an account, a group of accounts, or an accounting element to another account, group of accounts, or accounting element may be referred to as the *ratio*. For example, if the total current assets amount to twice as much as the total current liabilities, the ratio is said to be 2 to 1. Ratios may be expressed in percentages or on a unit basis. Fractions of units may be expressed by means of common fractions or decimals as, for example, 7¾ to 1 or 7.75 to 1.

In an enterprise in which capital invested is a material revenue-producing factor, such as is the case in a merchandising enterprise, the ratio of the current assets to the current liabilities may be important. Reference to the balance sheet shown on pages 242 and 243 reveals that the total current assets amount to $52,483.07 and the total current liabilities amount to $6,079.14, a ratio of a little over 8½ to 1. The total assets amount to $54,446.47 and the total liabilities amount to $6,079.14, a ratio of almost 9 to 1. These ratios are sufficiently high to indicate a very favorable financial condition.

Banks often consider the ratio of current assets to current liabilities when considering the advisability of making a loan. It is not expected that the long-lived assets will be sold to realize sufficient funds with which to pay a short-term loan. If the balance sheet seems to indicate that a sufficient amount of cash will not be realized from the collection of accounts receivable or from the sales of service or merchandise to repay a loan at maturity, the bank may consider the loan inadvisable. The excess of the amount of the current assets over the amount of the current liabilities is called *net current assets* or *working capital*.

It is difficult to estimate what the proper ratio of current assets to current liabilities should be, because of the variations in enterprises and industries. A 2 to 1 ratio of current assets to current liabilities may be more than sufficient in some enterprises but entirely insufficient in others. In the milk distributing business, for example, a 1 to 1 ratio of current assets to current liabilities is considered satisfactory. The reasons are that very little capital is tied up in inventory, the amount of accounts receivable is comparatively small, and the terms on which the milk is purchased from farmers are such that settlements are slow and comparatively large amounts are due to farmers at all times. Another reason is that a large amount of capital is invested in long-lived assets, such as equipment for treating the milk and for delivering it to customers.

Generally speaking, the ratio of the current assets to the current liabilities should be maintained in a range from 2 to 1 to 5 to 1. While a standard ratio cannot be established for all enterprises, a knowledge of the working capital requirements of a particular enterprise will be helpful in determining what the ratio of current assets to current liabilities should be.

A comparison of the relationships between certain amounts in the income statement and certain amounts in the balance sheet may be informative. The leading example of this type is the ratio of net income to owner's equity in the business. The owner's equity of The Adams Appliance Store was $47,789.42 on January 1. The net income for the year of $9,742.71 was over 20 percent of this amount. A comparison of this ratio with the ratio of net income to capital invested in prior years should be of interest to the owner. It may also be of interest to compare the ratio of the net income of The Adams Appliance Store to the amount of capital invested by Mr. Adams with the same ratio for others stores of comparable nature and size. It is important to note, however, that the net income of The Adams Appliance Store was computed without regard to any salary or other compensation for the services of Mr. Adams.

Inventory Turnover

A merchant is usually interested in knowing the rate of *inventory turnover* for each accounting period. This has reference to the number of times the merchandise available for sale is turned during the accounting period. The rate of turnover is found by dividing the cost of goods sold for the period by the average inventory. Where an inventory is taken only at the end of each accounting period, the average inventory for the period may be found by adding the beginning and ending inventories together and dividing by two. The turnover of The Adams Appliance Store for the year ended December 31 may be computed as follows:

Beginning inventory..	$28,842.45
Ending inventory..	31,604.50
Cost of goods sold for the period.................................	70,458.30

$28,842.45 + $31,604.50 ÷ 2 = $30,223.48, average inventory
$70,458.30 ÷ $30,223.48 = 2.33, rate of turnover

This calculation indicates that, on the average, the merchandise turns over a little more often than once every six months. A careful analysis of the theory involved in computing the rate of turnover will indicate that the greater the turnover the smaller the margin need be on each dollar of sales in order to produce a satisfactory total gross margin on sales.

Report No. 18

Complete Report No. 18 in the workbook and submit your working papers to the instructor for approval. After completing the report, you may continue with the textbook discussion in Chapter 10 until the next report is required.

chapter ten

adjusting and closing accounts at end of accounting period

As explained in the preceding chapter, the adjustment of certain accounts at the end of the accounting period is required because of changes that have occurred during the period that are not reflected in the accounts. Since the purpose of the temporary owner's equity accounts is to assemble information relating to a specified period of time, at the end of the period the balances of these accounts must be removed to cause the accounts to be ready to perform their function in the following period. Accounts of this type must be "closed."

adjusting entries

In preparing the work sheet for The Adams Appliance Store (reproduced on pages 232 and 233), adjustments were made to accomplish the
following purposes:

    (a) To transfer the amount of the merchandise inventory at the beginning of
the accounting period to the expense and revenue summary.

    (b) To record the calculated cost of the merchandise inventory at the end of
the accounting period.

    (c) To record the amount of interest accrued on notes receivable.

    (d) To record the amount of interest accrued on notes payable.

    (e) To record the amount of insurance premium expired during the year.

    (f) To record the cost of stationery and supplies used during the year.

    (g) To record the estimated amount of depreciation of long-lived assets for
the year.

    (h) To record the amount of bad debt losses expected to result from the sales
on account made during the year.

The effect of these adjustments was reflected in the financial statements
reproduced on pages 240, 242, and 243. To bring the ledger into agreement
with the financial statements, the adjustments should be recorded in the
proper accounts. It is customary, therefore, at the end of each accounting
period to journalize the adjustments and to post them to the accounts.

Journalizing the Adjusting Entries

Adjusting entries may be recorded in either a general journal or a combined cash journal. If the entries are made in a combined cash journal, the
only amount columns used are the General Debits and Credits columns.
A portion of a page of a combined cash journal showing the adjusting
entries of The Adams Appliance Store is reproduced on page 252. It should
be noted that when the adjusting entries are recorded in the combined cash
journal, they are entered in exactly the same manner as they would be
entered in a general journal. Since the heading "Adjusting Entries" explains the nature of the entries, a separate explanation of each adjusting
entry is unnecessary. The information needed in journalizing the adjustments was obtained from the Adjustments columns of the work sheet
reproduced on pages 232 and 233. The account numbers were not entered

in the Posting Reference column at the time of journalizing; they were entered as the posting was completed.

COMBINED CASH JOURNAL FOR MONTH OF *December* 19 —   PAGE 49

| DATE | | DESCRIPTION | POST. REF. | GENERAL | |
MO.	DAY			DEBITS	CREDITS
		AMOUNTS FORWARDED			
Dec.	31	*Adjusting Entries*			
		Expense and Revenue Summary	320	2 8 8 4 2 4 5	
		Merchandise Inventory	130		2 8 8 4 2 4 5
		Merchandise Inventory	130	3 1 6 0 4 5 0	
		Expense and Revenue Summary	320		3 1 6 0 4 5 0
		Accrued Interest Receivable	122	4 1 7	
		Interest Earned	710		4 1 7
		Interest Expense	810	8 0 6	
		Accrued Interest Payable	220		8 0 6
		Insurance Expense	619	2 1 5 5 5	
		Prepaid Insurance	140		2 1 5 5 5
		Stationery and Supplies Expense	615	2 1 0 7 0	
		Stationery and Supplies	150		2 1 0 7 0
		Depreciation Expense	611	9 5 4 5 0	
		Accum. Deprec.-Store Equip.	0180		2 0 8 5 0
		Accum. Deprec.-Del. Equip.	0190		7 4 6 0 0
		Bad Debts Expense	618	4 6 1 2 5	
		Allowance for Bad Debts	0120		4 6 1 2 5
				6 2 3 0 1 1 8	6 2 3 0 1 1 8

The Adams Appliance Store — Adjusting Entries

Posting the Adjusting Entries

The adjusting entries should be posted individually to the proper general ledger accounts. The accounts of The Adams Appliance Store that were affected by the adjusting entries are reproduced in type on pages 253 and 254. The entries in the accounts for December transactions that were posted prior to posting the adjusting entries are the same as appeared in the accounts reproduced in script on pages 217–222. The number of the combined cash journal page on which the adjusting entries were recorded was entered in the Posting Reference column of the general ledger accounts affected, and the account numbers were entered in the Posting Reference column of the combined cash journal as the posting was completed. This provided a cross-reference in both books.

Ruling the Merchandise Inventory Account

After posting the adjusting entry required to transfer the amount of the beginning inventory to the expense and revenue summary account, the merchandise inventory account was in balance. Since there was only one amount recorded on each side of the account, it was ruled by drawing a double line below the amounts across all columns except the Items columns. In posting the entry to record the inventory at the end of the period, the debit to the merchandise inventory account was recorded on the next horizontal line below the double line.

ACCRUED INTEREST RECEIVABLE		Account No. 122
19-- Dec. 31	CJ49 4.17	

	ALLOWANCE FOR BAD DEBTS	Account No. 0120
	19-- Dec. 1 Balance	√ 200.45
	31	CJ49 461.25
		661.70

MERCHANDISE INVENTORY		Account No. 130
19-- Dec. 1 Balance √ 28,842.45	19-- Dec. 31	CJ49 28,842.45
Dec. 31 CJ49 31,604.50		

PREPAID INSURANCE		Account No. 140
19-- Dec. 1 Balance √ 431.10 215.55	19-- Dec. 31	CJ49 215.55

STATIONERY AND SUPPLIES		Account No. 150
19-- Dec. 1 Balance √ 223.22	19-- Dec. 31	CJ49 210.70
31 CJ48 27.48		
40.00 250.70		

ACCUMULATED DEPRECIATION — STORE EQUIPMENT		Account No. 0180
	19-- Dec. 1 Balance	√ 646.50
	31	CJ49 208.50
		855.00

ACCUMULATED DEPRECIATION — DELIVERY EQUIPMENT		Account No. 0190
	19-- Dec. 1 Balance	√ 1,939.60
	31	CJ49 746.00
		2,685.60

		ACCRUED INTEREST PAYABLE				Account No. 220
			19-- Dec. 31		CJ49	8.06

		EXPENSE AND REVENUE SUMMARY			Account No. 320
19-- Dec. 31 Beg. inventory	CJ49 28,842.45	19-- Dec. 31 End. inventory	CJ49 31,604.50

		DEPRECIATION EXPENSE		Account No. 611
19-- Dec. 31	CJ49 954.50		

		STATIONERY AND SUPPLIES EXPENSE		Account No. 615
19-- Dec. 31	CJ49 210.70		

		BAD DEBTS EXPENSE		Account No. 618
19-- Dec. 31	CJ49 461.25		

		INSURANCE EXPENSE		Account No. 619
19-- Dec. 31	CJ49 215.55		

		INTEREST EARNED		Account No. 710
		19-- Dec. 1 Balance 31	✓ CJ49	32.15 4.17 *36.32*

		INTEREST EXPENSE		Account No. 810
19-- Dec. 1 Balance 31	✓ CJ49	46.05 8.06 *54.11*	

Report No. 19

Complete Report No. 19 in the workbook and submit your working papers to the instructor for approval. Continue with the following study assignment until Report No. 20 is required.

closing procedure

After the adjusting entries have been posted, all of the temporary owner's equity accounts should be closed. This means that the accountant must remove ("close out") **(1)** the balance of every account that enters into the calculation of the net income (or net loss) for the accounting period and **(2)** the balance of the owner's drawing account. The purpose of the closing procedure is to transfer the balances of the temporary owner's equity accounts to the permanent owner's equity account. This could be accomplished simply by debiting or crediting each account involved, with an offsetting credit or debit to the permanent owner's equity account. However, it is considered better practice to transfer the balances of all accounts that enter into the net income or net loss determination to a summarizing account called Expense and Revenue Summary (sometimes called *Income Summary, Profit and Loss Summary*, or just *Profit and Loss*). Then, the resulting balance of the expense and revenue summary account (which will be the amount of the net income or net loss for the period) is transferred to the permanent owner's equity account.

The final step in the closing procedure is to transfer the balance of the owner's drawing account to the permanent owner's equity account. After this is done, only the asset accounts, the liability accounts, and the permanent owner's equity account have balances. If there has been no error, the sum of the balances of the asset accounts (less balances of any contra accounts) will be equal to the sum of the balances of the liability accounts plus the balance of the permanent owner's equity account. The accounts will agree exactly with what is shown by the balance sheet as of the close of the period. Reference to the balance sheet of The Adams Appliance Store reproduced on pages 242 and 243 will show that the assets, liabilities, and owner's equity as of December 31 may be expressed in equation form as follows:

$$\text{ASSETS} = \text{LIABILITIES} + \text{OWNER'S EQUITY}$$
$$\text{\$54,446.47} \qquad \text{\$6,079.14} \qquad \text{\$48,367.33}$$

Journalizing the Closing Entries

Closing entries, like adjusting entries, may be recorded in either a general journal or a combined cash journal. If the entries are made in a combined cash journal, only the General Debits and Credits columns are used. A portion of a page of a combined cash journal showing the closing entries for The Adams Appliance Store is reproduced on page 257. Since the heading "Closing Entries" explains the nature of the entries, a separate explanation of each closing entry is not necessary. The information required in preparing the closing entries was obtained from the work sheet illustrated on pages 232 and 233.

The first closing entry was made to close the sales, purchases returns and allowances, purchases discount, and interest earned accounts. Since these accounts have credit balances, each account must be debited for the amount of its balance in order to close it. The debits to these four accounts are offset by a credit of $120,249.17 to Expense and Revenue Summary.

The second closing entry was made to close the sales returns and allowances, purchases, and all of the expense accounts. Since these accounts have debit balances, each account must be credited for the amount of its balance in order to close it. The credits to these accounts are offset by a debit of $113,268.51 to Expense and Revenue Summary.

Since the posting of the first two adjusting entries and the first two closing entries causes the expense and revenue summary account to have a credit balance of $9,742.71 (the net income for the year), the account has served its purpose and must be closed. The third closing entry accomplishes this by debiting the expense and revenue summary account, with an offsetting credit to R. L. Adams, Capital, for $9,742.71.

The fourth closing entry was made to close the R. L. Adams drawing account. Since this account has a debit balance, it must be credited to close it. The offsetting entry is a debit of $9,164.80 to R. L. Adams, Capital.

The account numbers shown in the Posting Reference column were not entered at the time of journalizing the closing entries — they were entered as the posting was completed.

Posting the Closing Entries

Closing entries can be posted in the usual manner — that is, exactly as each journal entry indicates. However, if it is considered desirable to have the expense and revenue summary account provide the details of the expense and revenue elements it summarizes, posting to that account can be in detail with a notation of the nature of each amount. This "posting in detail" practice is followed in the case of The Adams Appliance Store. In any case, proper cross-references are provided by using the Posting Reference columns of the combined cash journal and the ledger accounts. After all the closing entries have been posted in the manner described, the accounts affected appear as shown on pages 259 to 262.

It may be observed that the first two adjusting entries described and illustrated earlier in the chapter actually qualify both as "adjusting" and as

DATE		DESCRIPTION	POST. REF.	GENERAL	
MO.	DAY			DEBITS	CREDITS
		AMOUNTS FORWARDED			
Dec.	31	Closing Entries			
		Sales	410	11 9 1 8 4 1 2	
		Purchases Returns and Allow.	0511	6 0 5 1 3	
		Purchases Discount	0512	4 2 3 6 0	
		Interest Earned	710	3 6 3 2	
		Expense and Revenue Summary	320		12 0 2 4 9 1 7
		Expense and Revenue Summary	320	11 3 2 6 8 5 1	
		Sales Returns and Allow.	0410		3 6 7 4 0
		Purchases	510		7 4 2 4 9 0 8
		Rent Expense	610		6 0 0 0 0 0
		Depreciation Expense	611		9 5 4 5 0
		Salaries and Commissions Exp.	612		2 2 7 7 6 5 7
		Payroll Tax Expense	613		1 1 9 2 8 3
		Heating and Lighting Exp.	614		6 4 3 1 0
		Stationery and Supplies Exp.	615		2 1 0 7 0
		Telephone and Telegraph Exp.	616		2 4 0 2 0
		Advertising Expense	617		4 7 0 8 3 7
		Bad Debts Expense	618		4 6 1 2 5
		Insurance Expense	619		2 1 5 5 5
		Truck Expense	620		5 3 2 1 0
		Charitable Contributions Exp.	621		2 8 5 0 0
		Miscellaneous Expense	622		3 7 7 7 5
		Interest Expense	810		5 4 1 1
		Expense and Revenue Summary	320	9 7 4 2 7 1	
		R. L. Adams, Capital	310		9 7 4 2 7 1
		R. L. Adams, Capital	310	9 1 6 4 8 0	
		R. L. Adams, Drawing	031		9 1 6 4 8 0
				25 2 4 2 5 1 9	25 2 4 2 5 1 9

"closing" entries. They serve to adjust the merchandise inventory account by removing the amount of the beginning inventory and by recording the amount of the ending inventory. They facilitate the closing process in that they cause two amounts that enter into the calculation of net income or net loss to be entered in the Expense and Revenue Summary. It matters little which descriptive term is applied; the important thing is to be sure that needed adjustments are made and that the temporary owner's equity accounts are closed as of the end of the accounting period.

Ruling the Closed Accounts

After posting the closing entries, all of the temporary owner's equity accounts of The Adams Appliance Store were in balance and they were ruled in the manner illustrated on pages 259 to 262. Following is the recommended procedure:

    (a) Where there are two or more items posted to either side of an account, foot the amounts to be sure that the total debits are equal to the total credits.

    (b) Rule a single line across the debit and credit amount columns immediately below the last amount entered on the side with the most entries.

    (c) Enter the totals of the debit and credit amount columns in ink on the next line.

    (d) Rule a double line immediately below the totals extending through all but the Items columns.

If an account has only one item on each side, double ruling is sufficient. Note the ruling of the account with Depreciation Expense on page 260. If an account page is not filled, it may be used for recording the transactions of the following period.

Balancing and Ruling Open Accounts

After the temporary owner's equity accounts have been closed, the open accounts may be balanced and ruled in order to prepare them to receive entries for the next accounting period. The open accounts include the asset accounts, the liability accounts, and the permanent owner's equity account. Prior to ruling an open account, its balance should be entered on the side which has the smaller total. The effect of this entry is to equalize the total debits and credits. The account should then be ruled with single and double lines in the manner shown on page 263. The balance should then be brought down below the ruling on the proper side of the account. However, if the page is filled, the balance may be carried forward to the top of a new page. In carrying the balance down or forward, as the case may be, care must be taken to be sure that it is entered on the side which originally had the larger total.

There is no need for balancing and ruling an open account that has entries on only one side of the account. To illustrate the procedure in balancing and ruling open accounts, the following accounts of The Adams Appliance Store are reproduced on page 263:

Columbia National Bank, Account No. 111
Accounts Payable, Account No. 230
R. L. Adams, Capital, Account No. 310

In the case of the account with the Columbia National Bank, the balance of the account, $10,419.60, was entered on the credit side, the totals

ACCOUNT R. L. Adams, Capital   ACCOUNT NO. 310

DATE	ITEMS	POST. REF.	✓	DEBITS	DATE	ITEMS	POST. REF.	✓	CREDITS
19– Dec. 31		CJ50		9 1 6 4 80	19– Dec. 1	Balance	✓		4 7 7 8 9 42
					31		CJ50		9 74 2 71

ACCOUNT R. L. Adams, Drawing   ACCOUNT NO. 031

DATE	ITEMS	POST. REF.	✓	DEBITS	DATE	ITEMS	POST. REF.	✓	CREDITS
19– Dec. 1	Balance	✓		8 1 5 4 80	19– Dec. 31		CJ50		9 1 6 4 80
21		CJ47		1 0 0 0 00					
31		CJ48		1 0 00					
				9 1 6 4 80					
				9 1 6 4 80					9 1 6 4 80

ACCOUNT Expense and Revenue Summary   ACCOUNT NO. 320

DATE	ITEMS	POST. REF.	✓	DEBITS	DATE	ITEMS	POST. REF.	✓	CREDITS
19– Dec. 31	Beg. inventory	CJ49		2 8 8 4 2 45	19– Dec. 31	End. inventory	CJ49		3 1 6 0 4 50
31	Sales R + A.	CJ50		3 6 7 40	31	Sales	CJ50		11 9 1 8 4 12
31	Purchases	CJ50		7 4 2 4 9 08	31	Pur. R + A.	CJ50		6 0 5 13
31	Rent Exp.	CJ50		6 0 0 0 00	31	Purch. Disc.	CJ50		4 2 3 60
31	Depr. Exp.	CJ50		9 5 4 50	31	Int. Earned	CJ50		3 6 32
31	Sal + Com. Exp.	CJ50		2 2 7 7 6 57					15 1 8 5 3 67
31	Pay. Tax Exp.	CJ50		1 1 9 2 83					
31	Htg + Ltg. Exp.	CJ50		6 4 3 10					
31	Sto. + Sup. Exp.	CJ50		7 1 0 70					
31	Tel + Tel. Exp.	CJ50		2 4 0 20					
31	Adv. Exp.	CJ50		4 7 0 8 37					
31	Bad Debts Exp.	CJ50		4 6 1 25					
31	Ins. Exp.	CJ50		2 1 5 55					
31	Truck Exp.	CJ50		5 3 2 10					
31	Char. Cont. Exp.	CJ50		2 8 5 00					
31	Misc. Exp.	CJ50		3 7 7 75					
31	Int. Exp.	CJ50		5 4 11					
31	R. L. Adams Cap.	CJ50		14 2 1 0 96 9 74 2 71					
				15 1 8 5 3 67					
				15 1 8 5 3 67					15 1 8 5 3 67

ACCOUNT Sales   ACCOUNT NO. 410

DATE	ITEMS	POST. REF.	✓	DEBITS	DATE	ITEMS	POST. REF.	✓	CREDITS
19– Dec. 31		CJ50		11 9 1 8 4 12	19– Dec. 1	Balance	✓		10 5 8 3 5 52
					31		CJ48		6 4 9 1 85
					31		S44		6 8 5 6 75
									11 9 1 8 4 12
				11 9 1 8 4 12					11 9 1 8 4 12

The Adams Appliance Store — Partial General Ledger

ACCOUNT *Sales Returns and Allowances*   ACCOUNT NO. 0410

DATE	ITEMS	POST. REF.	✓	DEBITS	DATE	ITEMS	POST. REF.	✓	CREDITS
19— Dec. 1	Balance	✓		307 65	19— Dec. 31		CJ50		367 40
27		CJ47		59 75					
				~~367 40~~					
				367 40					367 40

ACCOUNT *Purchases*   ACCOUNT NO. 510

DATE	ITEMS	POST. REF.	✓	DEBITS	DATE	ITEMS	POST. REF.	✓	CREDITS
19— Dec. 1	Balance	✓		68911 14	19— Dec. 31		CJ50		74249 08
2		CJ47		42 19					
31		P32		5295 75					
				~~74249 08~~					
				74249 08					74249 08

ACCOUNT *Purchases Returns and Allowances*   ACCOUNT NO. 0511

DATE	ITEMS	POST. REF.	✓	DEBITS	DATE	ITEMS	POST. REF.	✓	CREDITS
19— Dec. 31		CJ50		605 13	19— Dec. 1	Balance	✓		565 13
					20		CJ47		40 00
									~~605 13~~
				605 13					605 13

ACCOUNT *Purchases Discount*   ACCOUNT NO. 0512

DATE	ITEMS	POST. REF.	✓	DEBITS	DATE	ITEMS	POST. REF.	✓	CREDITS
19— Dec. 31		CJ50		423 60	19— Dec. 1	Balance	✓		403 76
					23		CJ47		19 84
									~~423 60~~
				423 60					423 60

ACCOUNT *Rent Expense*   ACCOUNT NO. 610

DATE	ITEMS	POST. REF.	✓	DEBITS	DATE	ITEMS	POST. REF.	✓	CREDITS
19— Dec. 1	Balance	✓		5500 00	19— Dec. 31		CJ50		6000 00
2		CJ47		500 00					
				~~6000 00~~					
				6000 00					6000 00

ACCOUNT *Depreciation Expense*   ACCOUNT NO. 611

DATE	ITEMS	POST. REF.	✓	DEBITS	DATE	ITEMS	POST. REF.	✓	CREDITS
19— Dec. 31		CJ49		954 50	19— Dec. 31		CJ50		954 50

The Adams Appliance Store — Partial General Ledger (Continued)

ACCOUNT *Salaries and Commissions Expense*   ACCOUNT NO. 612

DATE	ITEMS	POST. REF.	✓	DEBITS	DATE	ITEMS	POST. REF.	✓	CREDITS
19— Dec. 1	Balance	✓		20 828 94	19— Dec. 31		CJ50		22 776 57
14		CJ47		925 96					
31		CJ48		1 021 67					
				22 776 57					
				22 776 57					22 776 57

ACCOUNT *Payroll Tax Expense*   ACCOUNT NO. 613

DATE	ITEMS	POST. REF.	✓	DEBITS	DATE	ITEMS	POST. REF.	✓	CREDITS
19— Dec. 1	Balance	✓		1 149 35	19— Dec. 31		CJ50		1 192 83
14		CJ47		21 74					
31		CJ48		21 74					
				1 192 83					
				1 192 83					1 192 83

ACCOUNT *Heating and Lighting Expense*   ACCOUNT NO. 614

DATE	ITEMS	POST. REF.	✓	DEBITS	DATE	ITEMS	POST. REF.	✓	CREDITS
19— Dec. 1	Balance	✓		578 20	19— Dec. 31		CJ50		643 10
28		CJ47		64 90					
				643 10					
				643 10					643 10

ACCOUNT *Stationery and Supplies Expense*   ACCOUNT NO. 615

DATE	ITEMS	POST. REF.	✓	DEBITS	DATE	ITEMS	POST. REF.	✓	CREDITS
19— Dec. 31		CJ49		210 70	19— Dec. 31		CJ50		210 70

ACCOUNT *Telephone and Telegraph Expense*   ACCOUNT NO. 616

DATE	ITEMS	POST. REF.	✓	DEBITS	DATE	ITEMS	POST. REF.	✓	CREDITS
19— Dec. 1	Balance	✓		217 15	19— Dec. 31		CJ50		240 20
28		CJ47		21 65					
31		CJ48		1 40					
				240 20					
				240 20					240 20

ACCOUNT *Advertising Expense*   ACCOUNT NO. 617

DATE	ITEMS	POST. REF.	✓	DEBITS	DATE	ITEMS	POST. REF.	✓	CREDITS
19— Dec. 1	Balance	✓		4 261 80	19— Dec. 31		CJ50		4 708 37
6		CJ47		53 37					
27		CJ47		382 40					
31		CJ48		10 80					
				4 708 37					
				4 708 37					4 708 37

The Adams Appliance Store — Partial General Ledger (Continued)

ACCOUNT Bad Debts Expense — ACCOUNT NO. 618

DATE	ITEMS	POST. REF.	✓	DEBITS	DATE	ITEMS	POST. REF.	✓	CREDITS
19— Dec. 31		CJ49		461 25	19— Dec. 31		CJ50		461 25

ACCOUNT Insurance Expense — ACCOUNT NO. 619

DATE	ITEMS	POST. REF.	✓	DEBITS	DATE	ITEMS	POST. REF.	✓	CREDITS
19— Dec. 31		CJ49		215 55	19— Dec. 31		CJ50		215 55

ACCOUNT Truck Expense — ACCOUNT NO. 620

DATE	ITEMS	POST. REF.	✓	DEBITS	DATE	ITEMS	POST. REF.	✓	CREDITS
19— Dec. 1	Balance	✓	473 60	19— Dec. 31		CJ50		532 10
18		CJ47		58 50					
				532 10					
				532 10					532 10

ACCOUNT Charitable Contributions Expense — ACCOUNT NO. 621

DATE	ITEMS	POST. REF.	✓	DEBITS	DATE	ITEMS	POST. REF.	✓	CREDITS
19— Dec. 1	Balance	✓	280 00	19— Dec. 31		CJ50		285 00
31		CJ48		5 00					
				285 00					
				285 00					285 00

ACCOUNT Miscellaneous Expense — ACCOUNT NO. 622

DATE	ITEMS	POST. REF.	✓	DEBITS	DATE	ITEMS	POST. REF.	✓	CREDITS
19— Dec. 1	Balance	✓	371 10	19— Dec. 31		CJ50		377 75
31		CJ48		6 65					
				377 75					
				377 75					377 75

ACCOUNT Interest Earned — ACCOUNT NO. 710

DATE	ITEMS	POST. REF.	✓	DEBITS	DATE	ITEMS	POST. REF.	✓	CREDITS
19— Dec. 31		CJ50		36 32	19— Dec. 1	Balance	✓		32 15
					31		CJ49		4 17
									36 32
				36 32					36 32

ACCOUNT Interest Expense — ACCOUNT NO. 810

DATE	ITEMS	POST. REF.	✓	DEBITS	DATE	ITEMS	POST. REF.	✓	CREDITS
19— Dec. 1	Balance	✓	46 05	19— Dec. 31		CJ50		54 11
31		CJ49		8 06					
				54 11					
				54 11					54 11

The Adams Appliance Store — Partial General Ledger (Concluded)

were entered in ink, the account was ruled with single and double lines, and the balance was brought down below the ruling on the debit side. Note that in bringing the December 31 balance down below the ruling, it was entered as of January 1 to indicate that it was the balance at the beginning of a new accounting period.

In the case of Accounts Payable, the balance, $4,481.80, was entered on the debit side, the totals were entered in ink, the account was ruled with single and double lines, and the balance was brought down below the ruling on the credit side as of January 1.

In the case of R. L. Adams, Capital, the balance, $48,367.33, was entered on the debit side, the totals were entered in ink, the account was ruled with single and double lines, and the balance was brought down below the ruling on the credit side as of January 1. The balance represents the owner's equity in the business on that date.

ACCOUNT Columbia National Bank   ACCOUNT NO. 111

DATE	ITEMS	POST. REF.	✓	DEBITS	DATE	ITEMS	POST. REF.	✓	CREDITS
19— Dec. 1	Balance	✓		865359	19— Dec. 31		CJ48		899931
31	10,419.60	CJ48		1076532 / 1941891	31	Balance	✓		1041960 / 1941891
19— Jan. 1	Balance	✓		1041960					

ACCOUNT Accounts Payable   ACCOUNT NO. 230

DATE	ITEMS	POST. REF.	✓	DEBITS	DATE	ITEMS	POST. REF.	✓	CREDITS
19— Dec. 31		CJ48		407575	19— Dec. 1	Balance	✓		212680
31	Balance	✓		448180 / 855755	31		CJ48		43500
				855755	31		P32	4,481.80	529575 / 855755
					19— Jan. 1	Balance	✓		448180

ACCOUNT R. L. Adams, Capital   ACCOUNT NO. 310

DATE	ITEMS	POST. REF.	✓	DEBITS	DATE	ITEMS	POST. REF.	✓	CREDITS
19— Dec. 31		CJ50		916480	19— Dec. 1	Balance	✓		4778942
31	Balance	✓		4836733 / 5753213	31		CJ50		974271 / 5753213
					19— Jan. 1	Balance			4836733

The Adams Appliance Store — Balancing and Ruling Open Accounts

At one time it was common practice to use *red ink* in balancing and ruling accounts. Any losses were also entered in red ink. This was the origin of the expression "in the red" to describe a loss.

Sometimes a balance-column account form is used for the general ledger accounts. In such case, the balance of each account is entered after each amount is posted. When an account is in balance, either a horizontal line or the symbol "–0–" is entered in the Balance column and no ruling of the account is required.

Trial Balance After Closing

A trial balance of the general ledger accounts that remain open after the temporary owner's equity accounts have been closed is usually referred to as a *post-closing trial balance*. The purpose of the post-closing trial balance is to prove that the general ledger is in balance at the beginning of a new accounting period. It is advisable to know that such is the case before any transactions for the new accounting period are recorded.

The post-closing trial balance should contain the same accounts and amounts as appear in the Balance Sheet columns of the work sheet, except that **(1)** the owner's drawing account is omitted because it has been closed, and **(2)** the owner's capital account has been adjusted for the amount of the net income (or net loss) and the amount of his drawings.

A post-closing trial balance of the general ledger of The Adams Appliance Store is shown on the next page. Some accountants advocate that the post-closing trial balance should be dated as of the close of the old accounting period, while others advocate that it should be dated as of the beginning of the new accounting period. In this illustration the trial balance is dated December 31, the end of the period.

Reversing Entries for Accrual Adjustments

In addition to balancing and ruling the open accounts at the close of an accounting period to make ready for recording the transactions of the succeeding accounting period, many accountants reverse the adjusting entries for accruals. The purpose of such reversing entries (sometimes called "readjusting entries") is to make possible the recording of the transactions of the succeeding accounting period in a routine manner and to assure that the proper amount of revenue will be credited to the period in which earned and that the proper amount of expenses will be charged to the period in which incurred.

When cash is received in payment of interest, the routine manner of recording the transaction is to debit Cash (or Bank) and to credit Interest

THE ADAMS APPLIANCE STORE
Post-Closing Trial Balance
December 31, 19--

Account	Acct. No.	Dr. Balance	Cr. Balance
Columbia National Bank...................	111	$10,419.60	
Petty Cash Fund...........................	112	125.00	
Notes Receivable.........................	121	2,000.00	
Accrued Interest Receivable...............	122	4.17	
Accounts Receivable......................	123	8,735.95	
Allowance for Bad Debts..................	0120		$ 661.70
Merchandise Inventory....................	130	31,604.50	
Prepaid Insurance........................	140	215.55	
Stationery and Supplies...................	150	40.00	
Store Equipment..........................	180	2,520.00	
Accumulated Depr. — Store Equipment.......	0180		855.00
Delivery Equipment.......................	190	2,984.00	
Accumulated Depr. — Delivery Equipment.....	0190		2,685.60
Notes Payable...........................	210		863.90
Accrued Interest Payable.................	220		8.06
Accounts Payable........................	230		4,481.80
Sales Tax Payable........................	240		398.68
FICA Taxes Payable......................	250		65.24
Employees' Income Taxes Payable...........	260		180.30
FUTA Taxes Payable......................	270		52.80
State Unemployment Taxes Payable.........	280		28.36
R. L. Adams, Capital.....................	310		48,367.33
		$58,648.77	$58,648.77

Earned. If any portion of such interest was accrued in the preceding accounting period and the adjusting entry had not been reversed at the beginning of the current accounting period, the amount credited to Interest Earned would not represent the proper amount earned in the current period. If, however, the adjusting entry at the end of the preceding period had been reversed, the interest earned account would be debited for the amount accrued and, after recording the interest collected in the current period as a credit to Interest Earned, the balance of the account would represent the correct amount of revenue applicable to the new period.

When cash is disbursed in payment of interest, the routine manner of recording the transaction is to debit Interest Expense and to credit Cash (or Bank). If any portion of such interest was accrued in the preceding accounting period and the adjusting entry had not been reversed at the beginning of the current accounting period, the amount debited to Interest Expense would not represent the proper amount of expense incurred in the current period. If, however, the adjusting entry at the end of the preceding period had been reversed, the interest expense account would be credited for the amount accrued and, after recording the interest paid in the current period as a debit to Interest Expense, the balance of the account would represent the correct amount of the interest expense for the current period.

Journalizing the Reversing Entries

Reversing entries, like adjusting and closing entries, may be recorded in either a general journal or a combined cash journal. If the entries are made in a combined cash journal, the only amount columns used are the General Debits and Credits columns. A portion of a page of a combined cash journal showing the reversing entries of The Adams Appliance Store is reproduced below. Usually the reversing entries are made immediately after closing the books at the end of an accounting period. However, it is customary to date the entries as of the first day of the succeeding accounting period. Thus, the reversing entries for The Adams Appliance Store are dated January 1. Since the heading "Reversing Entries" explains the nature of the entries, a separate explanation of each reversing entry is unnecessary. Following is a discussion of each of the reversing entries.

COMBINED CASH JOURNAL FOR MONTH OF *January* 19 —   PAGE *51*

| DATE | | DESCRIPTION | POST. REF. | GENERAL | |
MO.	DAY			DEBITS	CREDITS
		AMOUNTS FORWARDED			
Jan.	1	Reversing Entries			
		Interest Earned	710	4 1 7	
		Accrued Interest Receivable	122		4 1 7
		Accrued Interest Payable	220	8 0 6	
		Interest Expense	810		8 0 6
				1 2 2 3	1 2 2 3

The Adams Appliance Store — Reversing Entries

Accrued Interest Receivable. Reference to the adjusting entries reproduced on page 252 will reveal that Accrued Interest Receivable, Account No. 122, was debited and Interest Earned, Account No. 710, was credited for $4.17 to record the interest accrued on the 5 percent interest-bearing note of John F. White for $2,000. To reverse the adjusting entry it was necessary to debit Interest Earned, Account No. 710, and to credit Accrued Interest Receivable, Account No. 122, for $4.17. The accounts affected by this entry are reproduced at the top of page 267.

It will be noted that, after posting the reversing entry, the account with Accrued Interest Receivable is in balance and the account with Interest Earned has a debit balance of $4.17. If John F. White pays the amount due when his note matures on January 15, his payment will be $2,008.33

ACCOUNT *Accrued Interest Receivable*   ACCOUNT NO. *122*

DATE	ITEMS	POST. REF.	✓	DEBITS	DATE	ITEMS	POST. REF.	✓	CREDITS
19– Dec. 31		CJ49		4 1 7	19– Jan. 1		CJ51		4 1 7

ACCOUNT *Interest Earned*   ACCOUNT NO. *710*

DATE	ITEMS	POST. REF.	✓	DEBITS	DATE	ITEMS	POST. REF.	✓	CREDITS
19– Dec. 31		CJ50		3 6 3 2	19– Dec. 1	Balance	✓		3 2 1 5
					31		CJ49		4 1 7
									3 6 3 2
				3 6 3 2					3 6 3 2
19– Jan. 1		CJ51		4 1 7					

(principal of note $2,000, plus interest at 5 percent for 30 days, $8.33). To record this collection it is necessary only to debit Columbia National Bank for $2,008.33 and to credit Notes Receivable, Account No. 121, for $2,000 and Interest Earned, Account No. 710, for $8.33. After posting this entry the interest earned account will have a credit balance of $4.16 ($8.33 minus $4.17). This balance represents the amount of interest earned in the year in which the note matures. If the adjusting entry had not been reversed, it would be necessary to make an analysis before recording the collection from Mr. White on January 15 in order to determine the amount of interest accrued in the preceding year and the amount of interest earned in the current year. This would reveal that it would be necessary to credit Accrued Interest Receivable for $4.17 and Interest Earned for $4.16, so that each year might receive credit for the correct interest earned. When the adjustment is reversed, the need for this analysis is eliminated.

The reversal procedure is particularly useful if the year-end adjustment for interest earned but not collected related to interest accrued on several notes or other interest-bearing assets. When the adjustment is reversed, all future collections of interest can be credited to the interest earned account without any concern as to when the amount was earned. The portion of any collections that was earned in the new period will automatically emerge as the balance of the interest earned account.

Accrued Interest Payable. In the adjusting entries for The Adams Appliance Store, Interest Expense, Account No. 810, was debited and Accrued Interest Payable, Account No. 220, was credited for $8.06 to record the interest accrued on a 6 percent interest-bearing note for $863.90 issued November 5. To reverse the adjusting entry it was necessary to debit Accrued Interest Payable, Account No. 220, and to credit Interest Expense, Account No. 810, for $8.06. The accounts affected by this entry are reproduced at the top of the next page.

ACCOUNT *Accrued Interest Payable*   ACCOUNT NO. 220

DATE	ITEMS	POST. REF.	✓	DEBITS	DATE	ITEMS	POST. REF.	✓	CREDITS
19– Jan. 1		CJ51		8 0 6	19– Dec. 31		CJ49		8 0 6

ACCOUNT *Interest Expense*   ACCOUNT NO. 810

DATE	ITEMS	POST. REF.	✓	DEBITS	DATE	ITEMS	POST. REF.	✓	CREDITS
19– Dec. 1	Balance	✓		4 6 0 5	19– Dec. 31		CJ50		5 4 1 1
31		CJ49		8 0 6					
				5 4 1 1					5 4 1 1
					19– Jan. 1		CJ51		8 0 6

It will be noted that, after posting the reversing entry, the account with Accrued Interest Payable is in balance and the account with Interest Expense has a credit balance of $8.06. If the note for $863.90 plus interest is paid when due on May 5, the payment will be $889.82 (principal of note $863.90, plus interest at 6 percent for six months, $25.92). To record the payment it is necessary only to debit Notes Payable, Account No. 210, for $863.90 and Interest Expense, Account No. 810, for $25.92 and to credit Columbia National Bank for $889.82. After posting this entry the interest expense account will have a debit balance of $17.86 ($25.92 minus $8.06). This balance represents the amount of interest expense incurred in the year in which the note matures. If the adjusting entry had not been reversed, it would be necessary to make an analysis before recording the payment on May 5 in order to determine the amount of interest expense incurred in the preceding year and the amount of interest expense incurred in the current year. This would reveal that it would be necessary to debit Accrued Interest Payable for $8.06 and Interest Expense for $17.86 so that each year might be charged with the correct interest expense. When the adjustment is reversed, the need for this analysis is eliminated.

The reversal procedure is particularly useful if the year-end adjustment for interest expense incurred but not paid related to interest accrued on several interest-bearing obligations. When the adjustment is reversed, all future payments of interest can be debited to the interest expense account without any concern as to when each amount paid was incurred. The portion of any payments that is an expense of the new period will automatically emerge as the balance of the interest expense account.

From the foregoing discussion it will be seen that by reversing the adjusting entries made on December 31 for accrued interest receivable and accrued interest payable, it will be possible to record the interest collected on January 15 amounting to $8.33 and the interest paid on May 5 amounting to $25.92 in an ordinary routine manner.

The Accounting Cycle

The steps involved in handling the effect of all transactions and events completed during an accounting period, beginning with entries in the books of original entry and ending with the reversing entries, collectively comprise the *accounting cycle*. In Chapter 5 (page 128) nine steps were listed. A tenth step — journalizing and posting the reversing entries — needs to be added if the accrual basis of accounting is being followed.

Income and Self-Employment Taxes

The discussion of accounting for the revenue and expenses of a business enterprise has included frequent references to income tax considerations. It is important to note that an unincorporated business owned by one person is not taxed. The owner — not the business — is subject to income taxes. He, of course, must report the amounts of business revenue and expenses in his personal tax return regardless of the amount of money or other property he has actually withdrawn from the business during the year. As mentioned earlier, in the case of a sole proprietorship, there is no legal distinction between the business and its owner.

In order to bring a large class of self-employed individuals into the federal social security program, the law requires all self-employed persons (except those specifically exempted) to pay a self-employment tax. The rate of tax is 2 percent more than the prevailing FICA rate. (With a combined FICA tax rate of 4.5 percent, the self-employment tax rate is 6.5 percent.) The tax is applied to "self-employment income" up to a maximum of $6,600. The rate and base of the tax may be changed by Act of Congress at any time. In general, *self-employment income* means the net income of a trade or business conducted by an individual or a partner's distributive share of the net income of a partnership whether or not any cash is distributed. Earnings of less than $400 from self-employment are ignored.

A taxable year for the purpose of the tax on self-employment income is the same as the taxpayer's taxable year for federal income tax purposes. The self-employment tax is reported along with the regular federal income tax. For calendar-year taxpayers, the tax return and full or final payment is due on April 15 following the close of the year. Like the personal income tax, the self-employment tax is treated as a personal expense of the owner. If the taxes are paid with business funds, the amount should be charged to the owner's drawing account.

Report No. 20

Complete Report No. 20 in the workbook and submit your working papers to the instructor for approval. You will then be given instructions as to the work to be done next.

chapters 6-10

practical accounting problems

Problem 6-A

Mrs. Helen Maes decides to open a dress shop under the name of Helen's Shop. The books of original entry include a purchases journal, a sales journal, and a combined cash journal. This problem involves the use of the purchases journal and the combined cash journal only. The following selected transactions were completed during the month of October:

Oct. 2. Invested $5,000 in the business.
2. Received Invoice No. 262 dated Sept. 29 from New Modes, Inc., for merchandise purchased, $71.50. Terms, 30 days net.
3. Received Invoice No. 263 dated Sept. 29 from Emory Brothers for merchandise purchased, $142.18. Terms, 10 days net.
5. Purchased a cash register for cash, $49.13. (Debit Furniture and Fixtures.)
6. Received Invoice No. 264 dated October 4 from Towle, Inc., for merchandise purchased, $96.80. Terms, 30 days net.
10. Purchased merchandise for cash, $51.55.
11. Received Invoice No. 265 dated October 9 from New Modes, Inc., for merchandise purchased, $161.31. Terms, 30 days net.
12. Paid Emory Brothers $142.18 in full for Invoice No. 263 dated Sept. 29.
13. Returned defective merchandise to New Modes, Inc., $22.66.
17. Received invoice dated October 16 from the American Showcase Co. for showcases purchased, $1,823.14. Terms, 15 days net.

23. Received Invoice No. 266 dated October 18 from Emory Brothers for merchandise purchased, $286.47. Terms, 10 days net.
25. Purchased merchandise for cash, $96.18.
30. Received Invoice No. 267 dated October 26 from Kay Francis for merchandise purchased, $52.40. Terms, 30 days net.

REQUIRED: **(1)** Record each transaction in the proper journal using the following accounts:

11 Cash	31 Helen Maes, Capital
15 Furniture and Fixtures	51 Purchases
21 Accounts Payable	051 Purchases Returns and Allowances

For the purchases journal, use a sheet of paper ruled like that shown in the illustration on page 146. For the combined cash journal, use a sheet of paper like that shown in the illustration on pages 160 and 161. Number the pages of the journals. **(2)** Prove the combined cash journal by footing the amount columns; then total and rule this journal. Total the purchases journal and rule. **(3)** Open the necessary accounts using the standard account form of ledger paper. Post the purchases journal and combined cash journal entries for October, foot the accounts, and enter the balances. **(4)** Take a trial balance as of October 31, using a sheet of two-column journal paper.

Problem 6-B

A. K. Lein decides to open a men's clothing store under the name of The Westroads Store. The books of original entry include a sales journal, a purchases journal, and a combined cash journal. This problem involves the use of the sales journal and combined cash journal only. The following selected transactions were completed during the month of July:

July 3. Invested $7,500 in the business.
3. Sold merchandise on account to G. M. Zelenak, $15.60, tax 47 cents. Sale No. 204.
5. Sold merchandise on account to W. J. Morris, $49.65, tax $1.49. Sale No. 205.
6. G. M. Zelenak returned goods for credit. Sales price, $8.20, tax 25 cents.
10. Sold merchandise on account to J. R. Brooks, $28.31, tax 85 cents. Sale No. 206.
13. Received $7.62 from G. M. Zelenak in payment of account.
14. Sold merchandise on account to R. E. Foote, $25.02, tax 75 cents. Sale No. 207.
19. A customer returned some merchandise purchased earlier in the day for cash. Sales price, $9.75, tax 29 cents.
21. Received $29.16 from J. R. Brooks in payment of account.
26. Sold merchandise on account to William Dickey, $15.30, tax 46 cents. Sale No. 208.
28. Sold merchandise on account to J. D. Mitchell, $9.40, tax 28 cents. Sale No. 209.
31. Total cash sales for month, $685.10, tax $20.55.

REQUIRED: **(1)** Record each transaction in the proper journal using the following accounts:

11 Cash	31 A. K. Lein, Capital
12 Accounts Receivable	41 Sales
23 Sales Tax Payable	041 Sales Returns and Allowances

For the sales journal, use a sheet of paper ruled like that shown in the second illustration on page 153. For the combined cash journal, use a sheet of paper like that shown in the illustration on pages 160 and 161. Number the pages of the journals. (2) Prove the combined cash journal by footing the amount columns; then total and rule this journal. (3) Prove the sales journal by footing the amount columns and determining that the totals of the debit and credit columns are equal in amount. Enter the totals and rule. (4) Open the necessary accounts using the standard account form of ledger paper. Post the sales journal and combined cash journal entries for July, foot the accounts, and enter the balances. (5) Take a trial balance as of July 31, using a sheet of two-column journal paper.

Problem 6-C

Howard D. Harmon is engaged in a retail merchandising business operating under the name of The HDH Store. He keeps a purchases journal, a sales journal, and a two-column general journal as books of original entry. The standard account form of general ledger is used. Individual accounts with customers and creditors are not kept in ledger form; however, the purchase invoices and sales tickets are filed in such a manner that the amounts due to creditors and due from customers may be determined at any time. All charge sales are payable by the tenth of the following month. The trial balance taken as of March 31, 19—, is reproduced below.

THE HDH STORE
Trial Balance
March 31, 19--

Cash...	11	$ 2,148.00	
Accounts Receivable....................................	12	3,570.00	
Merchandise Inventory.................................	13	22,000.00	
Store Equipment..	15	1,160.00	
Accounts Payable.......................................	21		$ 3,736.62
Sales Tax Payable.......................................	22		77.07
Howard D. Harmon, Capital............................	31		6,124.31
Howard D. Harmon, Drawing...........................	031	1,400.00	
Sales...	41		48,800.00
Sales Returns and Allowances..........................	041	425.00	
Purchases...	51	26,800.00	
Purchases Returns and Allowances.....................	051		212.00
Rent Expense...	61	900.00	
Advertising Expense....................................	62	240.00	
Heating and Lighting Expense..........................	63	120.00	
Telephone and Telegraph Expense.....................	64	72.00	
Miscellaneous Expense.................................	65	115.00	
		$58,950.00	$58,950.00

NARRATIVE OF TRANSACTIONS FOR APRIL

Apr. 1. (Saturday) Paid the rent for April in advance, $300.
   3. Paid the following bills:
      Gas and electric bill, $42.50.
      Telephone bill, $21.75.
   4. Received Invoice No. 71 dated April 1 from B. F. Jackson, 124 Spring St., for merchandise purchased, $159. Terms, 30 days net.
   4. Sold merchandise on account to J. J. Schatz, 120 Main St., $25.60, tax 77 cents. Sale No. 41.

6. Sold merchandise on account to the Chase Hotel, 20 Broadway, $82.50, tax $2.48. Sale No. 42.
8. Sundry cash sales, $187, tax $5.61.
10. Paid the following creditors on account:
Chapman Bros., $163.50.
Schmidt & Co., $245.20.
11. Received the following remittances to apply on account:
Ramada Hotel, $75.60.
D. J. Wharton, $25.
Mrs. J. E. Campbell, $54.70.
12. Received Invoice No. 72 dated April 10 from Howard & Long, Detroit, for merchandise purchased, $320. Terms, 30 days net.
13. Paid $77.07 to State Treasurer for March sales tax.
13. Made sales on account as follows:
No. 43, Mrs. E. R. Carey, Kingston, $87.45, tax $2.62.
No. 44, Ramada Hotel, 200 Locust, $57.25, tax $1.72.
No. 45, Mrs. R. F. Lester, 125 E. Fourth St., $70, tax $2.10.
14. Paid $25.70 for newspaper advertising.
15. Sundry cash sales, $152.40, tax $4.57.
17. Howard D. Harmon withdrew $150 for personal use.
18. Made sales on account as follows:
No. 46, P. A. Benz, 604 Race St., $71.90, tax $2.16.
No. 47, Mrs. C. C. Morley, 25 E. Fourth St., $31.90, tax 96 cents.
No. 48, Chase Hotel, 20 Broadway, $75.16, tax $2.25.
19. Received Invoice No. 73 dated April 17 from Chapman Bros., City, for merchandise purchased, $252.40. Terms, 30 days net.
20. Gave the Chase Hotel credit for $12.36 on account of merchandise returned. (Sales price, $12, tax 36 cents.)
21. Received credit from Chapman Bros. for $18.70 on account of merchandise returned.
22. Sundry cash sales, $173.40, tax $5.20.
24. Received Invoice No. 74 dated April 22 from Schmidt & Co., Cleveland, for merchandise purchased, $95.20. Terms, 30 days net.
25. Made sales on account as follows:
No. 49, D. J. Wharton, 121 Elm St., $44.50, tax $1.34.
No. 50, Ramada Hotel, City, $75.16, tax $2.25.
25. Allowed credit for $4.33 to P. A. Benz for merchandise returned. (Sales price, $4.20, tax 13 cents.)
27. Paid Eberle Bros. $65.90 on account.
27. Received $123.60 from Chase Hotel to apply on account.
28. Purchased store equipment on account from the Clark Supply Co., 16 John St., $90. Terms, 60 days net.
28. Paid freight and drayage on merchandise purchased, $20.
29. Sundry cash sales, $165.40, tax $4.96.
29. Howard D. Harmon withdrew $100 for personal use.

REQUIRED: (1) Journalize the April transactions. Total the purchases journal and rule; foot the sales journal, enter the totals, and rule. Prove each page of the general journal by footing the debit and credit columns. (2) Open the necessary general ledger accounts. Record the April 1 balances as shown in the March 31 trial balance, complete the individual posting from the general journal, and complete the summary posting from the purchases and sales journals. Foot the accounts and enter the balances. (3) Take a trial balance using a sheet of two-column journal paper.

Problem 7-A

R. W. Newberry is a dealer in china and glassware. In accounting for notes, he uses a notes receivable register similar to the one reproduced on pages 176 and 177. Following is a narrative of transactions involving notes received from customers during the current year:

Mar. 6. Received from David Losh a 60-day, 6% note (No. 1) for $500 dated March 4 and payable at First National Bank, Cedar Falls.

April 26. Received from Burton J. Nissing a 90-day, 5% note (No. 2) for $400 dated April 25 and payable at Second National Bank, Mehlville.

May 3. Received a check for $505 from David Losh in payment of his note due today plus interest.

    19. Received from A. Bryant Foster a 60-day, 6% note (No. 3) for $425 dated May 18 and payable at Elmwood Park Trust Company, Elmwood.

July 17. Received a check for $429.25 from A. Bryant Foster in payment of his note due today plus interest.

    24. Received a check for $405 from Burton J. Nissing in payment of his note due today plus interest.

Oct. 2. Received from R. J. Crain a 90-day, 5% note (No. 4) for $640 dated October 2 and payable at Wellston State Bank.

    19. Discounted R. J. Crain's note for $640 at the Clayton Trust Company at 6% and received credit for the proceeds.

REQUIRED: (1) Prepare entries in general journal form to record the foregoing transactions. Foot the amount columns as a means of proof. (2) Make the required entries in a notes receivable register to provide a detailed auxiliary record of the notes received by R. W. Newberry.

Problem 7-B

B. F. Healy operates a department store. Sometimes he finds it necessary to issue notes to creditors to obtain extensions of time for payment of their accounts. Unless otherwise stated, all such notes are made payable at the Franklin County Bank, Franklin. Following is a narrative of transactions involving notes issued by Mr. Healy during the current year:

Feb. 1. Borrowed $600 from the bank on a 90-day, 5% note (No. 1).

Mar. 7. Issued a 60-day, 6% note (No. 2) for $375 to Allen & Donnelly Co.

April 20. Issued a 60-day, 5% note (No. 3) for $440 to A. E. Anderson & Sons.

May 2. Issued a check for $607.50 to the bank in payment of note due today plus interest.

    6. Gave Allen & Donnelly Co. a check for $3.75 in payment of the interest and a new note (No. 4) for $375, due in 60 days, with interest at 6%, in settlement of the note due today.

June 19. Issued a check for $443.67 to A. E. Anderson & Sons in payment of note due today plus interest.

July 1. Borrowed $2,000 from the bank on a 90-day, 5% note (No. 5).

    5. Issued a check for $378.75 to Allen & Donnelly Co. in payment of note due today plus interest.

Sept. 29. Gave Franklin County Bank a check for $25 in payment of the interest and a new note (No. 6) for $2,000, due in 60 days, with interest at 5%, in settlement of the note due today.

Nov. 28. Issued a check for $2,016.67 to the bank in payment of note due today plus interest.

REQUIRED: **(1)** Prepare entries in general journal form to record the foregoing transactions. Foot the amount columns as a means of proof. **(2)** Make the required entries in a notes payable register, similar to the one reproduced on pages 180 and 181, to provide a detailed auxiliary record of the notes issued.

There are no Practical Accounting Problems for Chapter 8.

Problem 9-A (see page 277)

Account	Acct. No.	Trial Balance Debits	Trial Balance Credits
Cash...	111	5,465.92	
Notes Receivable...........................	131	1,400.00	
Accrued Interest Receivable...............	132		
Accounts Receivable........................	133	4,324.00	
Allowance for Bad Debts...................	013		49.72
Merchandise Inventory.....................	141	10,728.00	
Prepaid Insurance..........................	151	560.00	
Stationery and Supplies....................	152	180.00	
Store Equipment...........................	161	4,400.00	
Accumulated Depreciation — Store Equipment..............	016		440.00
Delivery Equipment........................	171	3,600.00	
Accumulated Depreciation — Delivery Equipment............	017		900.00
Notes Payable..............................	211		2,200.00
Accrued Interest Payable..................	221		
Accounts Payable..........................	231		6,616.70
Sales Tax Payable..........................	241		80.00
Employees' Income Taxes Payable.........	251		205.00
FICA Taxes Payable.........................	261		187.50
J. R. Bachhuber, Capital...................	311		25,333.00
J. R. Bachhuber, Drawing..................	031	4,000.00	
Expense and Revenue Summary...........	321		
Sales.......................................	411		51,435.00
Sales Returns and Allowances.............	041	179.00	
Purchases..................................	511	36,231.30	
Purchases Returns and Allowances........	051		184.30
Rent Expense..............................	521	3,000.00	
Advertising Expense.......................	522	840.00	
Salaries Expense...........................	523	12,000.00	
Payroll Tax Expense........................	524	375.00	
Insurance Expense.........................	525		
Stationery and Supplies Expense..........	526		
Depreciation Expense......................	527		
Bad Debts Expense.........................	528		
Charitable Contributions Expense.........	529	250.00	
Miscellaneous Expense.....................	530	105.00	
Interest Earned............................	611		35.00
Interest Expense...........................	711	28.00	
		87,666.22	87,666.22

Note: Problems 9-B and 10-A are based on J. R. Bachhuber's work sheet. If these problems are to be solved, the work sheet should be retained for reference until after they are solved, when the solutions of all three problems may be submitted to the instructor.

Problem 9-A

J. R. Bachhuber is engaged in business as a retail plumbing and heating dealer. Merchandise is sold for cash and on account. On the preceding page is a reproduction of the Trial Balance columns of his work sheet for the current year ended December 31.

REQUIRED: Prepare a ten-column work sheet making the necessary entries in the Adjustments columns to record the following:

(1) Merchandise inventory, end of year, $12,754.
(2) Accruals:
Interest accrued on notes receivable, $14.
Interest accrued on notes payable, $18.34.
(3) Prepaid expenses:
Prepaid insurance unexpired, $280.
Stationery and supplies on hand, $60.
(4) Depreciation:
Store equipment, 10% a year, $440.
Delivery equipment, 25% a year, $900.
(5) Bad debts expense:
Increase allowance for bad debts $80 to provide for estimated loss.

Problem 9-B

Refer to the work sheet for J. R. Bachhuber (based on Problem 9-A) and from it prepare the following financial statements:

(1) An income statement for the year ended December 31.
(2) A balance sheet in account form as of December 31.

Problem 10-A

Refer to the work sheet for J. R. Bachhuber (based on Problem 9-A) and draft the general journal entries required:
(1) To adjust the general ledger accounts so they will be in agreement with the financial statements.
(2) To close the temporary owner's equity accounts on December 31.
(3) To reverse the accrual adjustments as of January 1.

Problem 10-B (Complete cycle problem)

A. B. Ransom is engaged in a merchandising business as a sole owner. He calls his business "Ransom's Store." He keeps a purchases journal, sales journal, combined cash journal, and general ledger. For his combined cash journal, he uses eight-column paper (8 columns divided — 2 left, 6 right) with headings arranged as follows:

Bank

    (1) Deposits Dr.
    (2) Checks Cr.

General

    (3) Debits
    (4) Credits
    (5) Accounts Payable Dr.
    (6) Accounts Receivable Cr.
    (7) Sales Cr.
    (8) Sales Tax Payable Cr.

The standard account form of ledger ruling is used. Individual accounts with customers and creditors are not kept in ledger form; however, the purchase invoices and sales tickets are filed in such a manner that the amounts owed to creditors and due from customers can be determined at any time. At the end of the eleventh month of this year, his trial balance appeared as shown below.

NARRATIVE OF TRANSACTIONS FOR DECEMBER

Dec. 1. (Friday) Purchased merchandise from Burrows Bros., Clinton, $1,300. Invoice No. 21, dated November 30. Terms, 2/20, n/30.
   2. Paid the December rent, $600. Check No. 64.
   2. Paid the telephone bill, $27. Check No. 65.
   4. Paid E. J. Kosy $932.50 in full of December 1 balance. Check No. 66.
   5. Sold merchandise on account to J. R. Cotton, 320 Main St., City, $450, tax $13.50. Sale No. 201.
   6. Purchased merchandise from the James Supply Co., Jamestown, $1,175. Invoice No. 22, dated December 5. Terms, 30 days.
   7. Received $275 from Russell Miller in full settlement of his account.
   8. Paid Burrows Bros. $1,274 in settlement of their invoice of November 30, less 2% discount. Check No. 67.
   8. Received $261.12 from Arno Becht in full settlement of his account.

RANSOM'S STORE
Trial Balance
November 30, 19--

Cash	111	$ 10,066.92	
Notes Receivable	121	3,600.00	
Accounts Receivable	123	5,479.80	
Allowance for Bad Debts	012		$ 139.20
Merchandise Inventory	131	41,600.00	
Prepaid Insurance	141	950.00	
Stationery and Supplies	151	160.00	
Store Equipment	181	3,800.00	
Accumulated Depreciation — Store Equipment	018		760.00
Notes Payable	211		2,400.00
Accounts Payable	231		3,104.50
Sales Tax Payable	241		304.30
Employees' Income Taxes Payable	251		239.20
FICA Taxes Payable	261		143.52
FUTA Taxes Payable	271		206.40
State Unemployment Taxes Payable	281		96.00
A. B. Ransom, Capital	311		63,800.00
A. B. Ransom, Drawing	031	7,400.00	
Sales	411		167,360.00
Sales Returns and Allowances	041	252.80	
Purchases	511	126,400.00	
Purchases Returns and Allowances	0511		282.20
Purchases Discount	0512		220.00
Rent Expense	611	6,600.00	
Advertising Expense	612	4,800.00	
Salaries and Commissions Expense	613	25,800.00	
Payroll Tax Expense	614	1,528.66	
Miscellaneous Expense	615	607.14	
Interest Earned	711		18.00
Interest Expense	811	28.00	
		$239,073.32	$239,073.32

Dec. 9. Sold merchandise on account to J. K. Andersen, Akron, $268.50, tax $8.06. Sale No. 202.

11. Purchased merchandise from the Heinz Mfg. Co., City, $1,921.60. Invoice No. 23, dated December 9. Terms, 30 days.

12. Sold merchandise on account to W. B. Leffingwell, 201 Prince St., City, $375.20, tax $11.26. Sale No. 203.

13. Issued Check No. 68 to the Third National Bank, a U.S. Depositary, in payment of the following taxes:

(a) Employees' income taxes withheld during November.............................		$239.20
(b) FICA taxes:		
On employees (withheld during November)	$71.76	
On the employer......................	71.76	143.52
Total................................		$382.72

14. Sold merchandise on account to R. V. Black, 738 Cliff St., City, $750, tax $22.50. Sale No. 204.

15. Issued Check No. 69 payable to State Treasurer for $304.30 for November sales tax.

18. A. B. Ransom withdrew $120 for personal use. Check No. 70.

19. Gave W. B. Leffingwell credit for $25.75 because a part of the merchandise sold him on the twelfth was returned. (Sales price, $25, tax 75 cents.)

20. Sold merchandise on account to J. R. Cotton, 320 Main St., City, $250.00, tax $7.50. Sale No. 205.

21. Purchased merchandise from the Green Mfg. Co., City, $1,874.25. Invoice No. 24, dated December 20. Terms, 30 days.

22. Received $360.71 from W. B. Leffingwell for balance of Sale No. 203.

23. Paid bill for advertising, $125. Check No. 71.

26. Sold merchandise on account to J. V. Kilgore, 159 Johnson St., City, $785, tax $23.55. Sale No. 206.

26. Purchased merchandise from Burrows Bros., Clinton, $945.70. Invoice No. 25, dated December 23. Terms, 2/10, n/30.

26. Received a check for $400 from J. R. Cotton to apply on account.

27. Sold merchandise on account to W. B. Leffingwell, 201 Prince St., City, $385.95, tax $11.58. Sale No. 207.

27. Sent the Heinz Mfg. Co. a check for $800 to apply on account. Check No. 72.

28. Sold merchandise on account to A. T. Nelson, 218 Sixth St., City, $943.15, tax $28.29. Sale No. 208.

28. Purchased store equipment from the Janesville Supply Co., Janesville, $240. Terms, 60 days net.

29. Received $276.56 from J. K. Andersen in payment of Sale No. 202.

29. Received credit from Burrows Bros. for $35 because a part of the merchandise purchased on the twenty-sixth was returned by agreement.

29. Sold merchandise on account to J. K. Andersen, Akron, $471.80, tax $14.15. Sale No. 209.

30. Sundry cash sales for month, $2,407.20, tax $72.22.

30. Issued Check No. 73 payable to Payroll for $1,273.30.

PAYROLL STATEMENT FOR MONTH ENDED DECEMBER 31

Total wages and commissions earned during period........		$1,500.00
Employees' taxes to be withheld:		
(a) Employees' income taxes.........................	$159.20	
(b) FICA taxes @ 4.5%.............................	67.50	226.70
Net amount payable to employees......................		$1,273.30

Employer's payroll taxes:
(a) FICA taxes @ 4.5% .... $ 67.50
(b) UC taxes —
State @ 2.5% .... $ 37.50
Federal @ 0.4% 6.00   43.50
Total .... $ 111.00

(In addition to recording the amounts withheld from employees' wages for income tax purposes and for FICA taxes, the social security taxes imposed on the employer should also be recorded.)

REQUIRED: **(1)** Journalize the December transactions. **(2)** Open the necessary general ledger accounts and record the December 1 balances, using the November 30 trial balance as the source of the needed information. Complete the individual and summary posting from the books of original entry. **(3)** Take a trial balance of the general ledger accounts. **(4)** Prepare a ten-column work sheet making the required adjustments from the information given below. Number the pages of the journals as follows:

Purchases Journal .... Page 34
Sales Journal .... Page 46
Combined Cash Journal .. Pages 49–51

(a) Merchandise inventory, end of year, $58,500.
(b) Accruals:
Interest accrued on notes receivable, $48.
Interest accrued on notes payable, $24.
(c) Prepaid expenses:
Prepaid insurance unexpired, $634.
Stationery and supplies on hand, $50.
(d) Depreciation:
Store equipment, 10% a year, $380.
(e) Bad debts expense:
Increase allowance for bad debts $211.36 to provide for estimated loss.

In recording the required adjustments on the work sheet, it will be necessary to add (in numerical order) the following account titles to those already appearing in the trial balance:

Accrued Interest Receivable, Account No. 122
Accrued Interest Payable, Account No. 220
Expense and Revenue Summary, Account No. 320
Insurance Expense, Account No. 616
Stationery and Supplies Expense, Account No. 617
Depreciation Expense, Account No. 618
Bad Debts Expense, Account No. 619

(5) Prepare an income statement for the year ending December 31 and a balance sheet in report form as of December 31. **(6)** Record the adjusting entries in the combined cash journal and post. **(7)** Record the closing entries in the combined cash journal and post. **(8)** Balance and rule the accounts that are in balance after the adjusting and closing entries have been posted; also balance and rule the following accounts: Cash, A. B. Ransom, Capital, Accounts Receivable, Accounts Payable, and Sales Tax Payable, and rule the merchandise inventory account. **(9)** Take a post-closing trial balance. **(10)** Record the necessary reversing entries as of January 1 in the combined cash journal. Post and rule the accounts that are closed.

appendix

automated accounting systems and procedures

Structure of Accounting Systems

The design of a system of books and records depends in large measure on the nature of the business by which the system is used. The number of transactions to be recorded in a given time period has much to do with the planning and arrangement of the chart of accounts and of the procedures for gathering and processing transaction information. Physical location of factory buildings and warehouses and the transaction volume at each location also influence the design of an accounting system.

The nature of the business, the kinds of transactions to be recorded and summarized, the transaction volume, and the location of physical facilities together comprise the *structure* of an accounting system. All of these factors together make careful systems planning essential.

The Language of Automated Accounting Systems

The original or immediate records of many kinds of business transactions have been presented in this textbook. The receipt has been discussed as the immediate record of a cash received transaction. The check stub has been discussed and illustrated as the immediate record of a cash payment transaction. Similarly, the invoice was presented as the immediate record of a purchase on account and the sales ticket as the immediate record of a sale on account. The immediate record is always the key record in an automated accounting system just as it is in a manual accounting system.

Whether an immediate record is prepared by hand or by machine, the data which it contains must be collected and recorded by people. In automated accounting the immediate record is usually referred to as the *source document*.

Some modern businesses are quite large, and this relative size affects their accounting systems. Modern systems for relatively large businesses include some equipment, called *automated equipment*, that operates without human guidance other than the press of a button. The use of such equipment in an accounting system makes it an *automated accounting system.*

Automated accounting has brought about the development of a new language as well as new procedures. In automated accounting, information such as ledger account titles, dollar amounts, and physical quantities is known as *data*. The use of these data in different ways for different business purposes is known as *data processing*. Accounting involves the processing of data in several different forms. In fact, the original preparation of the source document for a business transaction is a form of data processing. Likewise, the recording of transactions in books of original entry, posting to ledger accounts, taking trial balances, and preparing financial statements are also forms of data processing.

Those who use automated equipment to process accounting records must apply accounting principles to each step. The same principles of debit and credit apply whether the work is done with automated equipment, with conventional accounting machines, or by the manual bookkeeper. Equipment and machines are merely tools of the accountant. Such tools reduce routine manual work, increase the speed of producing records, and permit more accurate financial reporting.

Data processing is usually described in two ways. The processing of business transactions by the use of simple office machines with card punches or tape punches attached is known as *integrated data processing* (IDP). The processing of business transactions by the use of an electronic computer is known as *electronic data processing* (EDP).

The Write-It-Once Principle as a Laborsaving Device

A source document, such as a purchase invoice or a sales ticket, usually is prepared manually by handwriting or typing on the document at the time of the transaction. The first step in automated accounting is the preparation of a punched card or a punched paper tape by a machine operator from a source document.

If the operator types the source document on an office machine with a card punching or tape punching attachment, the card or tape is being punched at the same time that the source document is being typed. If the office machine used is not an integrated data processing machine, the card or tape must be punched later as a separate operation.

The process of recording the basic information about a business transaction in a form that makes later hand copying unnecessary has been called the *write-it-once principle*. This first step in automated accounting makes it possible to save labor in completing the later steps of the accounting cycle. Once a punched card or a punched paper tape has been prepared by a machine operator, the recorded information can be used over and over again when and where needed. The only further human effort needed is to feed the cards or tape into automatic machines. These machines then perform automatically the functions of journalizing, posting, taking trial balances, preparing financial statements, and adjusting and closing ledger accounts.

Importance of Locating Errors in the Write-It-Once Operation

If errors in the punching of cards or paper tape are not discovered before the cards or tape are fed into automated machines, such errors will be repeated in each step of the automated accounting cycle. The repetition of errors in this manner may pyramid with disastrous results.

Designers of automated accounting systems have recognized the seriousness of the error problem. Errors in automated systems are normally located in either of two ways:

    (a) Transaction information is verified as soon as it has been recorded.
    (b) Automatic error-locating procedures built into the automated accounting equipment are used later on in the accounting cycle.

Verifying transaction information already punched into cards or tape is a process of running the cards or tape through manually operated machines a second time. A different machine operator reads the information from the source document and goes through the same punching motions as did the original operator. If each punching stroke hits a hole in the card or tape, the card or tape passes right on through the machine. If a punching stroke hits a solid section of card or tape, an error is indicated, and the machine notches the edge of the card or tape next to the error. Notched cards or tapes are set aside and corrected later.

Businesses that find errors very difficult to control may decide not only to verify source document information before cards or tape are processed but also to use automatic error-locating procedures later in the accounting cycle. Automated accounting equipment also may be set up to locate certain errors electronically. When such errors are so located, an error light on the equipment usually goes on, and the equipment stops running.

Basic Phases of Automated Data Processing

The automated processing of any data in the completion of the accounting cycle consists of five basic phases. These five phases are common to all automated equipment, regardless of manufacturer. They are:

(a) Input   (d) Arithmetic
(b) Control   (e) Output
(c) Storage

A diagram of a basic automated data processing machine is shown below:

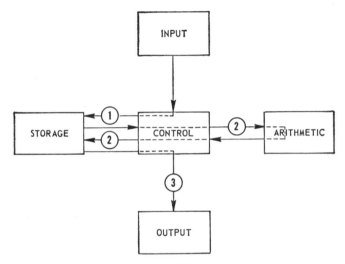

Diagram of Basic Automated Data Processing Machine

Input. In order that automated equipment may complete the accounting process, the immediate record must be rewritten in a form that the equipment can interpret. Information about a business transaction in a form acceptable for use in automated data processing equipment is known as *input*. Any acceptable means for presenting this information to an automated machine is known as an *input device*.

Input devices are fed into automated data processing machines to provide them with information about individual business transactions. The process by which an automated data processing machine receives information is similar in function to the intake of food by the human body.

Control. *Control* is the nerve center, or "action central" of the automated data processing system. It is like the central hall in a home or the lobby of a hotel. People must pass through the lobby of a hotel to get to their rooms. In the same way, transaction information must be routed through control in each step of automated data processing. Transaction information received as input is sent by control to storage, as shown by the flow line labeled "1" in the diagram on page A-4.

Storage. Transaction information stops in *storage* to await further use in automated accounting. Because storage holds information for future use just as does the human mind, it is often referred to as "memory." But unlike the human mind, storage must be told in great detail what to do with each item of transaction information that it holds. A detailed list of steps to be followed in completing the automated accounting cycle is known as a *program*. A person who designs programs is called a *programmer*. The detailed work of arranging transaction information in the most efficient manner for automated processing is called *programming*.

Arithmetic. The primary work of automated accounting is done in the *arithmetic* phase. Transaction information is routed from storage through control to arithmetic. In the arithmetic phase, addition, subtraction, multiplication, or division is performed as needed; and the result is returned by control to storage. This round trip is shown by the flow line labeled "2" in the basic automated machine diagram. Arithmetic also can compare two numbers and tell whether the first number is smaller than, equal to, or larger than the second number. This feature is useful in controlling inventories and expenses.

Output. When ledger account balances, financial statement items, or other data are desired, they are obtained from the automated data processing system in the output phase. Business information in a form acceptable for human use is known as *output*. Any acceptable means for converting coded machine information into English language is known as an *output device*.

Business information requested by management from the data processing system is routed from storage through control to output, as shown by the flow line labeled "3" in the basic automated machine diagram. Output devices are prepared which are used later to print in English the particular business information requested.

The Punched Card as an Input Device

At present, the punched card is the most frequently used input device. One form of punched card is the IBM (International Business Machines Corporation) card, illustrated at the top of page A-6.

Utility companies, oil companies, magazine publishers, and mail order houses use punched cards as statements of account. The federal govern-

Standard IBM Card

ment and many large private companies use punched cards for payroll checks and other remittance checks.

The small figures on the IBM card above show that it has 80 columns, numbered from left to right. The large figures on the card show that it has ten rows, numbered 0 to 9 inclusive from top to bottom. In addition, as the above illustration shows, the blank space at the top of the card provides room for two more rows, called the twelve row and the eleven row.

As shown by the punches in the illustration, a single numerical digit may be formed by punching a small hole in a column at one of the ten positions numbered zero through nine. A single letter or symbol may be formed by punching two holes in a column. One of these holes is punched through a position numbered one through nine. The other hole is punched through a position numbered twelve, eleven, or zero, as shown in the illustration above. The three top rows on the card are called the "zone" rows, and a hole punched in one of these rows is called a "zone" punch.

Planning the Use of the Punched Card. The first step in the use of a punched card as an input device is to plan the arrangement of the information on the card. A punched card that is to be used as a statement of account will contain the following information:

(a) Customer's name and address (e) Current sales to the customer
(b) Customer's account number   (f) Amount received on account
(c) Billing date   (g) Sales returns and allowances
(d) Customer's previous balance (h) Customer's new balance

Each item of information requires that several holes be punched into the card. An estimate is made of the longest group of letters or numbers required for each of the eight items to be placed on any statement of account. The punched card (or cards if two are needed) is then subdivided into eight groups of columns of sufficient size.

A group of columns used for a single item of information on a punched card is known as a *field*. There is a field for the customer's name and address, and a field for each of the other seven items of information.

Punching Information Into the Punched Card. After the information for preparing a customer's statement of account has been provided by the automated accounting system, a machine operator enters this information into a machine which in turn punches information holes into the card. One field on the card is used for each of the eight information items.

A machine used to punch information holes into punched cards from source documents is known as a *key punch*. The machine used has a keyboard very similar to a typewriter. An IBM key punch machine is illustrated below:

IBM Key Punch

Verifying the Information on the Punched Card. As soon as a batch of cards has been punched, the cards are checked in an attempt to avoid errors. A machine that looks exactly like a key punch and is used to find punching errors is called a *verifier*. As mentioned earlier, another operator reading from the same source document as the key punch operator enters the data into the verifier. The IBM verifier machine "feels" each card electronically to determine whether the correct holes have been punched. Each correct card is notched in a special "verify" position. If the verifier machine "feels" a missing hole or a hole in the wrong position, it notches a special "error" position on the card and the keyboard on the machine locks up.

Printing the Information on a Punched Card. The punched information on each IBM card is printed on a two-part statement card consisting of a statement and a stub. The printing is done by running the punched cards through a special printing machine. An automatic printing machine that lists, totals, and prints information previously punched onto cards is called a *tabulator* or *high-speed printer*. The information may either be printed on the same punched card from which it comes or on a separate sheet of paper.

Completing a Punched Card Statement of Account. After each of the two-part statement cards has been tabulated, the customer's account number and balance due are punched into the stub portion of the card. The statement card is then ready to be mailed to the customer. A completed two-part statement card is illustrated below:

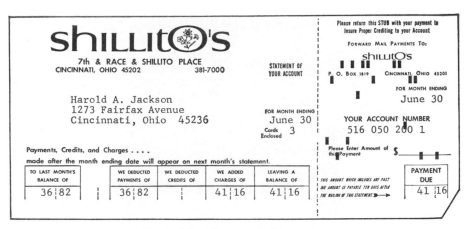

Punched Card Statement of Account

Sorting Customer Remittance Stubs. When the customer receives a statement like the one illustrated above, he detaches the stub and returns it with his remittance. When a remittance arrives, the amount received is keypunched into the stub that comes with the remittance. The stubs are then grouped into piles and run through a machine which sorts them by customer's account number.

A machine that automatically groups all punched cards of a similar kind and arranges them in some order is called a *sorter*. A sorter in common use is illustrated at the top of page A-9.

The stubs received from customers are placed in the hopper of the sorter. The hopper can be seen to extend from the upper right hand portion of the machine. The sorted stubs drop into the pockets that can be seen across the front of the machine. There is a "reject" pocket for cards that the machine is unable to sort.

IBM Sorter

Posting Customer Remittance Stubs. The final process in accounting for customer remittances is to run the stubs through the printer or tabulator in account number order. This machine process posts the remittances to individual customers' ledger account cards and determines the new account balances.

The same basic operations are followed in processing punched card checks, except that cash payment transactions are involved rather than cash receipt transactions. The transaction information must still be keypunched, verified, printed, sorted, and posted. These are basic data processing operations in automated accounting.

Punched Paper Tape as an Input Device

Punched paper tape is used as an input device almost as much as the punched card. Punched paper tape was originally used in sending telegrams. A section of five-channel paper tape is shown on page A-10.

It can be seen from the illustration that holes are punched the length of the tape to record and store transaction data. Data can be stored more tightly on paper tape than on punched cards. This is because the holes are smaller and closer together. Reels of paper tape are easier to carry and require less storage space than punched cards.

Punched cards are better for arranging data in different ways, because they can be sorted in different ways. Once data is punched into paper tape, the arrangement of the data on the tape cannot be changed.

Friden Five-Channel Punched Paper Tape

A	-	Q	1
B	$	R	4
C	N.P.	S	/
D	Tab	T	5
E	3	U	7
F		V	Punch Off
G	&	W	2
H		X	
I	8	Y	6
J	Error	Z	
K	P.R.	Space	
L		Carriage Return	
M		On 1, On 2	
N	,	Stop Code	
O	9	Letters Shift	
P	0	Figures Shift	

Punched Paper Tape and IDP

Tape punching attachments often are found on typewriters, adding machines, and bookkeeping machines in modern offices. At the same time that an immediate record is being prepared, the punching attachment records the transaction information on tape for later automated processing.

An electric typewriter with a tape-punching attachment is called a *flexowriter*. One model of flexowriter is shown below:

Friden Flexowriter

The flexowriter illustrates a practical application of IDP and the write-it-once principle. A tape can be punched along with the manual typing of a permanent record. Or, a permanent record can be automatically typed from a tape previously punched.

Magnetic Tape as an Input Device

Magnetic tape usually is used as an input device in EDP systems. It is prepared for input by depositing small magnetized spots on reels of tape. This tape comes from the factory coated with a magnetic metal substance.

The chief advantage of magnetic tape is the speed with which it can be used as input. Like paper tape, it is easy to carry and compact to store.

Magnetic Ink Symbol Numbers as Input Devices

As discussed in Chapter 3, the American Bankers Association recommends the use of symbol numbers printed in magnetic ink on each bank check. The use of these magnetic ink symbol numbers permits the automated processing of checks.

The use of magnetic ink symbol numbers in the processing of bank checks is called *magnetic ink character recognition*. The common abbreviation for this process is *MICR*. A bank check with magnetic ink symbol numbers printed across the bottom of the check is illustrated below:

Bank Check with Magnetic Ink Symbol Numbers

Note that the symbol numbers at the bottom of the check use a style that is different from regular Arabic numerals. This is because these numbers are read by a device that "feels" the surface area of each number and recognizes its shape. Regular Arabic numerals, especially 2, 5, 6, and 9, are too much alike to be easily distinguished one from the other by an electronic reading machine.

Encoding Symbol Numbers on Bank Checks. Magnetic ink symbol numbers are printed on checks using special printing machines. A special machine for printing magnetic ink characters on checks is called an *encoder*.

Encoding may be done by the company that prints the blank checks, or by the bank that supplies the blank checks to its depositors. Most banks have their check suppliers encode the appropriate symbol numbers on the checks.

Clearing Encoded Bank Checks Through the Federal Reserve System. The first series of encoded numerals in the check illustration (0810-0459) is adapted from the ABA number in the upper right-hand corner of the check. Notice that the number 80, which represents the State of Missouri, has been dropped from the encoded symbol number. This is because 0810 locates the bank in the Eighth Federal Reserve District (08) and the Greater St. Louis area (10), and the State of Missouri is understood.

The Federal Reserve system sorts checks encoded with magnetic ink symbol numbers as follows:

Step 1. The bank in which the check is deposited forwards it to the Federal Reserve clearing house in its district.

Step 2. The Federal Reserve clearing house sorts the check along with other checks received from banks in its district on special sorting equipment using the first two encoded symbol numbers (08 in the illustration). This results in twelve batches of checks for the twelve Federal Reserve districts.

Step 3. Each Federal Reserve clearing house forwards the checks drawn on banks in other Federal Reserve districts to the proper districts. In this process, the check illustrated on the previous page is forwarded to the Eighth Federal Reserve District clearing house in St. Louis.

Step 4. The clearing house in St. Louis sorts on the next two encoded symbol numbers (10 in the illustration) for distribution of the checks to regional clearing houses. Since the bank on which the illustrated check is drawn is a Greater St. Louis bank, this check is not forwarded to a regional clearing house.

Step 5. Each district or regional clearing house sorts on the next four symbol numbers (0459 in the illustration) for distribution to individual banks. These four symbol numbers are individual bank numbers.

Step 6. Batches of sorted checks are forwarded to the banks on which they were drawn. The illustrated check is sent to St. Louis County National Bank.

Processing Encoded Bank Checks in Individual Banks. The second series of encoded numerals on the illustrated check (121-077-3) is the account number of the individual depositor at his bank. The depositor's bank sorts its own checks by account number. It uses the same type of MICR sorting equipment as that used in the Federal Reserve clearing houses. This equipment can sort as many as 90,000 checks per hour, which is about 20 times faster than manual sorting.

In smaller banks, checks sorted by depositor's account number are posted by using conventional bank posting machines. Larger banks having encoders of their own print the amount of each check in magnetic ink under the signature line. This is done before the checks are sorted by depositor's account number. Encoding amounts of individual checks makes it possible to sort and post electronically to depositors' ledger accounts in one operation.

The Control Phase in Automated Accounting

The control phase of an electronic system receives commands from input devices and sees that they are carried out. These commands are received electronically. Each command refers to some item of transaction information which is in storage. The control phase searches storage locations one by one in carrying out commands from input devices.

The commands received from input devices are steps in the program to complete the automated accounting cycle. The control phase keeps track of the location of each command as it is carried out. This avoids skipping program steps.

The Storage Phase in Automated Accounting

In manual accounting, the journal, the ledger, and the trial balance are methods of storing transaction information. The journal in which a transaction is first recorded stores the transaction information temporarily awaiting posting. After a journal entry has been posted, the ledger accounts to which it has been posted store the transaction information temporarily awaiting the taking of a trial balance. After a trial balance has been taken, the trial balance stores the information temporarily awaiting financial statement preparation. The information is stored permanently on the financial statements.

In automated accounting, means of storage must be used which make it possible to complete the accounting cycle automatically. Means of storing journal entries, ledger account balances, and trial balance information must be found. Any means of storing accounting information in between the steps of the automated accounting cycle is known as a *storage device*.

External Storage Devices. Storage devices physically removed from an automated data processing system that can be fed into the system when desired are known as *external storage devices*. Punched cards, punched paper tape, and magnetic tape have already been discussed as input devices. All three of these input devices are able to retain transaction information for long periods of time. For this reason, in conjunction with the fact that they can be physically removed from the system, punched cards, punched paper tape, and magnetic tape are used also as data (external) storage devices.

Externally Stored Journal Entries. External storage devices may be used either for temporary storage or for permanent storage of transaction information. Punched cards are excellent storage devices for journal entries. This is because a separate punched card can be used to record each debit part of a journal entry and a separate punched card can be used to record each credit part of a journal entry. The cards can then be machine sorted by ledger account titles for machine posting.

Journal entries may also be stored on punched paper tape or magnetic tape. However, reels of tape cannot be sorted in the same way that punched cards are sorted. Journal entries on reels of tape must be machine posted in the order in which they were recorded. This is the same order in which journal entries would be posted manually. The only advantage that the posting of tape reels by machine has over manual posting is that machine posting is faster and relatively free of error.

Internal Storage Devices. The storage phase of an electronic system is contained within the machinery. The storage phase receives instructions from control, which have been passed on from input. These instructions are of four types:

(a) Take data from input   (c) Receive data from arithmetic
(b) Send data to arithmetic   (d) Send data to output

As mentioned earlier, each individual computer storage location is known as a storage address. Devices for storing accounting information within a computer are known as *internal storage devices.*

Accounting information may be stored internally on tiny doughnut-shaped metal cores, on cylinder-shaped metal drums, or on large metal disks. Metal cores, metal drums, and metal disks must all be magnetized for use as internal storage devices. Electronic transistors may also be used as internal storage devices.

Internally Stored Ledgers. Internal storage devices are used in automated accounting to keep ledger accounts up-to-date. Each account in the ledger is assigned a storage address. Debits and credits are fed in on punched cards or reels of tape. Control instructs input to transfer a debit or a credit amount into storage.

The incoming debit or credit amount must go to a storage address different from the address assigned to the related ledger account. Since this address is needed only for the current posting operation, it is not permanently assigned. However, the accountant must keep a chart of storage addresses in order to know at all times which addresses are assigned and which are open. This chart corresponds to the chart of accounts in manual accounting.

Automatic Posting. Automatic posting requires the following steps:

Step 1. Control instructs storage to transfer the old balance of the ledger account from its assigned address to the arithmetic unit.
Step 2. Control instructs storage to transfer the related debit or credit amount, which has just come into storage, to arithmetic.
Step 3. Control instructs arithmetic either to add the debit amount to or subtract the credit amount from the old balance of the ledger account.
Step 4. Control instructs storage to receive the new ledger account balance from arithmetic and to store it in the assigned storage address for the particular ledger account. This is the same address in which the old ledger account balance was stored.

In an automated accounting system, when a new item is stored electronically in the same storage address as a previous item, the new item replaces the old item at that address.

To illustrate the automated posting process, suppose that the cash account is assigned storage address number 10. The beginning cash balance, a debit of $1,200, becomes input by means of a punched card and is sent to address number 10 by the control unit. Suppose also that a debit to the cash account, in the amount of $50, is placed in input by means of another punched card and is sent by control to address number 100 for temporary storage. (There are 2,000 internal storage addresses in the automated data processing system that we are using to illustrate automatic posting.)

The posting process will proceed as follows:

Step 1. Control instructs storage to transfer the beginning cash balance of $1,200 from address number 10 to arithmetic.

Step 2. Control instructs storage to transfer the $50 debit to the cash account from address number 100 to arithmetic.

Step 3. Control instructs arithmetic to add the $50 cash debit to the beginning balance of $1,200.

Step 4. Control instructs storage to receive the new cash balance, $1,250, and to store it back in address number 10, the address permanently assigned to the cash account.

This process is repeated for each succeeding debit and each succeeding credit to the cash account. A similar process is used for all automated posting.

Limitations of Internal Storage. The illustration of automated posting demonstrates that internal storage is used both for permanent storage of ledger account balances and for temporary storage of debits and credits to ledger accounts. A small business having relatively few ledger accounts could get along with a rather small amount of internal storage. However, a large business having a great many ledger accounts would need a rather large amount of internal storage. Internal storage either must be large enough to handle the ledger accounts and the posting operations of the automated accounting system in which it is used, or ledger account balances will have to be stored externally on magnetic tape or punched cards.

The Arithmetic Phase in Automated Accounting

The arithmetic phase of an electronic system receives instructions from control to add, subtract, multiply, divide, or to compare two numbers. Arithmetic works with only two numbers at a time, having received them from different storage locations. To avoid returning subtotals or partial products to storage, however, arithmetic has a temporary electronic storage unit of its own. The electronic storage device in the arithmetic phase of a computer system used to store subtotals and partial products for further processing is known as an *accumulator*.

The Output Phase in Automated Accounting

In many ways, the output phase in automated accounting is just the reverse of the input phase. Punched cards, punched paper tape, and magnetic tape have already been described as input devices and as storage devices. Cards and reels of tape may also be used effectively as output devices.

Upon request, control will instruct storage to punch out cards or tape or to write on magnetic tape any information desired. This information might be journal entries, ledger account balances, trial balances, or financial statements. The cards or tapes must then be converted to English language information.

The Tabulator as an Output Device. The tabulator has already been discussed in connection with the use of the punched card. As indicated, it can list, total, or print journal entries, ledger account balances, trial balances, or financial statements whenever desired. The tabulator prints a line at a time and can handle up to 90 lines a minute.

The Flexowriter as an Output Device. The flexowriter has already been discussed in connection with the use of punched paper tape. As indicated, it can be used to prepare any accounting record or statement automatically from a tape punched by the output unit of an electronic computer or punched by itself.

The High-Speed Printer as an Output Device. High-speed printing machines are now available into which punched cards, paper tape, or magnetic tape may be fed. These machines use electronic grids or type wheels in the printing process instead of the type bars used by the tabulator. High-speed printing machines are capable of printing in excess of 900 lines of information per minute.

index

Inventory turnover, 248
Investments, permanent, 244; temporary, 244
Invoice, purchase, 143; purchase illustrated, 144; terms on, 193
Invoice method, 145

J

Journal, 22; defined, 21; purpose of, 31
Journal, cash disbursements, 51
Journal, cash payments, 51
Journal, cash receipts, 51
Journal, cashbook, 51
Journal, check register, 51
Journal, combined cash, 51, 105, 200; The Adams Appliance Store, 212–215; adjusting and closing entries, 121; Howard C. Miller, architect, 110–113; posting from, 160; The Rodgers Store, 160–161; special columns in, 51
Journal, four-column, 46; footing and ruling, 49; illustrated, 47; posting from, 50; proving, 48; special columns in, 51, 52; The Whitman Advertising Agency, 48
Journal, purchases, 142, 145, 201; The Adams Appliance Store, 216; model, 146; posting from, 147, 160; The Rodgers Store, 160
Journal, sales, 148, 152, 201; The Adams Appliance Store, 216; posting from, 154, 160; The Rodgers Store, 161; with sales tax, 153; without sales tax, 153
Journal, two-column, 22; illustrated, 23; posting from, 32; proving, 31; The Whitman Advertising Agency, 29–30
Journal entries, externally stored, A-13
Journalizing, 21, 24; the adjusting entries, 251; the closing entries, 255, 257; compound entry, 58; employers' payroll taxes, 95; payroll transactions, 91; petty cash disbursements, 58; procedure illustrated, 26, 47; reversing entries, 266; transactions, 21, 159

L

Ledger, accounts receivable, 202, 222–224; posting to, 31, 32; subsidiary, 31, 194; *see* General ledger
Ledger account, with bank, 70; with creditors and customers, 194
Ledger account method, 145, 147, 152; posting to accounts, 154
Ledgers, internally stored, A-14
Liabilities, 4; business, 5; current, 245; fixed, 245; long-term, 245; nonbusiness, 5
Liability, contingent, 172, 174; decrease in, 8, 15; increase in, 7, 14
Long-lived assets, 119, 244; depreciation of, 191
Long-term liabilities, 245
Loss from bad debts, 189

M

Magnetic ink character recognition (MICR), 66, A-11; equipment, 66
Magnetic ink symbol numbers, bank check with, A-11; as input devices, A-11

Magnetic tape, as an input device, A-10
Mail deposits, 63
Maker, of note, 168
Management services, 2
Margin, gross, 141, 239
Marketable securities, 244
Merchandise, accounting for, 140–166; purchased on account, 141, 201
Merchandise inventory, 141, 165
Merchandise inventory account, ruling the, 253
Merit-rating system, 95
Mortgage, 245

N

Narrative of transaction, The Adams Appliance Store, 203; Howard C. Miller, architect, 106; J. K. Jenkins' petty cash disbursements, 55; The Rodgers Store, 157; The Whitman Advertising Agency, 26
Nature of business accounting, 1–20
Negotiable instruments, 167
Net current assets, 248
Net income, 6, 16; calculation of, 141
Net loss, 16; calculation of, 141
Net operating income, 239
Net purchases, 141
Net sales, 141, 239
Net worth, 4
Night deposits, 63
Normal operating cycle, 121
Note, accounting for, 167–185; calculating interest on, 168; collected at maturity, 174; contingent liability on discounted, 174; discounted prior to maturity, 173; discounting a, 171; dishonored, 175; endorsement of, 178; interest-bearing, 168; issued to creditor in return for extension of time for payment, 179; issued in exchange for merchandise, 179; issued as security for cash loan, 179; non-interest-bearing, 168; notice of maturity, 180; paid at maturity, 180; present value of, 170; promissory, 167; received from customer for extension of time of payment of account, 172; received in exchange for merchandise, 172; received as security for cash loan, 173; renewed at maturity, 175, 181
Notes and interest, accounting for, 167–185
Notes payable, 4, 168; accounting for, 178
Notes payable account, 182; proving the, 182
Notes payable register, 181; illustrated, 180–181
Notes receivable, 4, 168; accounting for, 172
Notes receivable account, 176; proving the, 177
Notes receivable register, 176; illustrated, 176–177
Notice of maturity of note, 180
NSF check, 62

O

Old-age, survivors, and disability insurance (OASDI), 80
Open accounts, balancing and ruling, 126, 258; illustrated, 126, 263

Operating cycle, normal, 121
Operating statement, 9, 238
Original entry, book of, 22, 44
Output, in automated accounting, A-16; in electronic data processing, A-5
Output device, A-5; flexowriter, A-16; high-speed printer, A-16; tabulator, A-16
Overdraft, 65
Owner's equity, 4, 245; decrease in, 8, 16, 18; increase in, 7, 8, 14, 15, 17, 18; temporary accounts, 17, 122

P

Paper tape, punched, A-9
Passbook, 61
Paycheck, machine prepared, 86; manually prepared, 82
Payee, 168, 184
Payroll, accounting, 74–100; automated systems, 85; employee's earnings record, 83, 84, 88; employer-operated systems, 86; journalizing transactions, 91; records, 80; service bureaus, 85; types of compensation, 75; withholding allowances, 78; write-it-once principle, 85–86
Payroll register, 81; machine prepared, 89; manually prepared, 80–81
Payroll taxes, 92; application for social security and tax account number, 77; deductions from total earnings, 77; employee's income taxes withheld, 77; Employer's Quarterly Federal Tax Return and Quarterly Report (Form 941), 99; expense of employer, 93; FICA taxes payable, 93; filing returns and paying, 96; FUTA taxes payable, 93, 94; imposed on employer, 92; journalizing employer's, 95; state unemployment taxes payable, 94, 95; wage-bracket method of determining, 78; withholding exemption certificate, 78; withholding tax statement, 87
Periodic summary, 228–249
Permanent investments, 244
Personal service enterprise, 101–128; accounting cycle, 127; adjusting entries, 121; auxiliary records, 105; balancing and ruling open accounts, 126; books of account, 104; cash basis of accounting for, 102; chart of accounts, 103; closing the accounts, 122; closing entries, 122; combined cash journal, 105, 110–113; financial statements, 119, 120; general ledger, 105, 114–116, 123–125; narrative of transactions, 106; post-closing trial balance, 127; ruling the closed accounts, 126; types of, 101; work at close of fiscal period, 112; work sheet, 113, 117
Petty cash disbursements record, 54; of The Adams Appliance Store, 214–215; of J. K. Jenkins, 56–57; proving the, 56
Petty cash disbursements statement, of The Adams Appliance Store, 211; of J. K. Jenkins, 57; of Howard C. Miller, architect, 110
Petty cash fund, 53; imprest method, 58; journalizing disbursements, 58; operating a, 53; writing check for, 64
Petty cash transactions, of J. K. Jenkins, 55

Petty cash voucher, 54
Post-closing trial balance, 127, 264; The Adams Appliance Store, 265; Howard C. Miller, architect, 128
Postdated checks, 63
Posting, 32; the adjusting entries, 252; automatic, A-14; from books of original entry, 196; the closing entries, 256; from combined cash journal, 160; in detail, 122, 256; from four-column journal, 50; to individual accounts with creditors, 196; to individual accounts with customers, 197; to the ledger, 31; from purchases journal, 147, 160; from sales journal, 154, 160; summary, 50, 147; from vouchers or other documents, 196
Posting reference column, 23
Practical accounting problems, Chapters 1–5, 129–139; Chapters 6–10, 271–280
Prepaid expenses, accounting for, 191
Prepaid interest, 168
Present value, 170
Present worth, 170
Professional enterprises, 101
Profit, gross, 141, 239
Profit and loss, 255
Profit and loss statement, 9, 238
Profit and loss summary, 255
Program, in automated data processing, A-5
Programmer, A-5
Promissory note, 167; endorsement of, 178; illustrated, 168
Proprietorship, 4
Proving, cash, 52, 71; the four-column journal, 48; the petty cash disbursements record, 56; the two-column journal, 31; the work sheet, 236
Public accountants, 2
Punched card, as an input device, A-5; planning the use of, A-6; printing information on, A-8; punching information into, A-7; standard IBM, A-6; statement of account, A-8; verifying the information on, A-7
Punched paper tape, A-9; Friden five-channel, A-10
Purchase, defined, 142
Purchase invoice, 143; illustrated, 144
Purchases, and the purchases journal, 142
Purchases account, 142
Purchases discount, 193
Purchases journal, 142, 145, 201; The Adams Appliance Store, 216; model, 146; posting from, 147, 160; The Rodgers Store, 160
Purchases returns and allowances account, 143

Q

Quarterly Federal Tax Return and Quarterly Report, Employer's (Form 941), 99
Quick assets, 247

R

Rate of inventory turnover, 248
Ratio, of assets to liabilities, 247
Readjusting entries, 264
Receipt, Federal Depositary (Form 450), 97
Receipts, cash, 45; recording, 46

Receivable, accounts, 151
Reconciling the bank statement, 68
Record, petty cash disbursements, 54, 56–57, 214–215
Recording, in accounting, 3; bank transactions, 66; cash receipts and disbursements, 46
Records, auxiliary, 58, 83, 202; of cash receipts and disbursements, 45; employee's earnings, 83, 84, 88; kept by bank, 67; payroll, 80
Red ink, in balancing and ruling accounts, 264
Reducing-charge method of depreciation, 192
Registered accountants, 2
Remittance stubs, posting customer, A-9; sorting customer, A-8
Report of earnings, 238
Report form, of balance sheet, 119, 242; illustrated, 120
Restrictive endorsement, 61
Retail business, accrual basis of accounting applied to, 186–227
Retail sales tax, 149
Retail store, accounting for, 186–227; adjusting entries, 251; closing procedure, 255; reversing entries, 266; work sheet, 229
Revenue, defined, 16; and expense, 15; use of revenue accounts, 17
Revenue and expense statement, 238
Reversing entries, for accrual adjustments, 264; The Adams Appliance Store, 266; journalizing the, 266
Ruling, and balancing open accounts, 126, 258; the closed accounts, 126, 258; and footing the four-column journal, 49; the merchandise inventory account, 253

S

Salary, defined, 75
Sales, on account, 167; charge, 167; net, 141, 239; and the sales journal, 148
Sales account, 148
Sales journal, 148, 152, 201; The Adams Appliance Store, 216; posting from, 154, 160; The Rodgers Store, 161; with sales tax, 153; without sales tax, 153
Sales returns and allowances account, 149
Sales tax, retail, 149
Sales tax payable account, 150
Sales ticket, 150
Sales ticket method, 152
Savings account, 72
Schedule of accounts payable, 164; The Adams Appliance Store, 226; The Rodgers Store, 164
Schedule of accounts receivable, 163; The Adams Appliance Store, 226; The Rodgers Store, 164
Securities, marketable, 244
Self-employment income, 269
Self-employment taxes, 269
Service bureaus, and payroll accounting, 85
Service charges, 70
Sight draft, 184
Signature card, 59
Social security and tax account number, application for, 77

Sorter, in automated data processing, A-8, A-9
Source document, A-2
Standard form of account, 12
State unemployment taxes, 94; merit-rating system, 95; payable, 95
Statement, balance sheet, 9; bank, 68; financial, 9, 39, 119; income, 9, 39, 40, 120, 238, 240; income analysis, 239; operating, 9; profit and loss, 9; reconciling the bank, 68; withholding tax, 87
Statement of account, 198; illustrated, 199, A-8; posting remittance stubs, A-9; punched card, A-8; sorting remittance stubs, A-8
Statement of assets and liabilities, 241
Statement of condition, 241
Statement of financial condition, 10
Statement of financial position, 10, 241
Statement of petty cash disbursements, for The Adams Appliance Store, 211; for Howard C. Miller, architect, 110; for J. K. Jenkins, 57
Stock in trade, 142
Storage, in automated data processing, A-5, A-13; limitations of internal, A-15
Storage devices, external, A-13; internal, A-14
Straight line method, of depreciation, 192
Subsidiary ledgers, 31, 194
Summarizing, in accounting, 3
Summary account, 17
Summary posting, 50, 147; from sales journal, 154

T

"T" account form, 13
Tabulator, A-8; as an output device, A-16
Tax, retail sales, 149
Tax account number and social security, 77
Taxes, federal income, 77; FICA, 80, 87, 91, 92, 93; filing returns and paying payroll, 96; FUTA, 92, 93, 94; journalizing employers' payroll, 95; merit-rating system, 95; payable, 4; payroll imposed on employer, 92; state income, 79; state unemployment, 94; state unemployment payable, 95; wage-bracket method of withholding, 78; withholding allowances, 77
Temporary investments, 244
Temporary owner's equity accounts, 17
Terms, of trade discounts, 193
Ticket, deposit, 59, 60; sales, 150
Time draft, 184
Trade acceptances, 184
Trade discount, 171, 193; terms of, 193
Transactions, 6; analyses of, 14–18; dual effect of, 11; effect of, on the accounting equation, 7; journalizing, 21; journalizing payroll, 91; narrative for The Adams Appliance Store, 203; narrative for Howard C. Miller, architect, 106; narrative of petty cash, 55–56; narrative for The Rodgers Store, 157; narrative for The Whitman Advertising Agency, 26; typical, 6, 7
Transit numbers, American Bankers Association, 60
Transposition errors, 107

Trial balance, 19, 31, 36, 163; The Adams Appliance Store, 227, 265; adjusted, 254; after closing, 264; Howard C. Miller, architect, post-closing, 128; illustrated, 20; model, 38; post-closing, 127, 264; preparing the, 37; purpose of, 36; The Whitman Advertising Agency, 38

Trial balance columns, of ten-column work sheet, 230

Turnover, inventory, 248

Two-column journal, 22; illustrated, 23; posting from, 32; proving, 31; The Whitman Advertising Agency, 29–30

U

Use of revenue and expense accounts, 17

V

Verifier, A-7

Voucher, petty cash, 54

Vouchers, posting from, 196

W

Wage-bracket method, 78

Wage deductions, accounting for, 90

Wages, 75; accounting for, 90; defined, 75; expense account, 91

Wages and hours law, 76

Withdrawals, making, 63

Withholding, FICA taxes, 80; state taxes, 79; tables illustrated, 79; wage-bracket method, 78

Withholding allowances, 78

Withholding Exemption Certificate (Form W-4), 78

Withholding tax statement, 87; illustrated (Form W-2), 90

Work at close of fiscal period, 112

Work sheet, for The Adams Appliance Store, 230, 232–233; adjusted trial balance columns, 234; adjustments columns, 230; balance sheet columns, 236; completing the, 236; eight-column illustrated, 117; end-of-period, 113, 229; for Howard C. Miller, architect, 117; income statement columns, 235; proving the, 236; for a retail store, 229; ten-column illustrated, 232–233; trial balance columns, 230

Working capital, 248

Write-it-once operation, locating errors in, A-3

Write-it-once principle, 85, A-3; as a labor-saving device, A-2

Y

Year, calendar, 16; fiscal, 16